DESIGNING
THE MIND

THE PRINCIPLES OF PSYCHITECTURE

CONTENTS

Introduction

The year is 2084. You're playing a game of four-dimensional basketball, and one of your teammates makes a backhanded insult about your free throw skills. Immediately, a few things happen in your mind.

1. You feel pain.

2. You have the urge to reach through your virtual reality brain implant and make the guy regret his smug little comment.

3. Your self-esteem spends the next few days/weeks in a tailspin, causing you to ruminate over the insult, imagine and reimagine how you wish you had responded, and suffer.

But in the midst of this process, you think to yourself, "Wait a minute - it's 2084. We have technology for this."

So you open up an application through your neural interface that allows you to quickly modify your own brain. You sit through a few mind advertisements, try not to think any thoughts the government wouldn't like, and then you're in.

With just a few brain clicks, you are able to tell the software to remove your tendencies to suffer, seek revenge, and ruminate when someone insults you. You even add a feature that allows you to actually feel joy when you are insulted and to quickly respond with a witty and good-natured retort. Your new automatic response allows you to diffuse hostile situations and look like a rockstar, instantly making that awful sting of an insult a thing of the past.

By the year 2084, it is entirely plausible that we could have a method for directly modifying our brains to remove the maladaptive tendencies that hold us back. But unless this book has stood the test of time unreasonably well, you are most likely reading in an era in which this process will sound like science fiction. We can't just remove our mental bugs with a few clicks. Our ingrained psychological limitations are set in stone for the time being, right?

We are not as powerless as you may think. With the right cognitive tools, it is possible for anyone to make modifications to their own psychological software: their mind. Our unwanted psychological tendencies really do break down into what can be compared to software algorithms that can be reprogrammed. In this case, the insult is an input which triggers a kind of mental program. This program initiates a distorted thought cycle that causes you to reevaluate your self-worth in response to disrespect from your peers. This thought cycle then outputs emotional and behavioral responses which cause you to feel terrible and react impulsively.

Because these responses were programmed into us eons ago, humans have had a very long time to study them. Though they lacked our modern technological metaphors, ancient thinkers began examining and developing counter-algorithms for many of our problematic mental modules. These thinkers had the forethought to write their insights down for posterity, and their wisdom, however scattered and diverse, is the open-source code we can use to program our own minds.

My long-term goal is to curate and systematize these tools of software self-optimization and distribute them to as many people as possible. I want to do the next best thing to giving you an instant brain-modification implant. I want to provide you with a handbook for designing and optimizing your own psychological software.

Most people who read books to improve themselves do it because they want to advance their careers, lose weight, or make more money. "Why am I designing my mind?" you may ask, "What am I getting out of it?" If this is you, I will go ahead and weed you out by announcing that this book will not directly help you attain or achieve anything out there in the world. It won't turn you into a master of seduction or a champion of your conference room. It will not get you abs.

This book is for those who find the idea of building a better mind thrilling in and of itself. It is for those who are impassioned by the thought of cultivating greater wisdom, self-control, or tranquility - who are drawn to the philosophies of Buddhism and Stoicism or the fields of humanistic psychology and psychotherapy. We all want to be happier, healthier, better people. But only a few grasp that all of our highest aims can be reached by placing our focus directly on our minds.

If this describes you, you are what we will call a psychitect. You are among a collective of rare individuals who are excited by the idea of overcoming the seemingly fixed parts of themselves. You view the default state of your mind as an invitation to intervene and transmute. You want to unflinchingly look reality in the eye and find ways to alter it. You want to live a great life - not a normal one. If this is you, read on.

What do you dislike about your mind? Which patterns emerge when you examine your life - patterns you feel have held you back? Does fear prevent you from pursuing your ambitions? Does jealousy ruin your relationships? Do you allow distractions to rule your life? Do you have an inner critic whose expectations you are never able to meet?

This book will make the bold claim that the human condition as you know it - is optional. That it is possible for you to unplug from your own mind, examine it from above, and modify the very psychological code on which you operate, permanently altering these limiting patterns.

You will learn to build unshakable peace and levity into your mind so you can embrace whatever life throws at you while responding with effective action. You will develop the skills to think with razor-sharp clarity, overcome your own distortions of judgment, and cultivate wisdom so you can make the right decisions in your life. You will learn to build the habits, lifestyle, and character which will gradually enable you to become your ideal self.

And to begin this process, you won't have to wait one day for futuristic technology to arrive. You can rewire the default behaviors, emotional responses, and biases that hold you back. You can learn the principles and practices for building a mind better than you ever thought possible, one algorithm at a time. Most importantly, you can internalize a mindset that will allow you to take this process beyond what you read in this book. And as you scale the heights of self-mastery, you will gradually come to resemble the legendary figures who have unlocked radically superior states of mind.

This is not yet another book promising useful tricks for happiness like gratitude journals and cold showers or singing the praises of positive thinking, neuro-linguistic programming, or mindfulness meditation (although that one will have its place). I will refer to ideas and techniques which have been viewed through the lens of spirituality. But every mindset and method you find in this work is rational, psychological, and empirical. This book is based on the time-tested insights of ancient thinkers, the science of neuroplasticity, and findings within cognitive, affective, and behavioral science. It looks at the ways ordinary (and extraordinary) people can modify the "software" of their minds to dramatically impact their lives today. The ways we can structure our minds directly for wisdom, well-being, and character, and to reach toward our highest visions for ourselves.

The first catalyst for this book came about a decade ago. I don't remember the exact event, but ultimately, it was what happened right after that matters. The event was something bad, ostensibly. Some moderately-sized mistake or setback in my life. I had faced many of these before, just like everyone else. But this time was different. The negative emotion which was supposed to proceed from this setback didn't come - no grieving, no anxiety, no frustration. I did something in my mind that caused me to bypass the emotion I was supposed to have, and then I continued on with my life, responding to the event only in my actions.

What I did in my mind was not suppression or repression or denial, for you fellow armchair psychologists. It was a form of effective emotional self-regulation, and it turns out the ancient Greeks beat me to it a couple thousand years ago. No, I was not unique in this experience - only in the obsession I developed as a result of it. It became clear to me that this experience was only one example of what seemed to be a dark art one could master to become immune to problems some spend entire lives wrestling with - a path for continually upgrading the basic elements of my mind.

As I studied the human mind, its limitations, and its potential, I found a striking coherence. All the mental problems with which I struggled boiled down to automatic and systematic mental phenomena - chains of triggers and responses, inputs and outputs. More interestingly, the solutions to these problems that worked all fit into the same framework. I labeled these patterns **algorithms**, and the sum of these algorithms became **psychological software**. Within this software framework, my mental challenges began to make sense.

I started applying a new methodology to solving my problems - one centered less around changing my life circumstances and more on changing the psychological patterns at their source. I found that the problems which once seemed perpetual could be permanently extinguished. The version of my mind that once seemed out of reach could be iteratively approached, and ultimately, eclipsed by new, even better versions. I coined the term **psychitecture** to refer to this practice of designing and optimizing the software of one's mind. And concurrently with my practice, I was finding more and more evidence within cognitive, affective, and behavioral science that this framework wasn't just a metaphor. This was actually how the mind worked.

This discipline has grown beyond my initial sights. Lots of research has confirmed to me that the art of emotion regulation and restructuring is very real and very effective. But the pursuit of self-mastery has further developed to encompass three major components: cognitive, emotional, and behavioral. And the more I reflected on them, the more I realized that these three domains encompass the core competencies required for well-being and success in life.

Furthermore, incompetence in any of these three areas represents not only foolishness and weakness, but what some call evil. All of the "bad actors" in society can be explained in reference to deficiencies in one or more of these areas. This is why helping others to develop self-mastery in all its forms has become the greatest source of purpose in my life. The **self-mastery triad** will provide the organizational backbone of this book, and the chapters will teach you the principles and practices needed to master all three realms.

I am not the spiritual guru or venerated professor you may be seeking. My formal background is in the design of systems - physical, digital, and theoretical. But my most relevant credential is a lifelong appetite for introspective investigation, ravenous reading, and obsessive self-optimization. I don't tend to focus on myself in this book because I find the ancient teachers, practical philosophers, and cognitive scientists who have inspired it to be far more interesting.

My philosophical mentors have included Lao Tzu, Siddhārtha Gautama, Aristotle, Epicurus, Diogenes, Marcus Aurelius, Epictetus, Seneca, Michel de Montaigne, Rene Descartes, Friedrich Nietzsche, Abraham Maslow, Viktor Frankl, Aaron Beck, and many more. My contemporary influences are too many to name here, but you will be introduced to them along the way. Though they did not use the term themselves, I will refer to many of these individuals as psychitectural thinkers or visionaries. I'm no more a teacher of their wisdom than a student. My role has simply been to study, curate, and synthesize these insights into a modern framework, which I present to you in the following chapters.

You can join the community at designingthemind.org to receive more psychitectural insights and to participate in the discussion. This book, and DTM's growing community of psychitects, represents a living, breathing body of ideas which will continue to take shape over time. I invite you to take part in its evolution.

PSYCHITECT'S TOOLKIT

In addition to this book, verified readers can download a **free, 50-page guide on psychitecture**, which includes:

- An overview of the basic concepts of psychitecture and psychological algorithms
- A breakdown of 8 psychotechnologies you can start using to reprogram your mind
- 64 incredible book recommendations related to self mastery and psychitecture
- A list of 16 websites, blogs, and podcasts that can aid in self-optimization
- Quotes from the great psychitectural visionaries

Just go to designingthemind.org/psychitecture to get your Psychitect's Toolkit.

1

The Theory and Practice of Psychitecture

Mind as Machine

In the past, we humans have learned to control the world outside us, but we had very little control over the world inside us.

- **Yuval Noah Harari**, *21 Lessons for the 21st Century*

Every era attempts to explain the human mind in the terms and metaphors of its dominant technologies. For Plato, the mind was a chariot. For Descartes, it was a mechanical clock. For Freud, it was a steam engine. Today, the most common analogue for the mind is the computer. Although it's true that our brains are not literally digital computers, built on silicon circuits and binary logic, the modern metaphor of the mind as a computer is by far the most powerful and comprehensive one we've ever had.

Our hardware is the brain, the physical substrate made up of neurons, chemicals, and electrical impulses. Our software is the world of our experience - the mind. Our sensations, emotions, and thoughts are all experienced internally in the mind, but all have physical phenomena behind them and can be influenced by external events, chemicals, and technology.

Our minds don't generate emotions or cognitions arbitrarily: there are patterns coded into this software, inscribed by millions, or even billions of years of natural selection.[1] No word we speak or action we take is an isolated event, however spontaneous it may seem, and the same goes for the purely internal processes of thinking and feeling. They all flow from a determined system in the same way the outputs of a computer spring from the algorithms built into it by its programmers. The reason we cannot perfectly predict human behavior is that our minds are the most complex machines ever to exist (so far). They do not run a simple loop, but an intricate system which factors innumerable inputs and calculations into its behaviors.

> The brain, like it or not, is a machine. Scientists have come to that conclusion, not because they are mechanistic killjoys, but because they have amassed evidence that every aspect of consciousness can be tied to the brain.

> - **Steven Pinker**, "The Mystery of Consciousness"

The fact that our minds are machines does not preclude the vast richness of experience of which they are capable. It simply means that at its core, the ineffable complexity of human existence boils down to an operating system we can study and increasingly understand. Furthermore, to compare our minds to machines is not to suggest that they have been set in stone by evolution and are now doomed to iterate themselves perpetually until death. Our genes don't determine everything we will become, but they do determine how much we can be shaped by experiences during early childhood, adolescence, and adulthood, which, for all, is quite a bit.[2]

It is possible for you to alter your brain in ways that result in functional changes. Modern medicine has developed drugs and surgical procedures for treating diseases, disorders, and injuries to the brain. Prescription drugs are available to treat everything from ADHD to obsessive compulsive disorder to severe anxiety. Implants can even be placed into the brain to help rehabilitate stroke patients or stimulate nerves for treating Parkinson's or depression.[3]

Healthy people can also utilize technologies and practices to further improve their brains. Your lifestyle behaviors like sleep, diet, and exercise have a massive effect on brain health and function.[4] Growing evidence suggests that mindfulness meditation can increase concentration, self-awareness, and overall well-being.[5] Some evidence even suggests that devices such as the transcranial direct current stimulation (tDCS) which are now offered as consumer products are able to improve learning, sleep quality, and mood.[6]

You can take nootropics, which are typically readily available chemicals which have demonstrated an ability to enhance cognition, increase focus or memory, boost energy, or even heighten creativity.[7] You could even consume psychedelic drugs like psilocybin and LSD, which modern neuroscience indicates can stimulate new neural connection, ease anxiety related to death, and treat addiction and depression.[8]

There is an entire movement known as **transhumanism** concerned with modifying the human body, brain, and mind, and taking the evolution of human nature into our own hands. It is defined by the Humanity+ organization as:

> The intellectual and cultural movement that affirms the possibility and desirability of fundamentally improving the human condition through applied reason, especially by developing and making widely available technologies to eliminate aging and to greatly enhance human intellectual, physical, and psychological capacities.[9]

Transhumanist thinkers believe that some day in the not-so-distant future, we will be able to augment the brain and mind in ways nearly inconceivable today. Future pharmaceuticals and microscopic brain implants could rapidly repair, regenerate, and revamp brain cells. Genetic engineering could alter the mind biologically, increasing intelligence, creativity, or any other desired quality. Virtual or augmented reality technology may become so advanced as to be indistinguishable from reality, connect directly into our nervous systems, and allow us to live in worlds currently unimaginable.

Furthermore, an advanced understanding of the mind may allow us to perfectly simulate the human brain through digital computers and upload our consciousness to the cloud. Organizations such as DARPA[10] and Elon Musk's Neuralink[11] are already working to create brain-machine interfaces. These devices would allow our brains to connect directly to computers, convert our thoughts into bits and back again, and augment our intelligence, communication, and more. Theoretically, this could allow us to effectively merge with artificial intelligence, or with other people to form one radically intelligent and capable mind.

> When transhumanists refer to "technology" as the primary means of effecting changes to the human condition, this should be understood broadly to include the design of organizations, economies, polities, and the **use of psychological methods and tools**.
>
> - **Max More**, "The Philosophy of Transhumanism"

As fascinating as the potential for future modification of the mind may be, most of it is inaccessible to us today, leaving us only to wait and contemplate. But there is another type of modification, a kind of software transhumanism, which is already available. There are tools that can be unlocked right now, by anyone, without any external technology. We might call these tools **psychotechnologies**. The most powerful way to improve the brain at this point in history is through its software: Through your thoughts and actions.

Many of us would love to program our minds to work according to our preferences just as we might program computer software. Our organic brains, however, do not work in exactly the same way computers do. They don't simply do what they are told; we have to understand and work around their nature if we want to change their programming. Rather than keyboards and command lines, we have our cognition - which can be a robust tool if used properly.

Although it may seem like common sense to anyone who has ever learned something new or developed a skill, the idea that the brain can change has become fashionable in recent years. **Neuroplasticity** refers to the brain's ability to change and reorganize throughout the life of an individual. The ability to adapt to changing conditions has always been crucial to our survival, so this capacity has been hardwired into the mind of all higher life forms. You can build new neural pathways, and reinforce or diminish old ones through learning, conditioning, and practice. In fact, it would be impossible to prevent the modification of your mind.[12]

Everything you do or experience alters your mind. Even sharing pictures of your food is a form of practice that will strengthen the connections between certain neurons at the expense of others. Multi-linguists, professional musicians, and academics with encyclopedic knowledge are living proof of the incredible human capacity for neuroplasticity. Even more so are the victims of brain injury whose brains amazingly find ways to rewire themselves so that another part of the brain takes over the functions of a damaged area.[13]

All animals have software which is modified on a daily basis. Every animal learns. However, most animals don't try to learn. No creatures besides humans are familiar with any kind of deliberate practice. It is doubtful that a chimpanzee or a dolphin ever determined that there was something wrong with its own mind and attempted to modify it. But humans do. We modify our minds because our software lacks some desired function (speaking Italian), or because it has undesirable functions (speaking with a stutter). The capacity for this modification appears to be virtually limitless, but few people utilize it to its full potential.

The modern fascination with neuroplasticity has led many to try to optimize their intelligence, memory, and concentration. People obsessively track and optimize their sleep, nutrition, and exercise regimens. But people who obsessively and directly optimize the structure of their minds for flourishing are less common. This book is less concerned with intellectual learning or general competency development and more with psychological adaptivity and well-being.

The default human mind is an inherently disorderly place to be. The odds of being well adapted to this world by default are virtually none. The reason kids cry and scream so much more than adults is not just because their brains are less developed. It is because experience in the real world forces you to develop coping strategies over time that give you increased control over your mental state. The tantrums, agony, irrationality, and impulsiveness of child-hood represent the epitome of being a slave to one's own default software.[14][15]

Societal pressures work to pull you up to the line of psychological ade-quacy, and psychotherapy can be used when society falls short. But these aims are far too low. Falling within the current normal range of psychological health is nothing to aspire to. We are interested in far exceeding this line - in psycho-logical greatness. We want to structure our minds in the ways that will lead to our deepest fulfillment. But there is no such force that naturally pulls you above this line. That is why we have to carve out the path toward the peaks of psycho-logical well-being ourselves.

A New Vision of Enlightenment

Any man could, if he were so inclined, be the sculptor of his own brain.

- **Santiago Ramon y Cajal**, *Advice for a Young Investigator*

You probably fall into one of two camps. In one camp, we have those who believe there is an experiential state we might call spiritual enlightenment. This state represents a complete transcendence of ego, illusion, attachment, and/or suffering. After its attainment, the enlightened can finally see "the true nature of existence," break free from the limited survival mode of the mind, and blow out the candle of suffering. It is typically thought to be achieved through years of dedicated meditation, and eventually, a sudden click into a radically new state.

In the other camp, we have those who think this is bullshit. No such liberated state exists, and anyone who thinks it does is drinking the generic fruit beverage of spiritual lunatics and charlatans. We may be able to get a little better at dealing with life, but not radically transformed. The realities of ongoing suffering and dissatisfaction are inevitable, and the ancient claim of enlightenment is mythology.

My goal is to propose that perhaps both of these camps are wrong... or right. **We've just been thinking about it all wrong.** Imagine, if you will, that we live in an alternate world in which there is only one musical instrument. The instrument is called the piano pod, and in this alternate world, everyone has one in their living room. The piano pod is exactly like a piano, except that in order to play it, you have to open a door on the front of it, sit down inside a room only large enough for one, and shut the door behind you. You'll have to set your claustrophobia aside for this one. The piano pod has completely opaque and soundproof walls, so only the person inside can see or hear her own performance.

Being that the piano pod is otherwise exactly like a piano, most people who sit down to play find that it is incredibly difficult to create music that doesn't cause them to envy the deaf. You may find that even when you persist for months, you remain in a state of frustrating incompetence.

To make matters worse, the piano pod world is full of obvious con-men claiming they can help you become amazing at the instrument overnight if you'll just hand over some hard-earned money. While some seem more credible than others, it is clear that anyone who claims to have achieved piano pod greatness could be lying opportunistically, trying to impress others, or delusional.

Unlike in our reality, it is entirely reasonable within the piano pod world to believe frustrating incompetence to be the only possible state. Not being able to witness someone playing the instrument with incredible artistry and skill makes it easy to believe such people do not exist.

The piano pod world represents our current reality, and our minds are the instruments. We don't know what is going on in other people's heads. We don't ever know for sure how another person's subjective experience compares with ours. The most we can do is observe their behavior and take their word for it. But neither our frustrating incompetence nor the quick fixes promised by sleazy gurus are proof that the rabbit hole of psychological optimization does not exist. And the great innovation of pod-less pianos in our world reveals just how musically masterful it is possible to be. We have all heard brilliant musicians who make it very hard to let ourselves off the hook.

Having heard the work of great musicians, you may still conclude that these virtuosos have some kind of genetic gift the rest of us lack, and that playing this instrument skillfully simply isn't possible for you. Although it's true that genetics plays some role in musical ability, we simply don't observe regular people putting thousands of hours into musical practice and not getting really, really good. We know it is possible to become great on the keys by practicing diligently and applying the right methods. And we can see that the path of artistic mastery goes deeper and deeper, never really reaching a limit besides the laws of physics.

The "10,000 hour rule" popularized by Malcolm Gladwell suggests that the great talents of people like Albert Einstein, Bill Gates, and the Beatles are not simply the innate gifts they are often assumed to be. They can be understood as the result of many hours of development, often falling around 10,000 hours.[16] It may not be a mathematical theorem which infallibly dictates success in any field, but the rule goes a long way to explain just how crucial practice and diligence are, even for seemingly supernatural ability. It has even been demonstrated that the very belief in neuroplasticity, in the idea that our abilities are not fixed, can be the determining factor in our success. People who view their strengths as malleable are found to be more successful in their endeavors and more fulfilled in life.[17]

I see no reason the principles of neuroplasticity should not apply to the improvement of our subjectivity. Our neurons don't play favorites in terms of the tasks which can be improved. It would require more of a leap of faith to believe that the principles of human psychology made an exception for this particular area. If our sights are clearly set on the reworking of our own thoughts, emotional reactions, and behaviors, what is stopping us from gradually rerouting the neural pathways of well-being?

No, neuroplasticity does not prove we can suddenly click into a state of undisturbed bliss. The story of the ego and its transcendence is seductive enough to warrant careful scrutiny. We all love single-cause explanations of our problems and their solutions. But this sudden shift beyond our limits simply is not consistent with a modern understanding of human psychology. I think some of the ancient mystics may have been right about their own radically superior subjective experience. They were just wrong in the particular way they conceived of it.

Psychological mastery can be systematically pursued in fully rational terms without any difficult concepts, or the transcendence of concepts entirely. Just as the concept of suddenly snapping into a state of musical mastery after years of practice seems incompatible with current psychological understanding, doing the same with our minds seems implausible. The Buddha may have been the Beethoven of his psychological state, but Beethoven got to where he was gradually, and still fell somewhere on the endless continuum of musical mastery by the end of his life.

Our mental behaviors were selected to serve specific functions. We get jealous because it helped our ancestors retain mates.[18] We dogmatically accept flawed beliefs because it allowed our predecessors to bond with their tribes.[19] We get addicted to substances because the compounds within them offered a higher chance of survival.[20] There doesn't have to be a core defect at the root of all of our problems or a single solution to free us from it. We can modify and optimize the individual functions, features, and flaws of our minds a la carte, and this process, when practiced over time, can lead to the algorithmic enlightenment I'm proposing.

Neuroplasticity gives us the ability to gradually improve at things through consistent and sustained effort, and mastery is a relative term which does not indicate that one can reach a point at which no further progress can be made. By becoming intimately aware of the mistakes that we would like to relinquish - by working out the disadvantageous habits and building advantageous ones, **we can develop the ability to increasingly determine our own subjective experience**.

Although humans did not in any way evolve to play any instrument, it has been shown that with enough deliberate practice, we can overcome our incompetence and move closer and closer to mastery. The trained musician can play music in a way that looks and feels so natural that the audience would swear it was what she was made to do. And the biological forces which developed our minds, though our values and well-being were not their concern, have placed no barriers to reprogramming our psychological operating system toward a new purpose. The path of self-mastery can be followed to great heights with enough practice. The only problem is that until now, **we haven't known what we were practicing**.

Overture to Psychitecture

To make ourselves, to shape a form from various elements – that is the task! The task of a sculptor! Of a productive human being!

- **Friedrich Nietzsche**, unpublished notes

The central practice and framework of this book is called psychitecture. **Psychitecture** is self-directed psychological evolution - the act of deliberately reprogramming your own psychological operating system. We will see that psychitecture applies to everything from breaking a bad habit to rebuilding an entire worldview.

Though it is a new term, psychitecture is not a new practice. For millennia, thinkers such as Aristotle, Siddhārtha Gautama (the Buddha), the Stoics, and many others have directed their pupils to place their focus on optimizing their minds and consciously constructing their character. But this book attempts to provide a modern vocabulary and framework for understanding these internal battles. As stated above, we all engage in psychitecture at certain points in our lives. But calling it out and giving it a name can change our perspective on it.

The mind's software can be understood as a system of interconnected and interacting behaviors and tendencies. This system determines who you are and how you live your life. And when delusion, distortion, or tampering affect parts of it, the resulting problems can corrupt the entire operating system. But making improvements can have a chain reaction as well, and we will look at the mechanisms for consciously embedding positive functions and programming out the undesirable functions.

The process of psychitecture, and the structure of the following chapters, is organized into a triad: cognitive, emotional, and behavioral. The cognitive realm will deal with beliefs and biases, introspection, and wisdom. The emotional realm will deal with coping mechanisms, feelings, and desires. And the behavioral realm will look at actions, temptations, and habits. We can actually see this same division in the work of Descartes, in which he outlined the goals of an ideal life.

1. [Cognitive] Use reason for its highest purpose: to evaluate and judge the best possible course of action, as free as possible from passion and bias.

2. [Behavioral] Have an unwavering will for executing whichever actions were judged to be the best.

3. [Emotional] Understand that beyond clear reasoning and a resolved will, everything is outside of one's power, and should be no cause for stress or regret.

- **Rene Descartes**, Letter to Princess Elisabeth

We will use the concept of the algorithm to model our automatic thoughts, emotions, and actions. For those who don't know anything about algorithms, except perhaps that they are apparently coming for your job, an **algorithm** can be defined as "a step-by-step procedure for solving a problem or accomplishing some end."[21] In our minds, the problems our algorithms were meant to solve are biological problems. A person with an algorithm causing him to be afraid of presenting in front of large crowds would be less likely to publicly embarrass himself, alienate himself from his social group, and lower his chances of passing on his genes.[22] But like many others, this genetically useful algorithm can act against our own highest goals, preventing some from becoming the inspiring TEDx speakers they are capable of being.

Perfectly clear reasoning and stable emotions may have gotten in the way of our survival and reproduction. **But the "solutions" these default algorithms provide are actually the source of most of our psychological problems today**. Our thoughts, emotions, and behaviors can all be understood in terms of algorithms, and this model will serve you well in your attempts to optimize your mind.

Our goal is not freedom from the algorithms that make up our minds, but the autonomy to transform the algorithms which don't serve us into algorithms which do. In order to make these transformations, we must learn to think about our psychological problems algorithmically. We can't be vague about our issues. What specific habit or emotion or error of judgment is the problem? What does the whole chain look like? How can it be programmed out?

This algorithm model is not a superficial metaphor. Our bad habits and harmful behaviors are effectively if-then programs triggered by real-world inputs that result in undesirable outputs.[23] Our cognitive biases and fallacies are reflexive inferences which flow systematically from preprogrammed rules below our ordinary level of awareness.[24] And modern psychology tells us that our emotions are mechanically generated by automatic thoughts which can be restructured.[25]

These reflexes all chain together to result in our habitual state of existence. Although some of these tendencies may vary from one individual or culture to another, by and large the bad algorithms that plague us are found across our species. Confirmation bias, procrastination, and thanatophobia (death anxiety) are all universal enough that we can understand our own minds by studying these ubiquitous human tendencies.[26] And promisingly, **there is strong evidence that we can deliberately reprogram these bad algorithms.**[27][28][29]

Here is how we will visually represent an algorithm:

if this

then that

An algorithm is made up of dots representing inputs and outputs, and a line connecting them. Simple enough, right? Eventually, we will look at algorithms that look more like this:

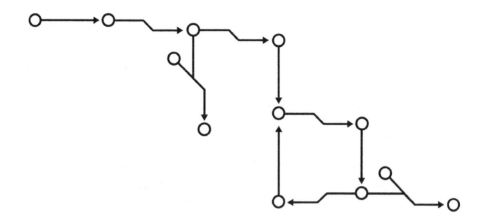

But we'll work our way there gradually. Modern self-help books often center around a few major algorithms to be banished - automatic tendencies like blaming yourself when things go wrong, making assumptions without evidence, or retreating whenever you experience fear. But the psychitectural perspective takes a step back. Instead of simply providing you with a few key algorithms to optimize your mind, this book attempts to provide you with a framework to codify the wisdom you come across in other books or stumble upon yourself. It offers you a new perspective and a methodology to become the collector, curator, and programmer of adaptive algorithms. And this new way of looking at your own mind will remain with you long after you have finished this book.

It is important to emphasize the "system" part of "psychological operating system." Aristotle viewed a person as the sum of his habits. This understanding of habit far exceeded the narrow notion of morning routines and ingrained compulsions. An individual's entire being could be represented by his habits. A person's disposition was not decided at every moment and in every isolated action. His words and actions flowed from his habits, which in turn were reinforced or broken by his actions. In this way, his disposition could be cultivated and perfected. [30] The aggregate of all his habits was his character.[31]

It is not hard to imagine that if Aristotle had possessed our software framework, he would have found it even more useful than his habit model. What are habits, after all, if not a collection of if-then statements determining one's behavior? The sum of these habits, what Aristotle called character, we call software. The way your mind is structured will determine the person you become, the life you live, and the fulfillment you realize. When you modify your mind, you edit the operating system at your core and change your personal trajectory. And when you make a persistent occupation of this endeavor, **you become the architect of your own character**.

If you want to take on this project, you have to orient yourself toward gradual optimization. Psychitecture is an often slow process of recognizing and iteratively compensating for errors in perception and action. Your great satisfaction should be the feeling of making one tiny optimization, inching one step closer to your ideal. This perspective is not unlike the best dieting advice available. Trying to constantly muster willpower to bring about a result can't compare to gradual and habitual optimization.

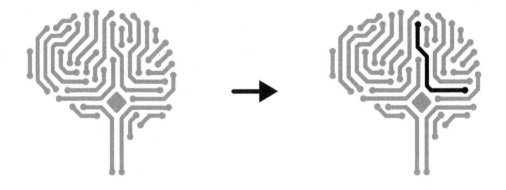

Kaizen is a Japanese term often used in business, meaning continuous change for the better - an ongoing endeavor for incremental optimization. This concept can be applied to the psychological operating system just as easily. Individual thoughts, emotions, and actions are never the problem, in the same way that the individual drops of water leaking through your roof are not the problem. **We are interested in the source - in the structural patterns**.

Psychitecture is a kind of self-improvement, but not the vague self-improvement that leads people to take up yoga or yo-yoing for no particular reason. When you engage in psychitecture, you begin by acknowledging the current state of your mind and envisioning the ideal one. You work backwards from this vision, through broad strategies - all the way down to individual algorithmic optimizations, each of which is one small step toward that vision. When you practice psychitecture, you design your mind's structures such that your goals come about naturally. You move to the adjacent possible using your highest ideals as your beacon.

Psychitecture's aim is to reform biologically ingrained habits and tendencies of all forms. Its goal is to rewire the mental biases, distortions, and assumptions that cause us to make mistakes, the unnecessary suffering we fall victim to on a regular basis, the mentalities that hold us back in life, and the impulses that lead us away from our ideals. It is a high-level design and implementation process - creative problem-solving for the subjective experience. When utilized persistently, **it can take a mind that is like a prison and gradually transform it into a palace.**

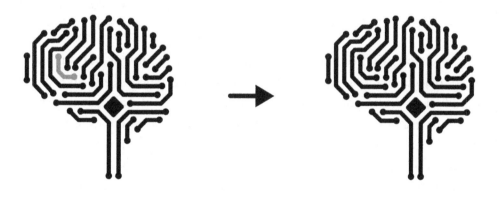

Unplugging from Your Software

When you have cultivated mindfulness, life becomes richer, more vivid, more satisfying, and you don't take everything that happens so personally. Attention plays a more appropriate role within the greater context of a broad and powerful awareness. You're fully present, happier, and at ease, because you're not so easily caught up in the stories and melodramas the mind likes to concoct. Your powers of attention are used more appropriately and effectively to examine the world. You become more objective and clear-headed, and develop an enhanced awareness of the whole.

- **Culadasa**, *The Mind Illuminated*

Before we dive into the many methods for modifying our minds, we need to acquire a tool that will be indispensable for our progress. In order to modify the structure of our minds, we need to observe and analyze their rules and patterns. We need to closely examine our thoughts, emotions, values, and drives, as well as the relationships among them, and correct the misperceptions which have been built into us.

It's as if you have just taken a job as a programmer where your role is to redesign a poorly built program. The original programmer failed to comment the function of each part of the software, and he is not available for questioning. So you have to figure out how this thing is structured by studying it. You have to go through the algorithms one by one and figure out how they work to determine how they can be reworked.

In order to effectively analyze our software, we have to step outside of it. And the tool that allows us to do this is called metacognition. **Metacognition** has been defined as "knowledge and cognition about cognitive phenomena".[32] You could view it as thinking about your thinking or awareness of your own field of awareness, and the metacognitive perspective is the foundational viewpoint for psychitecture.

Redesigning the mind without stepping outside of it would be like trying to repair your glasses without taking them off. Although you obviously never actually exit your own mind, when you practice metacognition, you essentially lift yourself up out of the system on which you normally operate so you can look down on the tangled mess of wires and begin the process of rewiring.

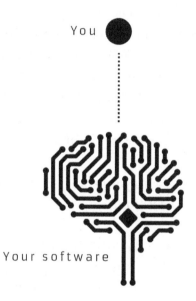

Closely related to metacognition is the now-popular concept of **mindfulness**. Mindfulness is a metacognitive strategy which has been defined as "the awareness that emerges through paying attention on purpose, in the present moment, and non-judgmentally to the unfolding of experience moment by moment."[33] Though the term is often misunderstood, and has lost some of its meaning in the process of becoming a cultural fad, it is a crucial method of psychitectural intervention. Mindfulness allows us to press pause on our software so we can step in and reprogram it.

We will look at methods for increasing mindfulness, but I have found that making a priority of objective introspection and metacognitive awareness can be enough to cultivate it. Simply deciding to start noticing your thoughts without judgment or engagement may cultivate this habit in the same way that deciding to enter the housing market causes you to start noticing "for sale" signs in suburban lawns.

If mindfulness does not come easily to you and you are not accustomed to noticing the thoughts and emotions you experience in any given moment, you may need a practice for cultivating it. Vipassana meditation is one of the most common of such practices, and many people, as well as some preliminary research, have found it to be beneficial.[34]

This practice will gradually guide you to a non-attached awareness of your own internal processes, often beginning with physical sensations like the breath and working up to thoughts and emotions. It trains you to notice when your attention gets sucked back into the captivating narrative your cognition presents to you. Many books have been written describing how to meditate, so I will only include a concise guide from Sam Harris's *Waking Up*:

1. Sit comfortably, with your spine erect, either in a chair or cross-legged on a cushion.

2. Close your eyes, take a few deep breaths, and feel the points of contact between your body and the chair or the floor. Notice the sensations associated with sitting— feelings of pressure, warmth, tingling, vibration, etc.

3. Gradually become aware of the process of breathing. Pay attention to wherever you feel the breath most distinctly— either at your nostrils or in the rising and falling of your abdomen.

4. Allow your attention to rest in the mere sensation of breathing. (You don't have to control your breath. Just let it come and go naturally.)

5. Every time your mind wanders in thought, gently return it to the breath.

6. As you focus on the process of breathing, you will also perceive sounds, bodily sensations, or emotions. Simply observe these phenomena as they appear in consciousness and then return to the breath.

7. The moment you notice that you have been lost in thought, observe the present thought itself as an object of consciousness. Then return your attention to the breath— or to any sounds or sensations arising in the next moment.

8. Continue in this way until you can merely witness all objects of consciousness—sights, sounds, sensations, emotions, even thoughts themselves—as they arise, change, and pass away.[35]

Possibly the most important benefit of mindfulness is that developing it causes your mental processes to become direct objects of examination. It trains you to suspend judgment on your own thoughts and emotions and view them as the reflexive instincts they are, rather than as incontestable facts.[36][37]

Meditation seems to train you to stop automatically identifying with all of your thoughts, so that, for example, when the thought 'John's a jerk' pops into your head, you don't assume that John necessarily is a jerk. You take the thought as something your brain produced, which may or may not be true, and may or may not be useful.

- **Julia Galef** [38]

As we will soon explore, the thoughts your brain outputs are generated automatically in response to real-world events, generally without your consent. The chains these thoughts form are stories which often embody both the emotional dramatization and banality of a soap opera. The default mind accepts these repetitive tropes as legitimate, and often even identifies with them.[39]

Attention will be represented by the gaps between points in an algorithm. The less attention you are paying to your own mind in any given scenario, the more powerful the links will be. The more attention you are paying, the weaker the links will be. This means that mindfulness can always serve as a psychitectural tool, as awareness of the active algorithms at any time is the first step to modifying them.[40][41] Although his work contains its fair share of new age pseudoscience, Eckhart Tolle captures and distills some of the wisdom which the ancient Eastern sages taught:

> The mind is a superb instrument if used rightly. Used wrongly, however, it becomes very destructive. To put it more accurately, it is not so much that you use your mind wrongly - you usually don't use it at all. It uses you. This is the disease. You believe that you are your mind. This is the delusion. The instrument has taken you over.

> - **Eckhart Tolle**, *The Power of Now*

Siddhārtha Gautama and others have argued that our perceptions of self are illusory - that you are not the self you typically identify as, or even that there is no self at all.[42] The self, like all concepts, is a fluid, man-made construct, and it is best not to take it as a rigid reality. This book will urge you, however, not to eliminate your sense of self, but to **choose to identify as the designer of your mind rather than as your mind itself.** Imagine looking down on your own mind, observing, analyzing, and ultimately shaping and rewiring it.

Stepping off of our rogue psychological roller coaster often provides momentary relief, which is what people mean when they talk about "living in the present." But more importantly, it gives us the distance and clarity needed to actually observe the function of this roller coaster. It allows us to increasingly cease to identify with our minds, and to see our inner experiences for what they are.[43]

Before you unplug, beliefs are simply the truth. Values are good and bad. Goals are automatically worth pursuing. Emotions unconsciously color our experience. Desires are in control. But after unplugging, you gain the ability to step back and observe what is really going on. Once you've unplugged, notice how things look from here. Notice that thoughts are just thoughts, beliefs just beliefs, emotions just emotions. **All are simply the reflexive algorithms of a robotic mind - not reality.**

The mindfulness/meditation movement stops with what I consider to be the prerequisite step of psychological optimization. It tells you to cultivate the objective, non-attached awareness of your own internal processes... and then do it some more. I would speculate that a leading reason some people seem not to benefit from meditation is that they are not instructed to analyze and modify the automatic processes they observe during meditation. **This is exactly what we are going to do.**

The following nine chapters will examine the most commonly problematic algorithms in the cognitive, emotional, and behavioral realms. They will teach you the methods for reprogramming them and nearing your ideal software. You will become a skilled psychitect, and by aiming your constructive efforts toward the structure of your mind, you will learn to terraform it into a truly habitable, delightful place for its sole inhabitant.

Key Takeaways

•   Our minds can be meaningfully compared to computers, consisting of hardware and software.

•   Patterns have been programmed into our psychological software through millions of years of natural selection.

•   Our thoughts, feelings, and actions are not one-off experiences, but flow from a complex, determined system and operate according to reliable principles.

•   There are many ways to alter these default patterns through your hardware using anything from exercise to surgical procedures to psychedelic drugs.

•   But the most powerful and reliable way of optimizing your mind is through its software, through **psychotechnologies,** which are unlocked by your thoughts and actions.

•   Once we have learned the methods, which have been uncovered by both ancient philosophers and cognitive scientists, we can become the designers and programmers of our own minds.

•   Psychological modification is made possible by **Neuroplasticity** - the brain's ability to change and reorganize throughout the life of an individual.

•   You can build new neural pathways and reinforce or diminish old ones through learning, conditioning, and practice. Everything you think and do changes these pathways in some way.

•   Movements like transhumanism, quantified self, and biohacking focus on enhancing intelligence, focus, and energy, but the same spirit of self-optimization can be applied to well-being, adaptivity, and wisdom.

•   By default, our minds are poorly adapted to this world and we lack control over their patterns. Over time, most people become adequate at operating their minds, but it is possible to go far beyond the norm.

•   It is up to us to carve out the path toward the peaks of psychological well-being ourselves.

•   Most people view enlightenment as a mystical state which suddenly appears after years of dedicated practice, but this book proposes that psychological mastery can be approached as a gradual and systematic process like the mastery of a musical instrument.

•   Our mental mistakes and maladaptive tendencies don't stem from a single source, but were selected for different biological purposes, and we can modify and optimize these individual functions, features, and flaws of our minds a la carte.

• Much like playing a musical instrument, we were not built to be enduringly happy, wise, or altruistic, but there are no barriers to reprogramming our psychological operating system toward a new purpose.

• **Psychitecture** is self-directed psychological evolution. The act of deliberately reprogramming your psychological operating system.

• The process of psychitecture, and the structure of the following chapters, is organized into a triad: cognitive, emotional, and behavioral.

• The tendencies and patterns built into our psychological software are called **algorithms**.

• Algorithms are triggered by real-world inputs and chain together to form our habitual state of existence.

• Many of our algorithms serve our genes, but don't serve us, and there is strong evidence that we can deliberately reprogram and restructure these bad algorithms.

• The way your mind is structured will determine the person you become, the life you live, and the fulfillment you realize. When you modify your mind, you edit the operating system at your core and change your personal trajectory. And when you make a persistent occupation of this endeavor, you become the architect of your own character.

• **Metacognition** and the closely related **mindfulness** allow us to step outside of our software and analyze it, and vipassana meditation is one of the best methods for cultivating these qualities.

• Mindfulness weakens the links between algorithms and provides an opportunity to intervene and restructure them. It allows you to pause and examine your algorithms for what they are, rather than simply being subject to them.

• You can choose to identify as the designer of your mind, cultivate metacognition, and begin the process of designing your mind.

2

Cognitive Biases and How to Rewire Them

Understanding Cognitive Bias

Dogmatism is the greatest of mental obstacles to human happiness.

- **Bertrand Russell**, *The Conquest of Happiness*

We begin our psychitectural journey in the cognitive realm. Without mastery of this realm, our minds are riddled with false beliefs, recurring biases, and dissonance between our models of reality and reality itself. But the importance of the cognitive realm does not stop here. **Cognition is the gatekeeper of virtually every function of our software.**

Our decisions, emotions, and actions are all rooted in our beliefs, so if we do not first work to develop clear and objective thinking, our distorted thoughts and beliefs will sabotage our psychitectural efforts.[1][2][3] We will see why a lack of self-awareness and rationality will result in bad decisions and a faulty compass for navigating your life. We will learn why failing to detect and correct false beliefs and distorted cognition is detrimental to emotional well-being. And we will come to understand why a lack of clarity into your values will prevent you from realizing the deep well-being you are capable of attaining.

Our chief cognitive concern is to perceive reality as clearly and accurately as possible. To develop a functional map which aligns as closely as possible to the territory it aims to portray. This chapter will cover many of the mechanisms behind our beliefs and cognitive tendencies, as well as the methods for optimizing and reprogramming them, and many of the concepts and methods covered here will be foundational to those in later chapters.

There may be some things you just know are true. If someone asked you how sure you are, you would answer one-hundred percent. But the truth is the feelings of absolute certainty we have about some things are completely independent of the actual property of truth. **These feelings are experienced in entirely different brain regions from our rational faculties**. We determine what we are sure of intuitively, and then we use reason to justify it.[4]

> Despite how certainty feels, it is neither a conscious choice nor even a thought process. Certainty and similar states of "knowing what we know" arise out of involuntary brain mechanisms that, like love or anger, function independently of reason.
>
> - **Robert A. Burton**, On Being Certain

Though it may be the most brilliantly complex thing in the universe, the human mind is riddled with false assumptions, perceptions, and beliefs. Everyone knows this, but few people recognize the full extent of distortion in their thinking. If you are like most people, you look around and see others who are confused, dogmatic, and irrational. You, on the other hand, have mostly found the correct beliefs and learned to think clearly. If everyone else would just listen to you, the world would be a much better place. But we tend to see the distorted thinking in everyone but ourselves. Even when we genuinely want to think and see clearly, our desires and emotions dominate us beneath our awareness.

We feel strongly that some things are true and others are false. The problem is that truth can be tricky. Everyone has had the disorienting experience of finding out they were wrong about something of which they felt certain. And many have grappled with the fact that every statement of apparent truth can be made "more true" by providing a more comprehensive and detailed explanation. In order to get to the bottom of this thing we call truth, it can be helpful to make a distinction between the map and the territory. The territory represents what is real independent of our beliefs and interpretations.[5]

Territory

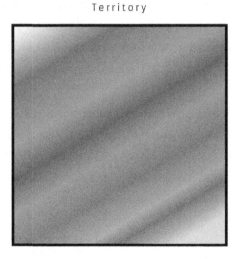

The territory is infinitely and incomprehensibly complex. In order to grapple with it, humans have to convert it to a form of lossy compression called concepts, and we organize these concepts into our belief system, or map.

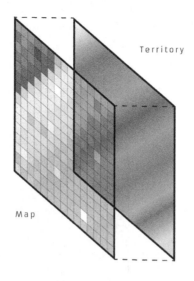

Just as a geographical map would be useless if it contained every single detail of the territory it portrays, our belief system must simplify the territory to be comprehensible or useful, compromising accuracy in the process. A child's belief system is crude and pixelated compared to an adult's.

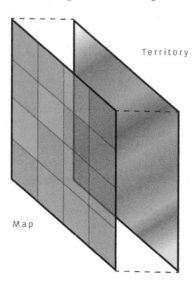

As we develop cognitively, we continually reassess our beliefs, sharpen our distinctions, and accumulate more refined and less pixelated concepts. But concepts and models, even the most sophisticated, are always inherently pixelated, and our beliefs are always incomplete. So it's possible for us to develop models which more and more closely approximate the truth without ever reaching "perfect truth."

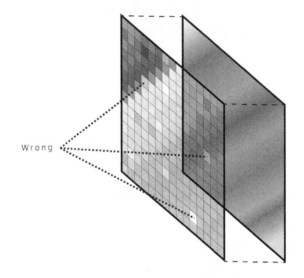

But beliefs can also be wrong. And often when they are, they are the product of a systematic mental cause. Cognitive algorithms are sometimes known as **inferences**. Here is how we will represent cognitive algorithms in their most basic form:

input

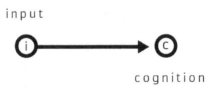

cognition

It can be read either as "if x then y," or "x, therefore y." The input is a starting premise or raw perception about the world. The output is a cognition - a thought or belief. These algorithms are triggered and run automatically, and the rules they follow are uniform. Sometimes that is perfectly fine, useful even. But many of these algorithms are fundamentally flawed and distorted, which can have consequences ranging from amusing to catastrophic. These faulty algorithms will be shown with an angled portion representing the distortion:

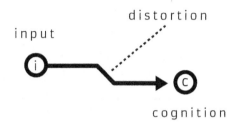

These bad algorithms are generally called **biases**, or systematic flaws in our thinking. Biases are reflexive inferences which invalidly flow from premises without our conscious awareness - hidden patterns which result in mistaken beliefs and faulty decisions and will continue to result in the same mistakes indefinitely unless they are identified and programmed out. We will cover many biases and the principles behind them throughout this chapter, so feel free to skim for the main ideas and come back to the specifics later.

Some of the simplest and easiest to recognize biases fall into the category of logical fallacies. Take this argument:

All humans are mammals
Ryan Seacrest is a mammal
Therefore, Ryan Seacrest is a human.

This is called the **fallacy of the undistributed middle**. Just because all humans are mammals doesn't mean all mammals are humans, and just because we know a conclusion to be true does not mean it logically follows from its premises (**belief bias**). Given our premises, it is entirely possible that the beloved television personality could be another type of primate, or even a large rodent. And it has been found that 70% of university students get this type of problem wrong when challenged with it.[6]

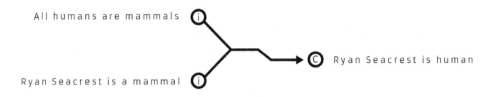

All humans are mammals

Ryan Seacrest is a mammal

Ryan Seacrest is human

We don't often hear such formal arguments in ordinary life, but anyone who follows politics or media is guaranteed to encounter informal fallacies regularly. These arguments often succeed in distracting the listener from the relevant aspects of an argument. An **ad hominem fallacy**, for example, attacks the character or authority of the person making an argument rather than the argument itself. An **appeal to consequences** distracts from the validity of an argument and focuses on whether the implications of that argument are desirable or not. And an **appeal to emotion** may use persuasive rhetoric and anecdotes to stir up fear, indignation, or sympathy in the listeners - glossing over bad logic or insufficient evidence.

There are many other common logical fallacies. A **slippery slope** argument claims that a small step will inevitably lead to a whole chain of undesirable consequences, such as parents arguing that if they let their daughter learn a card trick, there will be no stopping her from pursuing a career as an illusionist. A **false dichotomy** claims that if one extreme is rejected (capitalism has no flaws), another extreme must be the only alternative (communism it is). And the **post hoc fallacy** causes us to assume that correlation equates to causation, such as the belief that the sun rising actually *causes* your drinking problem.

Once you have familiarized yourself with the full list of common fallacies, they start appearing everywhere. It is hard to imagine what political debates would look like if candidates knew they would be called out for every red herring or faulty generalization committed.

Not all of our biases are errors in logic per se, and some of the trickiest mistakes occur in the places we don't even think to look. Our view of the past, for example, is far less accurate than we generally assume. We all know our memory declines as we age, and we frequently fail to recall things we once knew. But contrary to popular belief, memories do not neutrally depict events as they happened, but reconstruct and change those events every time they are evoked.[7]

Have you ever looked back at your emails or social media posts from years ago and found it hard to believe that was you? **Consistency bias** causes us to conform our views of our past actions and attitudes to those of our present. We remember events that are humorous, disturbing, or otherwise emotionally salient much more easily than those that are mundane, even when these qualities don't align with the importance of the issue. Memories can be fabricated, or even intentionally implanted in another person's mind.

Our view of the future is even more distorted, as we are also imperfect in our assessments of probability and prediction. We tend to think past events affect future odds when they don't, such as believing a streak of flipping heads or scoring in basketball makes it more likely (**hot hand fallacy**) or less likely (**gambler's fallacy**) that we will do so again in the future. And have you ever heard someone defend dangerous behaviors by making the argument that some people are killed because they were wearing seatbelts, or some smokers live to be 100? We sometimes **neglect probability** entirely and make decisions based only on anecdotal evidence.

Our present evaluations, even the ones we reflect deeply on, are much less coherent than we tend to think. We overvalue information which is readily available (**availability bias**), presented first (**primacy bias**), frequently (**frequency bias**), or recently (**recency bias**). And various expressions of loss aversion, such as the **endowment effect** cause us to demand more to give something up than we would pay to acquire it.

> Homo sapiens is a storytelling animal, that thinks in stories rather than in numbers or graphs, and believes that the universe itself works like a story, replete with heroes and villains, conflicts and resolutions, climaxes and happy endings.

> - **Yuval Noah Harari**, *21 Lessons for the 21st Century*

Our minds were built to find patterns. Pattern recognition is highly advantageous from a biological perspective, as we would not be able to identify predators, find food, or recognize our family members without it.[8] But our brains have limited bandwidth, so they have to cut corners. We make hasty judgments, oversimplify the factors at play, and quickly construct narratives and explanations for the complex outcomes in our world. Of course every story, including the one this book is telling, is false - in the sense that it necessarily oversimplifies reality, but we have a tendency to cling to our stories as if they were perfect representations of reality. In pathological extremes, this delusional over-recognition of patterns manifests in disorders like schizophrenia.[9]

Some light examples of pattern recognition gone haywire are found in optical illusions and **pareidolia**, the tendency to see patterns like faces in abstract images or hear voices in noise. We hear our house creak and believe we've encountered a ghost, attributing agency where there is none. Some more concerning examples are some of the heuristics and generalizations we regularly employ. We **stereotype**, assuming that all individuals in a group share certain characteristics which may only be true of the group on average or may be completely fictional.

The **clustering, frequency, and recency illusions** cause us to find meaning in a repetition or grouping of similar things, such as a man who believes the universe wants him to apply for a new job because he hears the words "multi-level marketing" three times in one week. Our tendency to seek meaning in things which may be entirely devoid of it is at the root of superstition and conspiracy thinking. It is also at the root of the most destructive ideologies in history. **Far too many wars and atrocities have been committed because powerful people were overly confident in the oversimplified narrative systems to which they subscribed**, whether in the form of a political system, a prejudice, or a religion.

The most concerning aspect of these biases is that they can chain together, and their effects can be compounded. Beliefs don't exist in isolation. They are entangled with one another, so changing one belief may threaten a large portion of the full map. Belief systems are essentially complex chains of cognitive algorithms, and when those algorithms are heavily biased, **they make up massively warped worldviews.** When people take action according to their distorted worldviews, they can cause great damage and harm in the name of doing good. (Belief systems may be simplified for demonstration purposes)

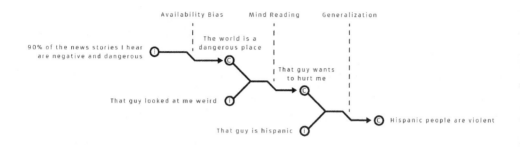

Methods for Cognitive Debiasing

You should take the approach that you're wrong. Your goal is to be less wrong.

- Elon Musk

Perhaps as you read over these biases you accepted consistently irrational tendencies we all share. Or maybe, you thought to yourself, "Well, I can see that most people would have that bias, but I don't think I have that one." Well, I've got another one for you. **Bias blind spot** refers to the tendency to believe one is immune to the same biases which plague others.

The question you may be wondering now is, how can we program out our faulty cognitive algorithms? Removing biases is not a simple task, but there are a few leverage points which allow us to intercept and reprogram these algorithms.

If you want to overcome distorted cognitive algorithms, the first and most obvious step is to familiarize yourself with the most common biases found across the human race. This chapter only provides a primer on cognitive biases - not an exhaustive list by any means. You can find a more exhaustive list in the Wikipedia entry for cognitive biases,[11] and John Manoogian III and Buster Benson created a nice diagram that breaks them down.[12]

But even these excellent resources remain hopelessly incomplete. Spending some time on the blog LessWrong will demonstrate to you just how complex the web of human bias really is. You will need to make a discipline of studying the biases you discover from a variety of sources, as well as uncovering them within your own mind. Memorize them until you can recite them in your sleep, and learn the types of situations which can trigger them. **But do not assume that awareness of a bias makes you immune to it**. In some, but not all cases, being aware that a certain bias exists has proven to counter the bias.[13][14]

Correcting a bias will typically require an awareness that a bias-triggering situation has arisen in your life. You need to build the habit of noticing these situations, which is largely a function of metacognitive awareness. Mindfulness has been found to decrease cognitive bias by bringing deliberate attention to otherwise habitual cognitive patterns.[15] Being aware of times when you might be particularly prone to mistakes, such as when you are tired, angry, or even hungry can also help you counteract your biases, or at least postpone decisions until you are in a more optimal state.

Before you can question your intuitions, you have to realize that what your mind's eye is looking at is an intuition—some cognitive algorithm, as seen from the inside—rather than a direct perception of the Way Things Really Are.

- **Eliezer Yudkowsky**, "How An Algorithm Feels From Inside"

Once you are aware of a bias or bias-triggering situation, your next goal will be to design a better alternative algorithm to the faulty one. Let's look at an example algorithm known as the **planning fallacy**, which causes us to (often greatly) underestimate the amount of time certain tasks will take to complete. This algorithm will lead you to habitually underestimate timelines for your entire life and turn you into a perpetual deadline-misser. But it is possible to program this bias out and solve it for good. "When do you think you can have this done by?" someone asks you.

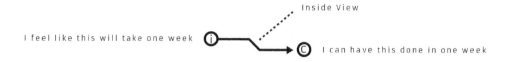

Under normal circumstances, the planning fallacy would be activated: You would consult your intuitions and output the conclusion "one week from now." We'll call this mode of reasoning the "inside view." But if you have sufficient metacognitive awareness and familiarity with this bias, you will have the opportunity to step in, design a counter-algorithm, and rewire the bias, which we call **cognitive revision**.

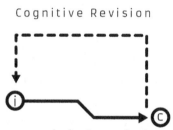

Daniel Kahneman, a psychologist and pioneer in cognitive bias research, suggests a workaround for this particular bias:

> Using such distributional information from other ventures similar to that being forecasted is called taking an 'outside view' and is the cure to the planning fallacy.

> - **Daniel Kahneman**, *Thinking Fast and Slow*

In other words, if you have to determine how long a project will take you, don't look at how long you feel like it will take. Look at how long this type of project typically takes you, how long other people take to do the same type of task, and how these compare with your intuitions.[16] If you feel that you will be done in a week but experience says it will actually take you three, this will probably be a much closer guess. In this case, you are replacing the algorithm "If I feel like it will take one week, then I believe it will" with the algorithm, "If this type of project usually takes me three times longer than my intuitions suggest, then I believe it will take three weeks."

Eventually, this outside view will become your habitual approach to estimating deadlines, and the original algorithm will have officially been reprogrammed.

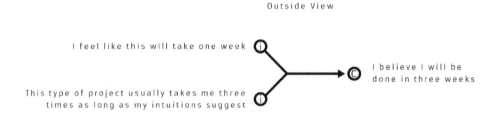

Outside View

I feel like this will take one week

I believe I will be done in three weeks

This type of project usually takes me three times as long as my intuitions suggest

This example makes the process seem simple, but every bias is different and may require you to design a different creative solution. Though lots of research has been done on cognitive biases, the process of removing them is fairly new territory. Numerous studies have confirmed the efficacy of debiasing methods, but no single process has been shown to be universally effective.[17][18][19]

There are many thinking tools you can add to your arsenal of alternate algorithms. By internalizing models and principles for specific domains of reasoning, you can replace old bias patterns with better, more accurate ones. There are many logical, statistical, and economic principles you can learn to maximize accurate beliefs and good decisions. Coming to grasp principles like **probability theory**, counterintuitive ideas like **compound interest**, and cognitive tools like **systems thinking** can transform the quality of your judgments.

Bayesian reasoning has been called the gold standard of rationality. Although there is a formal theorem for calculating Bayes' rule when precise numbers are available, the type of reasoning it can be most readily applied to is far less formal. The root of many biases is the failure to take prior probabilities into account when forming beliefs. A commonly given example is that when trying to predict the profession of a shy and timid individual, people assign a far higher likelihood to the possibility that he is a librarian than a salesman. The reasoning goes something like this:

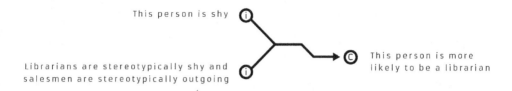

This person is shy

Librarians are stereotypically shy and salesmen are stereotypically outgoing

This person is more likely to be a librarian

This default algorithm is biased, as it fails to consider how common librarians are compared to salesmen. As it turns out, there are seventy-five times as many salesmen in the population as there are librarians.[20]

With Bayes' Rule in your thinking toolkit, you can replace this type of algorithm with a more accurate one. To make use of **Bayesian revision**, or updating, you would assign a likelihood to an existing hypothesis or belief and probabilities to reflect those likelihoods. When you come across new evidence, you try to determine how much this new information should alter your confidence.

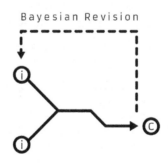

Bayesian Revision

In the case above, you would first estimate the ratio of librarians to salesmen, and then adjust this estimate based on the person's temperament.

I would estimate there are 50x more salesman than librarians

I would estimate that a shy person is 2X more likely to be a librarian than average

This person is more likely to be a salesman

In each case, you must be aware of the relevant faulty bias, pause and notice that you are in a bias-triggering scenario, and design and implement a better alternative algorithm. You need to make it so the *same* type of input will trigger a *different* algorithm in the future. Once you have programmed out a certain type of bias in a few different scenarios, the more rational algorithm can become your habitual response. You can internalize the better pathways of reasoning and gradually restructure your worldview to resemble reality more and more.

You need to work to build the habit of noticing the indicators of flawed thinking and beliefs. The feelings of confusion, surprise, and lack of clarity surrounding some views should sound alarm bells, triggering you to further investigate. Consider the reasons why your initial judgments might be flawed before forming important views. Simply adding the prompt "**consider the opposite**" to the default algorithm has been found to counter anchoring, overconfidence, and hindsight bias.[21] Some biases can be mitigated or eliminated by finding outside factual information, so take every opportunity to distance yourself and put your reasoning and beliefs to objective tests to remove as much human bias from the equation as possible.

> Not-knowing is true knowledge.
> Presuming to know is a disease.
> First realize that you are sick;
> Then you can move toward health.

> -**Lao Tzu**, *Tao Te Ching*

Understanding Motivated Bias

Humans were not directly selected to process information, nor to store it, learn it, attend to it—nor even, in fact, to think.

- **Handbook of Evolutionary Psychology**

People who have learned of these biases and the methods for countering them often refer to themselves as critical thinkers, freethinkers, or rationalists. These people often make use of the debiasing methods we have covered to attempt to see the world more clearly, and these methods can be effective in the right circumstances. But the counterintuitive truth that has become clear to me is that **critical thinking skills are not enough to prevent being deeply biased.**

Most people recognize the need for critical thinking. Even most schools and universities try to teach these skills. But they miss the point. Learning critical thinking skills is no more likely to cause someone to think critically than it is to provide them with ammunition for arguing against whatever ideas they don't want to accept. **The tools of rationality are identical to the tools of rationalization.**

If you wish to program out your biased algorithms, you must understand their deeper underlying principles. Many of our biases, including some mentioned above, seem to be artifacts of the simple truth that our minds were not built to understand, remember, and predict complex, modern phenomena with perfect accuracy. These goals are all biologically beside the point. But some of our biases can be linked directly to biological pressures, meaning **it was in some way advantageous to our genes for us to systematically misperceive reality.**[22] The most pernicious biases have this in common: they stem from desire. I refer to these as **motivated biases.** We may want to develop an accurate view of reality, but this **will to genuinely understand is imperceptibly overpowered by other motivations.**

In these cases, we can modify our representation of the cognitive algorithm to include this role our motivations play. Here, a desire is playing a major direct role in the cognitive distortion.

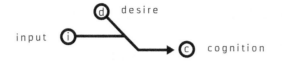

Desires are always present, but we don't show them in the diagram when they are in alignment with our explicit goals - in this case, clear reasoning. When shown in this type of diagram, the desire is misaligned with our goals to think clearly.

Many of our desires, or drives, relate to the world and how we view it. We desire for the world to make sense to us, so we strip it down and make our decisions based on our simplified simulations which may bear little resemblance to reality (**attribute substitution**).[23] We desire for the world to be fair and just, so we assume victims of injustice must have deserved their fate (**just-world hypothesis**).[24] And we desire a positive future, so we allow wishful thinking to determine our predictions (**optimism bias**), sometimes going to the extent of completely ignoring the negative (**ostrich effect**).

And as always, these biases can compound and result in harmful effects.[25]

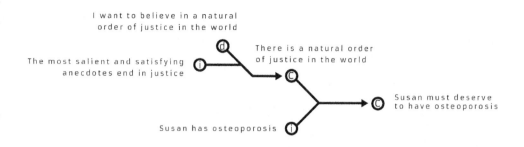

Another set of desires which colors our perceptions is of a social nature. We speak of young people being impressionable as if adults had all grown out of this trait. But we are all far more socially impressionable than we would like to admit to ourselves. Just as our brains are optimized to find useful patterns over accurate ones, we were built to seek companionship and community over truth.[26] The **bandwagon effect** refers to our tendency to come to conclusions and make decisions based on what is popular, though we often find ways to rationalize these decisions to ourselves. We are swayed by authority and social proof. We acquire our beliefs through dogmatic inheritance and imitation.

As a human being, you are embedded in the collective mesh of society. You are not wired to develop impeccably clear views, rational insights, and wisdom. You are built to inherit your views, values, and judgment from your tribe - to flow with the wave of your culture. We want to belong. We want to be accepted, respected, and liked, and this desire bends our beliefs to its will. The problem is that this desire, if unacknowledged and unchecked, can result in delusional decisions and deviation from our values.

Some of the most pervasive motivations behind our biases stem not from how we want to see the world, or how we want others to see us, but **how we want to see ourselves**. The desires related to our sense of identity can be the hardest to change.[27]

Our desires to be special and to maintain a positive view of ourselves result in the over-inflation of our own positive traits. The **fundamental attribution error** and **self-serving bias** cause us to attribute our own positive behaviors and successes, as well as the failure of others, to individual character. Correspondingly, we blame our negative behaviors and failures, and the successes of others, on luck and circumstance. **Illusory superiority** is the overestimation of one's positive qualities and the underestimation of negative ones.[27]

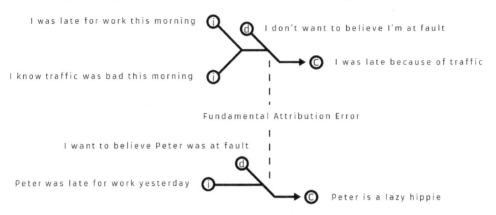

Our desire to be in control of our lives creates the **illusion of control**. An interesting finding is that people with clinical depression believe they have less control over external events, demonstrating a more accurate and less biased perception than healthy people in this regard. This may, however, be the effect of the **negativity bias** characteristic of depression counterbalancing the original bias.[27]

The desire which quite possibly distorts our view the most also has to do with our identity, but this one poses so well as the desire for genuine truth that it is incredibly hard to spot. I'm talking about **the desire to be right**. The minute we form a belief, we start developing attachments to it. From this point forward, it is our mind's default behavior to stack up the evidence in its favor. Our goal in an argument is almost never to determine what is correct, but to prove to ourselves and our opponent that we were right all along.[28]

Confirmation bias is responsible for the fact that we tend to look only for information that confirms our existing theories, beliefs, and worldview at the expense of those that conflict with them. We get so attached to these views that even when conflicting evidence is forced upon us, it often only makes us defensive, strengthening our original belief (**backfire effect**). This tendency ultimately results in groups on two sides of an issue slowly moving further and further apart, known as **attitude polarization**.

Worse, the modern world reinforces biases by structuring incentives so as to confirm our beliefs. Search engines, entertainment platforms, and social media websites are rewarded for getting clicks and views, so it is in their interest to pander to the desires of their readers rather than to determine the truth. The digital algorithms distributing information further distort our cognitive algorithms by **funneling us into reality tunnels and echo chambers.**[29]

Methods for Motivational Debiasing

> The truth may be puzzling. It may take some work to grapple with. It may be counterintuitive. It may contradict deeply held prejudices. It may not be consonant with what we desperately want to be true. But our preferences do not determine what's true.

> - **Carl Sagan**, *Wonder and Skepticism*

The second, deeper layer of cognitive psychitecture is motivational. Motivated biases are not little bugs in the system. They are the system functioning as intended. I am not just talking to conspiracy theorists or religious fanatics or political ideologues here. **Everyone has cherished beliefs.** And we can't simply will these beliefs away. **We have to unplug the desires that perpetuate them.**

In order to do this, you need the habit of not only noticing the triggers for common biases, but of taking stock of your desires to hold certain beliefs, and the intensity of these desires. Notice which ideas you are attached to and which ones you resist. The areas you tend to turn your curiosity away from - that make you defensive when they are called into question. Perhaps you feel highly resistant to questioning a certain belief because you are a part of a group which is based on that belief. Or maybe you feel like one belief provides you with a critical coping mechanism - one that you would be lost without. Write these observations down.

You can then use the method known as **Socratic questioning** to identify potential holes in your beliefs. Treat your beliefs as if they were someone else's beliefs you were arguing against. Build the best argument you can against them, and identify the assumptions and weak points of your views. What evidence do I have for this belief? Could I be misinterpreting the evidence? Can I think of any counter evidence? Continue to ask probing questions and flag the beliefs which may not be fully supported.[30]

A related approach to wrangling desires is called **counteraction**. This tactic entails attempting to cultivate an equal and opposite desire to balance the first one. When you have an equal desire for two opposing possibilities, you will be able to evaluate them objectively according to evidence because either possibility will suit you just fine.

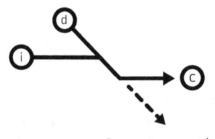

Counteraction

If you believe the world is fundamentally just, and you notice that you strongly *want* to hold this belief, consider possible advantages to the belief that there is no such innate justice. Though this belief forces us to confront our own vulnerability, it also opens up our ability to understand and empathize with victims of misfortune instead of blaming them. It can provide purpose by giving us something to work toward instead of lulling us into the impression that everything is as good as it can be.

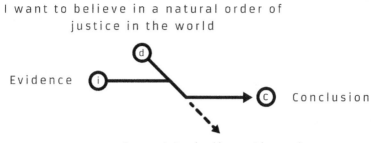

I want to believe in a natural order of justice in the world

Evidence — Conclusion

I want to believe there is no natural order of justice in the world

The goal here is not to switch to the alternate belief, but to confront it and realize that it wouldn't be so horrible, and might even be good if it were true. Then you can decide on beliefs based on what the evidence suggests is most likely. I am not here to tell you which specific beliefs are true or false. It is my goal to encourage you, on behalf of the many great psychitectural thinkers, to seek truth wherever it leads.

Evidence — Conclusion

There is a common conviction that some false beliefs may be worth believing in. It may be fun to check your horoscopes from time to time, even to believe them, but the ability to think for yourself and differentiate between fact and fiction has much higher stakes than your entertainment. Irrationality, dogmatism, and ignorance are the cause of a massive proportion of global problems.[31]

People are killed every year because they believe that completely untested medicine will heal them, or that proven medicine is more likely to harm them than help.[32] The reason our environmental problems haven't been solved is because people have been fed, and have swallowed the lie that these problems do not exist or pose no threat to us.[33] Major decisions are made for millions based on deeply flawed ideas and deliberate deception. And far too many atrocities have been caused by actors with perfectly good intentions and unquestioned ideologies.[34]

The dangers of not thinking clearly are much greater now than ever before. It's not that there's something new in our way of thinking – it's that credulous and confused thinking can be much more lethal in ways it was never before.

- Carl Sagan, 1996

As technology becomes exponentially more powerful, the consequences for faulty thinking and dogmatism will rise exponentially along with it. Nuclear weapons, bioengineering, nanotechnology, and artificial intelligence are all quickly advancing. All will become more powerful, less expensive to create, and easier to wield. And all will pose threats to the very existence of humanity. If we are unable to conquer the human tendencies to believe and act according to dogma and desire, **the same forces which cause destruction and war today will cause total extinction tomorrow.**[35]

But even the most selfish sociopath has plenty of reason to view the world as clearly as possible. Rationality is a core building block of wisdom. Good decisions in your life, your relationships, and your career or business depend on the ability to think clearly and learn properly. On his excellent blog, Wait But Why, Tim Urban provides an analysis of Elon Musk, the billionaire founder of Tesla and SpaceX.[36] He suggests a key factor of the entrepreneur's success is his ongoing endeavor to optimize his own mind:

> Musk sees people as computers, and he sees his brain software as the most important product he owns—and since there aren't companies out there designing brain software, he designed his own, beta tests it every day, and makes constant updates. That's why he's so outrageously effective, why he can disrupt multiple huge industries at once, why he can learn so quickly, strategize so cleverly, and visualize the future so clearly.

In this mindset, we see the essence of the psychitect. Most people strive to preserve their beliefs at all costs - to protect them from the constant threats that seek to undermine them. But if you are a psychitect, all beliefs are really just temporary experiments. Every day is a mental beta test - an opportunity to iterate, expand, and upgrade your cognitive software. To uncover and question assumptions, test new conceptual models, and throw the obsolete ones out. No belief is safe.

> The strength of a person's spirit [can be] measured by how much truth he could tolerate... to what extent he needs to have it diluted, disguised, sweetened.

> - **Friedrich Nietzsche**, *Beyond Good and Evil*

If your happiness is dependent on false beliefs, it means you have become reliant on coping structures which have been built on a bad foundation, and as soon as storms come in and reality crashes against your shoddy models of it, you'll be hit with pain and confusion. Anything that contradicts your beliefs, real world experiences or the arguments of others, will present a threat to your identity and will damage your balance of mind.[37]

You can choose to take on a slow and gradual process of rebuilding your foundational beliefs and replacing your current coping structures with those more closely resembling reality. Your mind is not a delicate garden that needs to be protected from all threats, but a powerful, antifragile immune system. And by questioning all of your beliefs and assumptions, **you can inoculate yourself against the pain and confusion of facing the facts, and your worldview can become more and more robust.**[38]

The conclusions you form can be troubling at first. But after you have taken your hard-to-swallow pills, you get to enjoy their invigorating effects. You will grow to find beauty, comfort, and joy in the understanding which is thought by some to be unbearable. You will not only learn to live with the truth, but to assimilate it. To make it a part of you and feel immense gratitude and awe for it.

The key to overcoming your biases is found deep within your intentions. Overcoming and optimizing yourself must be more deeply embedded in your desires, in your identity, than the desires that threaten to undermine it. The desires to be competent, to be unique, and even to be right, must all fall short of the desire for self-mastery. **You must come to pride yourself, not on the accuracy of your current beliefs, but on your willingness to abandon your beliefs for new, more accurate ones.** When you insist on finding the real truth first and learning to love it second, you can become the master of your own cognition.

Key Takeaways

• Our psychitectural journey begins in the cognitive realm, which is the gate-keeper of virtually every function of our software.

• The human mind is riddled with false assumptions, perceptions, and beliefs, and this affects not only our reasoning and wisdom, but our actions and emotional well-being.

• Cognitive self-mastery is embodied by a map of reality that aligns as closely as possible to that reality.

• Cognitive algorithms can be called **inferences**, and they can be perpetually distorted by **cognitive biases**.

• Biases can include formal and informal logical fallacies, but they also distort our memory of the past, our prediction of the future, and our perception of the present.

• Our minds were built to find patterns, so we make hasty judgments, over-simplify the factors at play, and quickly construct narratives and explanations for the complex outcomes in our world.

• Belief systems are essentially complex chains of cognitive algorithms, and when those algorithms are heavily biased, they make up massively warped worldviews.

• There are proven methods for removing and mitigating biases.

• Familiarize yourself with all of the common biases, which can be adequate to remove some but not all biases.

- Increase your awareness of bias-triggering situations by building metacognitive awareness and trying to identify these scenarios in your life.
- Once you are aware of a bias or bias-triggering situation, design a better alternative algorithm to the faulty one.
- **Cognitive revision** is the act of replacing a habitual cognitive response to an input with a better, less distorted conclusion or thought.
- One example known as the planning fallacy can be programmed out by replacing your intuitive prediction of timelines with objective data about how long certain activities usually take.
- Thinking tools like Bayesian reasoning can be used to revise certain sets of biased algorithms.
- Try to notice the feelings of confusion, surprise, and lack of clarity surrounding some views, consider the reasons why your initial judgments might be flawed, find outside factual information when possible, and remind yourself to consider the opposite to your default algorithms.
- Critical thinking skills are not enough to prevent being deeply biased, because some of our biases are perpetuated by our desires. If we strongly want to believe something, we will simply use our thinking tools to rationalize these beliefs.
- To correct these **motivated biases**, we have to identify and alter our desires to hold certain beliefs.
- We desire for the world to make sense to us, so we strip it down and make our decisions based on our simplified simulations.
- We want to belong and be accepted, respected, and liked by other members of our community, and this desire bends our beliefs to its will.
- We desire to maintain a positive view of ourselves, which results in the over-inflation of our own positive traits.
- And of course we all want to be right, so we stack up evidence that our current views are correct rather than objectively evaluating the evidence to see what is actually correct.
- To reprogram motivated biases, you must build the habit of taking stock of your desires to hold certain beliefs, and the intensity of these desires.
- You can then use **Socratic questioning**, treating your beliefs as if they were

someone else's beliefs you were arguing against and build the best argument you can against them.

• You can also use **counteraction** to cultivate an equal and opposite desire to balance the first one so you are indifferent to the conclusions the evidence leads you to.

• The stakes of clear thinking are high, as irrational and biased beliefs are responsible for most of the world's increasingly dangerous problems.

• Good decisions in your life, your relationships, and your career or business depend, among other things, on the ability to think clearly and learn properly.

• As a psychitect, you should be constantly beta-testing your belief system, taking every opportunity to iterate, expand, and upgrade your cognitive software.

• Though some people avoid considering uncomfortable possibilities, doing so will inoculate you against the pain and confusion of facing the facts, and your worldview can become more and more robust.

• If you come to pride yourself, not on the accuracy of your current beliefs, but on your willingness to abandon them for new, more accurate ones, you will not only learn to live with the truth, but to feel immense gratitude and awe for it.

3

Values and the Methods of Introspection

Do You Want What You Want?

It isn't normal to know what we want. It is a rare and difficult psychological achievement.

- **Abraham Maslow**, *Motivation and Personality*

So maybe our beliefs about the external world are flawed, but if there is one thing we know, surely it is what is best for us, right? We tend to take for granted that we know what we want. Much like the beliefs we examined in the previous chapter, we all like to think we are directing our lives well. But the evidence suggests it is surprisingly easy to be delusional about our own self-interest.

Though there is less research on them, ancient and modern thinkers have uncovered many errors we all share which limit our acquisition of wisdom. **The algorithms which most often lead people astray in life are not simply distortions of memory, prediction, or pattern recognition in the external world, but distortions of introspection.** And now that we have laid the groundwork for the mechanisms that bias our beliefs about the outer universe, we will build on it to reveal the biases of the inner universe.

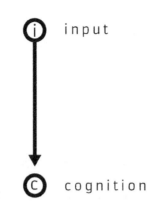

input

cognition

We saw in the previous chapter that the **illusion of control** causes us to believe we have more control over our circumstances than we actually do, and to attribute unrelated outcomes to our own actions.[1] But we are also wired to falsely believe we know which outcomes would make us happy. Anyone who has seen a film in which a protagonist's most desired wishes are granted by a genie or David Bowie can tell you the problem with this confidence. Our tendency to reduce complex situations to oversimplified simulations plays out in our pursuit of happiness, where it gives us a false confidence in our prediction of wanted or unwanted outcomes.

The butterfly effect states that there are certain systems which are so complex and sensitive to initial data that precise prediction of outcomes becomes impossible. This theory explains why our ability to predict the weather is still so mediocre despite our advancement in other areas. It has been said that "a butterfly flapping its wings in Brazil can cause a tornado in Texas."[2] But this difficulty in complex prediction applies to our happiness as well, and the bias here is our tendency to vastly simplify the complexity of these real-world events. Philosopher Alan Watts recounts a relevant Chinese parable:

> Once upon a time there was a Chinese farmer whose horse ran away. That evening, all of his neighbors came around to commiserate. They said, "We are so sorry to hear your horse has run away. This is most unfortunate." The farmer said,

"Maybe." The next day the horse came back bringing seven wild horses with it, and in the evening everybody came back and said, "Oh, isn't that lucky. What a great turn of events. You now have eight horses!" The farmer again said, "Maybe."

The following day his son tried to break one of the horses, and while riding it, he was thrown and broke his leg. The neighbors then said, "Oh dear, that's too bad," and the farmer responded, "Maybe." The next day the conscription officers came around to conscript people into the army, and they rejected his son because he had a broken leg. Again all the neighbors came around and said, "Isn't that great!" Again, he said, "Maybe."[3]

We often look back on past events and see them with the same wise perspective we see in the Chinese farmer. We see that the things we thought were so terrible at the time actually ended up being good for us in the long run. But almost no one talks about their lives in the moment with this type of insightful ambiguity. We are always sure of what is desirable or undesirable at the time. We insist on chasing what we want, oversimplifying the complex mechanics of the world to an absurd degree. Relying on our internal life-simulator to guide us through life is like relying on a child's crayon map to guide us through New York City.

Watts adds:

The whole process of nature is an integrated process of immense complexity, and **it's really impossible to tell whether anything that happens in it is good or bad** — because you never know what will be the consequence of the misfortune; or, you never know what will be the consequences of good fortune.

The psychological study of affective forecasting shows that we not only oversimplify the world, but our prediction of our own emotional state. Daniel Gilbert, a leading psychologist studying affective forecasting, discovered that humans share an algorithm he called **impact bias**, which causes us to poorly forecast how we will feel about a certain event or decision, how intense that feeling will be, and how long it will last. In other words, **our internal emotion-simulator is just as flawed as our life-simulator.**[4]

In his book, *Stumbling on Happiness*, Gilbert names several principles behind our shortcomings. The principle of **realism** is "the belief that things are in reality as they appear to be in the mind." Our brains constantly weave their biases and fabrications into reality, filling in the gaps so quickly and seamlessly that we don't even notice anything is off. If you are trying to decide between attending a college in San Francisco or Seattle, your brain will start conjuring mental images of both experiences. The image of sunny beaches and happiness in California may be so lifelike that you fail to consider that temperature isn't the only determinant of your well-being.[5]

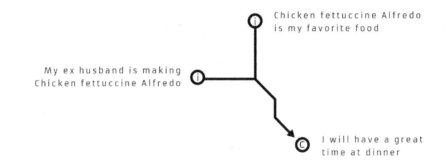

The principle he calls **presentism** is "the tendency for current experience to influence one's views of the past and the future." After we've eaten a massive stack of pancakes, we can't imagine being hungry again. When we are happy, we have a very hard time imagining what it would be like to be sad, and vice versa. So when you're having a blast cruising in your Hummer stretch limo, it will be hard to relate to your future self whose house is under water.[6]

Rationalization is "the act of causing something to be or to seem reasonable." We experience anxiety and dread around adversity and loss, believing they will cause us to feel worse and for longer than they actually will. Our emotional predictions don't account for the psychological defenses that allow us to reason away inescapable circumstances. Gilbert provides numerous examples of unlucky individuals, from twins conjoined at the head, to prisoners, to people paralyzed from the neck down. And he points out that despite how terrible we think all these fates are, all of these people he lists claim to be deeply satisfied. Studies have shown that one year after their respective incidents, lottery winners and paraplegics have roughly equal levels of life-satisfaction despite our deeply contrary intuitions.[7]

All of these findings tell us that we are bad at achieving our desired outcomes, bad at accounting for the complexity of those outcomes, and bad at predicting our emotional reactions to them. The human condition is starting to make perfect sense. We're just really bad at things.

The Right Way to Introspect

So what is the moral of this story? That we don't understand our own well-being and never will? It is momentarily tempting to simply stop striving in all of our endeavors after confronting all of these compounded biases. We may briefly consider becoming a Tibetan monk before realizing we're hungry and need to do something about it. But I don't think this story ends here. I agree that most people only stumble onto happiness, but I think there are tools and practices which can lead us, not only to wrap our minds around our delusion, but to overcome it and reverse its effects.

Introspection has gotten a bad rap in recent years. It has come to be viewed as an act of self-absorbed navel-gazing, and some have pointed out that it is often ineffective. In her book about self-awareness, *Insight*, Tasha Eurich points out some counterintuitive findings. Introspection appears to be generally correlated with lower well-being, higher anxiety, lower attitudes about oneself, and most surprisingly, lower self-awareness.[8]

In truth, introspection can cloud our self-perceptions and unleash a host of unintended consequences. Sometimes it may surface unproductive and upsetting emotions that can swamp us and impede positive action. Introspection might also lull us into a false sense of certainty that we've identified the real issue. Buddhist scholar Tarthang Tulku uses an apt analogy: when we introspect, our response is similar to a hungry cat watching mice. We eagerly pounce on whatever 'insights' we find without questioning their validity or value.[8]

But this "pouncing" problem is not unique to introspection. It is highly reminiscent of the "natural philosophers" who "pounced" on the belief that the earth was flat and was made up of only four elements. Scientists have to be trained not to take their initial hypotheses to be true until they are corroborated by evidence, but most of us are not scientists. We are never taught not to take our introspective hypotheses as reliable fact without good reason. We resort to the same types of oversimplified stories for understanding our own minds as we do when trying to understand the world. We form conclusions and explanations about ourselves and our lives based on intuitive hunches and narratives, failing to break our mental phenomena down into their basic algorithmic units and account for our biases.

Eurich says those who introspect by asking "what" questions are far more effective than those who ask "why" questions. But it isn't hard to change a question to start with a different word without really changing the question itself. The real key to the "what" questions is that they tend to be more objective than "why" questions. Although our self-reflections are necessarily subjective, we can work to make them far more objective.

It has actually been found that meditation experience predicts introspective accuracy by giving us the distance and objectivity necessary to see our own minds more clearly.[9] And just like the biases in the previous chapter, we can study the common errors in introspection that lead people astray.

Much like rationality, introspection can be problematic when done incorrectly. Yet failing to do it simply is not an option. You cannot live a coherent life without investigating your own internal variables and factoring them into your decisions. So like rationality, we must learn to use the tool of introspection properly. We must apply the same methods and principles that helped us overcome bias in the previous chapter to introspection.

All truly great thoughts are conceived by walking.

- **Friedrich Nietzsche**, *The Twilight of the Idols*

If the best position for meditation is sitting with an upright posture, the best position for reflection is walking. Walking doesn't just provide valuable exercise and vitamin D. It provides the perfect amount of stimulation while still allowing you to quietly reflect. It is difficult to simply sit and reflect for more than a few minutes without opening up a tab on your computer or pulling out your smartphone. Walking takes away the often irresistible temptation of constantly filling your attention with something.[10]

Bring a notepad, an app, or some other way to take down thoughts. The best introspection method I have used corresponds closely with a technique known as **focusing**, which was developed by philosopher Eugene Gendlin. Through his work with humanistic psychologist Carl Rogers, Gendlin came to believe that failing to focus on unclear body senses was the key reason some people seemed not to benefit from therapy.[11]

To practice it, begin your walk by listening to your mind without imposing any questions or topics. Relax, and see if anything comes to you automatically. If not, you can begin to ask yourself some basic questions about your current state. Gendlin suggests, "How is my life going? What is the main thing for me right now?" Talking through these questions out loud is a great way to ensure you won't be bothered by overly-friendly strangers. Rather than rushing to answer these questions, let a sense develop in your body.

Allow your attention to turn to a particular problem or area in your life. Maybe you will be drawn toward uneasiness about a forthcoming transition in your life, or maybe irritation toward a particular person. Take in all of the feelings that arise in your body. Try to generate words or images which describe the feeling, and continue doing so until you come across one that intuitively captures the feeling. Ask yourself what it is about this transition or person or idea that makes your chosen phrase or image resonate so closely. Gendlin says, "Be with the felt sense until something comes along with a shift, a slight 'give' or release." This shift should feel like an "ahah!" moment and is the sign of an introspective breakthrough. By repeating this process on your walks, you can develop a much clearer sense of your intuitions.

You can ask yourself about which qualities you admire, the current balance of your lifestyle, or your future aspirations. Get in touch with your "felt sense" in response to these questions, and be sure to take notes when you make a realization. You can develop enough clarity into yourself to build out conceptual maps of your sense of identity, passions, or ambitions.

Anything which can help you escape your habitual thoughts and conclusions can help you attain more insight. Altering your own state of consciousness through practices like meditation, chemicals like psychedelic drugs, or even changes to your routine like travel can unlock previously hidden depths of your mind.

> There is no light without shadow and no psychic wholeness without imperfection.
>
> - **Carl Jung**, *Dreams*

These depths can be disturbing when first encountered, and this causes some to avoid being left alone with their own thoughts whenever possible. But you must explore even the dark places in your mind and become your own friend. Failing to understand yourself, your flaws and vices, or your strengths and potential can hold you back immensely. Spending time alone is not just for introverts; it is one of the least discussed and most essential parts of any healthy life.[12] **The most important relationship in your life is your relationship with yourself.** And like any relationship, it will degrade if you don't ever dedicate quality time to it.

The best way to stunt your personal growth is to decide that you have made it - that your beliefs about yourself are correct now, and you don't need to upgrade them anymore. **This decision will disconnect you from the continual cycle of trial and error, learning and adaptation, that initiates your own personal evolution.**

Believing you are not the creative type will prevent you from taking on creative projects and proving yourself wrong.[13] If you believe money is a scarce resource, your risk-averse decisions will ensure you miss the abundant opportunities in front of you.[14] The belief that you are unattractive will make you far less secure and confident, and hence far less attractive.[15] **Your self-limiting beliefs might just be the single largest factor separating the best and worst versions of you.**

The Value System

This inner nature is not strong and overpowering and unmistakable like the instincts of animals. It is weak and delicate and subtle and easily overcome by habit, cultural pressure, and wrong attitudes toward it.

- **Abraham Maslow,** *Toward a Psychology of Being*

There is one area of our minds which we must understand deeply in order to live great lives - or even to know what that means. One of the great psychitectural guides, Abraham Maslow, thought each person had a biologically inscribed inner core in his mind, guiding him in the same way an acorn is guided toward becoming an oak tree. This inner core was partially unique to the individual and partially shared among all humans. And the inner core was the key to achieving deep satisfaction and the state he called self-actualization. Unlike the much louder forces of desire, this inner core could easily be ignored or neglected by the individual to his own detriment.[16]

I will use the term **value intuitions** to refer to the evaluative impulses which cause us to attribute "goodness" or "badness" to certain actions or outcomes. And getting deeply in touch with our felt sense of these intuitions will play a key role in the better alternative to the default approach to life. When we identify patterns in our value intuitions and arrange them into labeled concepts like "honesty," "compassion," or "discipline," they become **values**, or ideals. And the sum of these values is our **value system**, a full conceptual map of what matters to us.

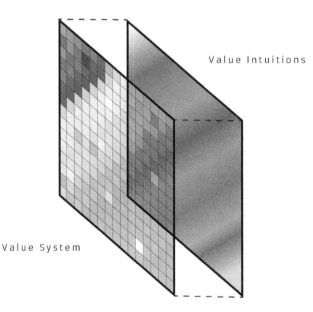

In the previous chapter, we saw that the aim of our belief system was to build a map of reality that corresponds to reality as closely and usefully as possible. When it comes to our value system, the goal is to build a map of our value intuitions which corresponds to those value intuitions as closely and usefully as possible. Just like with our belief system, our values can be more or less pixelated, and more or less accurate. And we can easily be deceived about our own core values by those around us.

If you have never engaged in deliberate introspection, self-examination, or philosophical inquiry, it can be said that none of the values with which you identify are actually your own. You initially inherited your moral framework and direction in life from those around you. Humans learn by imitation through childhood, and they do not develop the cognitive capacity to truly question what they have been taught until adolescence.[17]

Even after this point, though, there is no guarantee that a person will actually initiate this process of questioning. Maybe around this time you rejected the political views of your parents or the morally dubious actions of your friends. But you may have merely converted from one brand of dogma to another. To truly be able to claim that your values belong to you, you must go through an extensive process of uprooting the relics of your early indoctrination and examining them with critical rigor.

The unexamined life is not worth living

- **Socrates**, Plato's Apology

It is strange that the quote above is the quote most often associated with the field of philosophy, which today primarily consists of theoretical and linguistic analysis. But the word philosophy literally means "love of wisdom." Originally, philosophers were concerned above all with living a good life, and studying the ideas of these thinkers can vastly increase your capacity to do so. If you think philosophy is boring or irrelevant to your life, it is likely because your early encounters with it were exactly these things.

But the study of philosophy is an indispensable tool for anyone trying to live the best life possible. Studying the ideas and values of other thinkers may seem like it would only indoctrinate us to their ways of thinking, but the thoughts of others can give us great insight into our own minds. Although we all have our differences, there are many aspects of our minds which are more or less true of all people.[18] We can study the values acclaimed by the most reflective thinkers in history for guidance into our own. **The key to finding out which of your values are truly yours is the process of taking a philosophical wrecking ball to them and seeing what refuses to fall.**[19]

Philosophy, though unable to tell us with certainty what is the true answer to the doubts which it raises, is able to suggest many possibilities which enlarge our thoughts and free them from the tyranny of custom. Thus, while diminishing our feeling of certainty as to what things are, it greatly increases our knowledge as to what they may be; it removes the somewhat arrogant dogmatism of those who have never traveled into the region of liberating doubt, and it keeps alive our sense of wonder by showing familiar things in an unfamiliar aspect.

- **Bertrand Russell**, *The Problems of Philosophy*

The process of exploring what is truly important to you can be an incredibly rewarding experience and can save you from spending an entire life pursuing things that don't matter. This process of self-examination is never complete, but it is possible to construct a highly coherent path for your life without the confusion and conflict that most people never escape.

Cultivating Value Insight

You may be surprised by what you find when you subject what you thought were your values to critical rigor. Our capacity for self-deception does not stop short of our values. When we want or enjoy something enough, we frantically search for rationalized loopholes to justify it. Albert Speer, master architect of the Third Reich and top adviser of Adolf Hitler describes his own gradual corruption in his memoir:

In normal circumstances people who turn their backs on reality are soon set straight by the mockery and criticism of those around them. In the Third Reich there were not such correctives. On the contrary, every self-deception was multiplied as in a hall of distorting mirrors, becoming a repeatedly confirmed picture of a fantastical dream world which no longer bore any relationship to the grim outside world. In those mirrors I could see nothing but my own face reproduced many times over.[20]

You must ask yourself which historical atrocities you are contributing to today. Which of your actions have you been lulled into believing are benign? What has popular opinion or your own convoluted arguments convinced you is acceptable, or even positive? By popular opinion, I don't mean popular on the other side, I mean popular within your circles. What are the socially acceptable "concentration camps" of the modern day? Factory farms? Fracking sites? Immigration bans? Prisons? Fraternities? Abortion clinics?

Too far? Did I touch on something sacred for you? Were you hoping I would pick only practices which were already fashionable to condemn? Are you trying to figure out my political views? If you aren't finding uncomfortable truths about your values, you haven't gone far enough. **If you or your groups consider an issue to be obvious, ethically simple, and taboo to question, questioning it is exactly what you must do.**

Conformity will not just lead you to make bad life choices. The laughing spectators of the Roman Colosseum, the supportive majority in Nazi Germany, and the God-fearing and ruthless slave owners of the American south were all conformists. And if you had lived in these periods and regions, you likely would have found a way to justify these atrocities.[21]

Social influence can cause you to impose pseudo-values on top of your deepest intrinsic values.[22] It can bring about horrifying behaviors, and the unreflective individual will be ignorant to the source of his resulting self-hatred. Convincing yourself that something does not violate your values does not change the content of those values. You will slip away from your ideals no matter how intricate or eloquent your justifications.

Some of our value intuitions relate to how we treat others, but the majority of our values don't actually fall into the category we sometimes call "moral." They have to do with beauty, truth, originality, competence, discretion, etc.[23] When you observe another person taking an action, you may experience a positive emotional impulse of admiration, or you may have a negative emotional impulse letting you know that something has violated your values.

After enough life experience, you accumulate enough value intuitions to be able to find patterns within them. It is the ongoing task of each person to observe her value intuitions and synthesize her own values into a coherent system. In order to create a refined value system, you will need to sit down and map out your intuitions. Create a document, ideally a highly editable one so you can easily rearrange what you write down. Create a list of people you deeply admire. These can be people in your life, ancient historical figures, or even strangers you have only briefly observed. You do not have to admire everything about these people.[24]

Don't do any labeling yet; simply write down the particular tendencies or example situations with as much precision as possible. You might write down that you admire one person's tendency to manage difficult situations with levity, or another person's ability to captivate the attention of everyone in a room. Your list can be stream-of-consciousness at first, but eventually you will want to place similar examples into organized clusters. Don't stop until you find that you have covered the full territory of what is important to you. Create your own titles for each category, trying to avoid vague virtues like "kindness" or "honor."[25]

Ultimately, you will end up with an organized list of your highest individual values. Single words often fail to fully capture your values. It can be beneficial to express them in mission statement form, through key phrases such as "always act as if the whole world were watching, but tell the story as if I were the only one listening" or "accept, embrace, and adapt to all of life's challenges, and convert them into opportunities."

When done in parallel with philosophical investigation, you can sort out which of these values represent cultural dogmas and which ones are based on your genuine value intuitions. I find that a map of your value system needs to be updated about every three years. Over time, your experiences pile up and shed more light on your intuitions, enabling greater nuance and refinement in your categories.

You should never have total confidence in the value system you have constructed. This map represents an ever-evolving and improving draft. You always have to keep inquiring and synthesizing in order to get closer to your genuine value intuitions. You observe things you admire or disapprove of, try to extract the precise aspects you admire, and synthesize these observations into integrated principles.

The value systems you form are clunky early on, but you will develop a greater capacity for nuance as you accumulate observations. Perhaps you find that you admire Tiger Woods' perseverance but not his promiscuity, rather than idealizing or demonizing the man as a whole. Eventually, these isolated observations will coalesce into a unified understanding.

To get the most out of this value system you can anthropomorphize it as your **ideal self**. Your ideal self is a conglomerate of your highest value intuitions and admired qualities.[26] And this ideal is the north star in your psychitectural journey. Your ultimate goal, of course, will be to diminish the gap between your actual self and your ideal self to the highest degree possible. In order to do this, you need to develop a more coherent and comprehensive view of your actual self and integrate your experiences, character traits, values, and drives into a unified whole. And this ideal will serve a crucial guiding role in proper goal-setting.

Key Takeaways

• Much like our beliefs about the outer universe, our beliefs about our inner universe - our desires, goals, and values - can be distorted, which can lead us astray in our lives.

• Our internal life and emotion simulators are warped and vastly oversimplified, and overconfidence in them will cause us to continually make mistakes.

• Though we think we know what will make us happy, we often end up stumbling onto happiness rather than achieving it through deliberate efforts.

• The principle of **realism** explains why our brains constantly weave their biases and fabrications into reality, filling in the gaps so quickly and seamlessly that we don't even notice anything is off.

• **Presentism** is "the tendency for current experience to influence one's views of the past and the future" and assume we always have and will feel the way we do now.

• **Rationalization** causes us to experience anxiety and dread around adversity and loss, believing they will cause us to feel worse and for longer than they actually will.

• Through effective introspection, it is possible to become aware of and reprogram these internal biases and live more fulfilling lives.

• It is crucial to observe our internal phenomena objectively rather than imposing stories about "why" we may be experiencing something.

• Keep a log of your thoughts, feelings, and behaviors, as well as the real-world events that seem to trigger them. Try to notice the relationships and chains between them.

• One method, called **focusing**, has to do with connecting with your body's "felt sense" and paying attention to shifts that represent introspective breakthroughs.

• The most important relationship in your life is your relationship with yourself, which will degrade if you fail to dedicate quality time to it.

• Self-limiting beliefs may be the single largest factor separating the best and worst versions of you.

• One of the highest goals of introspection is to develop an accurate map of our values, based on intuitive impulses.

• We can easily be deceived about our own core values by those around us, and by default, none of the values with which you identify are actually your own.

• The key to finding out which of your values are truly yours is the process of taking a philosophical wrecking ball to them and seeing what refuses to fall.

- Be bold in questioning the values espoused by your culture and social circles.
- An exercise for getting more clarity into your values entails creating a document and listing the people and qualities you admire. Group similar entries, and eventually apply labels or statements that encompass each group.
- When done in parallel with philosophical investigation, you can sort out which of these values represent cultural dogmas and which ones are based on your genuine value intuitions.
- Your **ideal self** is a conglomerate of your highest value intuitions and admired qualities, and this ideal is the north star in your psychitectural journey.
- The ultimate goal of psychitecture is to diminish the gap between your actual self and your ideal self to the highest degree possible.

4

Cognitive Self-Mastery and Wisdom

The Decoys to Well-Being

The goals that you have set for yourself may be ones sold to you by the larger culture - 'Make money! Own your own home! Look great!' - and while there may be nothing wrong with striving for those things, they mask the pursuits more likely to deliver true and lasting happiness. In this case, your priority should be to discern which goals will make you happy in the long term and to follow them.

- **Sonja Lyubomirsky**, *The How of Happiness*

In the previous two chapters, we have looked at the methods for developing rationality and self-awareness. This chapter is about how these two qualities come together to form wisdom. Wisdom is the pinnacle of cognitive self-mastery, the first pillar of the self-mastery triad. Despite the dry manner in which it is normally portrayed, wisdom is not some consolation prize for aging. **The sooner you begin the endeavor to acquire wisdom, the greater your ability to increase your satisfaction in life.**

The word "wisdom" has been used to mean many things, including the acceptance of spiritual dogmas, the theoretical understanding of reality, and even the tendency to speak in the form of enigmatic riddles. Here, we use the term in a very specific way.

> Wisdom: The capacity for judging rightly in matters relating to life and conduct; soundness of judgment in the choice of means and ends.

- Oxford English Dictionary

Wisdom is practical insight - knowing what is good for you - strategic self-interest. Wisdom is about taking the most rational and insightful beliefs and forming goals based on them. Our culture is highly goal-oriented in that it advocates setting and pursuing goals as effectively as possible. But it places much less emphasis on ensuring that one is setting the *right goals*.

We naturally acquire beliefs about which goals are worth striving for from our culture just as we acquire beliefs about the world, and every culture has its own "success" narrative.[1] This narrative assigns arbitrary milestones that deem people "successful" after they meet them. And we've all heard our culture's success narrative a thousand times.

You are born, given a name, and also given a cow name and a goat name. You are given head massages to elongate your skull to make you appear to be a strong warrior. From an early age, culture tells you to herd goats. You are told to plow the fields, learn to raise beehives, and steal livestock from other communities.

If you are a man, you are told that in order to be "successful," you have to have your head partially shaved, get rubbed with sand to wash away your sins, and get smeared with cow dung. You are told to strip naked, jump onto the back of a cow, and then jump across the backs of a row of fifteen cows, which have also been smeared with dung. You must do this four times without falling, and are told that falling off will deem you a failure and a shame to your family. Success will allow you to marry a woman you have never met, but not before you accumulate 30 goats and 20 cattle in order to purchase the marriage from her family. The more wives you accumulate, the more you are deemed a "success" by your culture.

If you are a woman, you are expected to meet men who have gone through this process, and to beg them to brutally whip you, not showing any pain the whole time. Cultural narrative dictates that you marry a man twice your age who has been assigned without your vote. If your family fails to find you a husband, you have to watch all of your friends receive phallic-shaped necklaces, indicating their "success," while you wear only an oval, metal plate on your head. If you become pregnant outside of marriage, your child will be considered cursed, and your peers will encourage you to abandon it. If you do get married, your husband will beat you routinely for no apparent reason until you have had two to three children. The more scars you receive, the more "successful" you will be considered by your tribe.

Not the story you were expecting? Oh, you must not be a member of the Hamar community of southwestern Ethiopia. I guess I just assumed. Yes, these are all very standard practices in the Hamar community, and they are not even the most bizarre traditions we see in cultures around the world.[2] What is really hard to grasp is that the Hamar would likely view our culture's definitions of success to be just as strange and arbitrary as we find theirs.

The special thing about the western narrative is that every industry which can make itself vaguely relevant is fighting for a piece of it. Just as our culture builds onto our genes and creates new decoys to well-being, our economic system builds onto culture and introduces more diversions still. Businesses capitalize on the great tourist traps of life - the things which are presented as highly desirable by culture and industry, but are not necessarily good deals at all. And in order to sell these fantasies, they have to find ways to shape culture to tell us what it means to be "successful."[3]

My goal here is not to suggest that getting married, buying nice cars, or climbing corporate ladders are bad decisions, nor is it to offer a tired critique of capitalism, consumerism, or popular culture. None of these decisions are invalid in and of themselves, and if I told you they were, I'm sure you wouldn't listen anyway.

I do not regret my decision to attend college. I don't regret spending time working in order to make money, spending money on vacations, being in a relationship, or any of the other choices I've made that happen to mesh with the success narratives of my culture. And that is because I have not done these things out of blind conformity to a social script. **Being an unconditional non-conformist is no badge of honor.** What ultimately matters is the foundation underlying your aspirations.

The Goal Hierarchy

> We start trying to be wise when we realize that we are not born knowing how to live, but that life is a skill that has to be acquired.
>
> - **Alain de Botton**, *Essays in Love*

This is a goal:

 Goal

Goals are pretty simple on their own. But goals tend to chain together, like this:

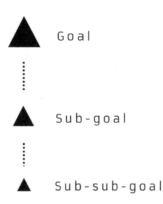

Some of our goals are end goals, and others serve as the instrumental means to reach them. The goal hierarchy is a structure of motivations with abstract goals like "raise financially responsible children" at the top, strategies like "teach children about Roth IRAs" in the middle, and individual actions like "figure out what a Roth IRA is" at the bottom.[4] As you can imagine, the interactions of our goals can form hierarchies far more complex than we could visualize, but we can capture the basic idea.

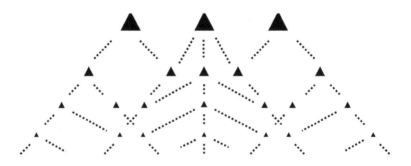

"Why am I doing this?" When you ask yourself this question, you are effectively examining your goal hierarchy.[5] And when you don't have a cogent answer, you are examining a goal hierarchy that needs work.

The goal hierarchy of most animals is hardly a hierarchy at all. All actions are taken because immediate drives compel the organism to take them.[6] This structure looks something like this:

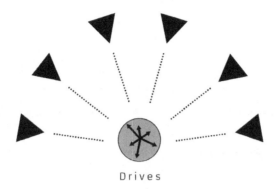

Drives

That symbol at the bottom represents a conglomerate of the organism's drives. Due to the incredible ability of humans to strategically orchestrate the satisfaction of their desires, the **default goal hierarchy** for humans is far more complex.

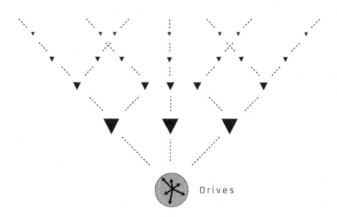

Drives

Basic drives determine which goals are to be pursued, but reason is used to determine effective methods for achieving them. Default goals are automatically set in a bottom-up fashion by our drives. By default, our goals are set up to serve genetic purposes, including everything from eating to keep ourselves from dying to doing favors for others to increase our social status. The default goal hierarchy does not result in a particularly coherent life - it is a patchwork of desires which is modulated by biology and the popular opinions of our culture and social circles.[7] Author Ted Chu cites a relevant story:

> There is a story about a reporter who went to a remote village and interviewed a young shepherd about the meaning of life. 'Why do you shepherd a herd of sheep?' asked the reporter. 'Because I want to accumulate wealth,' the shepherd answered. Then the reporter asked, 'Why do you want to accumulate wealth?' The reply: 'So that I will be able to get married.' 'Why do you want to get married?' 'So that I can have a son.' 'What do you need a son for?' The shepherd stopped and thought for a while, and answered, 'So he can continue to shepherd the sheep.[8]

None of us like the idea of having incoherent goals - of spending our entire lives working toward things that don't matter, even to us. We would prefer to have goals which make sense and connect together in a coherent fashion. Fortunately, goal construction is like breathing - it happens automatically by default, but can also be done reflectively and coherently.[9] So how do we go about setting good goals?

There has been a long-standing debate on the relationship between reason and the passions, a term which generally combines emotions and desires. Plato argued that reason was like a charioteer, and the irrational impulses and emotions were the horses which pulled in often conflicting directions. Desire for wealth may pull an individual in one direction, and the desire for social status may pull in another. Bodily impulses for food and sex may pull in other directions still. It was the role of reason to keep them in check and guide them in the right direction.[10] And it has been found that those who are capable of resisting the temptation of desire and delaying gratification in favor of a more rational choice are more successful and happy in life, suggesting that Plato may be right.[11]

Reason

Passions

But there were those who disagreed as well. David Hume argued that reason could not possibly be a motive for action, and that every act is ultimately motivated by emotion. He famously claimed that "Reason is, and ought only to be the slave of the passions."[12] What he meant by this is that reason can be used to determine the best means to a desired end, but cannot generate an end or motivate a person to action by itself. Other, later philosophers like Nietzsche have taken Hume's side of this debate.

Studies of people with neurological disorders, such as one famous patient named Elliot who suffered ventromedial prefrontal cortex damage, shed light on a life unmotivated by emotion and desire. These people fail to process emotions in their decisions, which results in a total inability to make decisions at all, even those as simple as which restaurant to go to for dinner.[13] Neuroscientist Antonio Damasio concluded that 'well-tuned and deployed emotion... is necessary for the edifice of reason to operate properly.'[14] These findings suggest that Hume's side is right.

Passions

:
:
:
:
:
:

Reason

So which is it? Should we follow our heads or our hearts?

The Dukkha Bias

For countless generations our biochemical system adapted to increasing our chances of survival and reproduction,
not our happiness. The biochemical system rewards actions
conducive to survival and reproduction with pleasant sensations. But these are only an ephemeral sales gimmick.

- **Yuval Noah Harari**, *Homo Deus*

During a trip to South America, I was once struck by how frequently the
word "quiero" appears in Spanish music. "Quiero" means "I want," and I would
guess that the phrase "I want" is no less common in American music. Television,
film, and music all reinforce the idea that we should get what we want. That our
desires are valid and there is something wrong if they are not satisfied. That our
only chances at true fulfillment lie in immediate pleasure, romantic passion,
material possession, power, and prestige. And we all know it would be nearly
impossible to create a great film in which everything is just as it should be and
everyone is pretty much cool with it.

Our software was programmed for specific genetic purposes, and it was very important for these purposes that we follow our desires without questioning them too much.[15] These drives have the nifty feature of automatically setting our goals for us, and biased cognitive algorithms convince us that their gratification will make us happy. But the major problem with this approach to life is this: **Desires don't point to happiness, and their gratification is no more likely to result in it than their denial**. It may seem strange that desires wouldn't be indicators of desirability, but we will see that it is true.

We find it incomprehensible that lottery winners and paraplegics would have the same levels of satisfaction because we *want* to win the lottery and *don't want* to lose the use of our legs. Our desires are very good at posing as guides to genuine satisfaction. We are programmed to tie these separate phenomena together. **We are built not to notice how little our actual emotional satisfaction corresponds to the objects of our desires.**

You may have heard of the neurotransmitter dopamine, which is strongly connected with desire and pleasure. Dopamine is a major part of the brain's reward system, so it is understandable to assume that it is the reward. It is popularly referred to as the pleasure chemical, after all. But this view is incorrect. Dopamine is the primary chemical behind desire and anticipation, but it isn't the pleasure chemical - it is better understood as the *promise* chemical.[16]

Dopamine is responsible for the anticipation of pleasure that compels us to act. The feeling we typically call "pleasure" is primarily caused by endogenous opioids and endorphins. Dopamine is the craving and the compulsion which causes us to take another hit or try our luck on the slots one more time. It has no obligation to deliver on its promise, and very often, it doesn't.

Mice are normally very eager to drink sugar water, but mice who have been modified to be incapable of producing dopamine do not seem to crave or actively pursue this delicious drink. Interestingly, when they are fed sugar water, they experience the same amount of pleasure and enjoyment as a normal mouse, but they will not mind when it is taken away.[17] Deep brain stimulation implants have allowed people to give themselves a hit of dopamine at the push of the button. Although these people do press the button many times per day, they have reported the feeling as being less one of pleasure and more of uncontrollable compulsion.[18] These findings lead us to the conclusion that wanting and enjoying are two entirely separate phenomena.[19]

Desire can be programmed by pleasure, but just like in the training of a dog, it is the immediate pleasures that reinforce these desires.[20] Even though we may leave the casino feeling deeply disappointed, the quick and immediate spikes of pleasure we feel each turn we take on the slot machine condition our desire to want to do it again. These all serve as examples that our cravings, short-term or otherwise, are decoys to well-being.

Around the 6th-century BCE, a man known as Siddhartha Gautama left a life of luxury to seek enlightenment. After apparent success, The Buddha, as he was thereafter known, began teaching and disseminating his path to liberation.[21] Siddhārtha taught that ordinary human life is inherently characterized by something called **dukkha**, or "unsatisfactoriness." He was partially referring to the "bad things" in life - the inevitable suffering we all face at some point or another in the hands of unpleasant living conditions, sickness, and loss. Losing or failing to attain what we want undeniably results in pain.[22]

He was also referring to the **impermanence** of even the "good things" in our lives. All things which seem to make us happy are impermanent. As soon as we attain something which brings us joy, we become dependent upon it. And when the tides inevitably shift, we become vulnerable to the suffering which comes with loss. When we long for things we do not have, or long not to lose the things we do, we are craving - grasping for control and permanence in a world in which these things can never be attained.[23]

But the Buddha argued that unsatisfactoriness was built into the very structure of desire. When it comes to satisfying our cravings, the pleasure we experience and the pain that comes later are inextricably tied together. Not only are many of the things for which we long impermanent, but even permanent achievements do not result in permanent satisfaction.[24]

We are built with a very clever mechanism which causes us to become quickly dissatisfied with our achievements and possessions and begin to look for ways to get even more (**hedonic adaptation**).[25] At some point, it is inevitable that even the luckiest person will have nowhere to go but down relative to her own expectations. In *Why Buddhism Is True*, Robert Wright outlines a basic principle of Buddhism:

> Humans tend to anticipate more in the way of enduring sat-
> isfaction from the attainment of goals than will in fact tran-
> spire. This illusion, and the resulting mindset of perpetual
> aspiration, makes sense as a product of natural selection, but
> it's not exactly a recipe for lifelong happiness.

> - **Robert Wright**, *Why Buddhism Is True*

So yes, loss or failure to attain desired outcomes results in very real spikes of pain. And success at attaining desired outcomes results in short spikes of pleasure, but this pleasure quickly turns to pain when we lose what we previously gained. And even when we manage to attain semi-permanent achievements, we quickly adapt to our success, and the failure to live up to our new expectations results in more pain. But the real essence of dukkha is not that life is suffering, as it has been interpreted before. It is that we are not built to reap real satisfaction from the attainment of our desired goals, but we *are* built not to notice this fact.

Most of us don't consider our lives to be all pain. Many of us do feel relatively satisfied with our lives. Hence Gilbert's book title, *Stumbling on Happiness*. We have to stumble onto happiness because our well-being fluctuates independently of desire gratification. We aren't just bad predictors. We're operating within a faulty framework - a false theory for how psychological well-being works.

In order to attain genuine fulfillment, **we have to learn to quit trusting our wants as valid indicators of what will genuinely satisfy us**. If we could learn to ignore our desires, or better yet, use them, and understand the real mechanics of satisfaction, we could take our well-being out of the hands of chance and maximize it.

Setting Defined Goals

Anyone who has not groomed his life in general towards some definite end cannot possibly arrange his individual actions properly. It is impossible to put the pieces together if you do not have in your head the idea of the whole... The bowman must first know what he is aiming at: then he has to prepare hand, bow, bowstring, arrow and his drill to that end. Our projects go astray because they are not addressed to a target. No wind is right for a seaman who has no predetermined harbour.

- **Michel de Montaigne**, *The Complete Essays*

The second type of goal archetype is called the **defined goal hierarchy.**

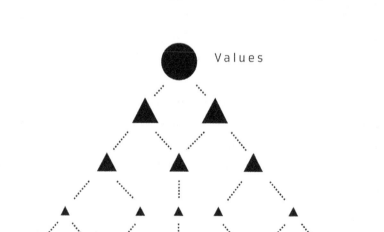

The defined goal hierarchy is constructed through a top-down determination in which our reflective mind calls the shots. It is developed consciously and shaped to be coherent, unified, and purposeful. The symbol at the top represents the preponderance of your values, and in this case, those ideals are the determinants of all other goals. Your goal hierarchy probably isn't adequately represented by either of these archetypes. It probably looks more like this:

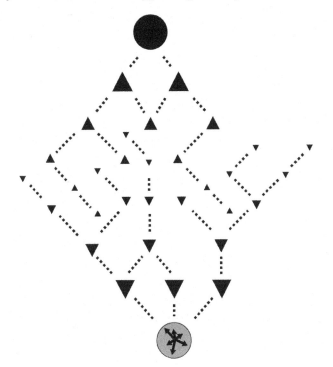

Our goals are typically a mixed bag - some have been set reflectively and others reflexively. But when you ask "Why am I doing this?" you take a step toward building a better goal hierarchy. When you realize that you are pursuing something arbitrary, the ends that your drives or peers or parents told you were worthwhile, you have the opportunity to take corrective measures.

The problem with the Plato-Hume debate is that it simplifies the passions a bit too far. There is a useful distinction to be made between drives, the "hot" motivational forces which compel us to act, and values, the intuitive ideals which tell us what is actually important to us. Both could be called "passions," but it is important to separate the two qualia.

Value intuitions and desires can be easily confused. Both could be described as preferences of an affective nature, but they are different in meaningful ways. When you reflect on your values, you don't feel a sense of craving, a motivational force pulling you toward them. They are always there, but unlike desires, they allow you to neglect them if you choose. **Desires are the screams you can't ignore, but values are the whispers it is often hard to notice.**[26]

In the ideal mind, desires are modulated: bent to our will so they serve our values (we will learn how to do this in a few chapters). Values are to be uncovered, worked toward, and embodied.

By reintroducing reason at this point, we can reconcile the two seemingly correct views espoused by philosophers. Our values are at the top. Reason is in the middle, and is used to determine which goals will most effectively serve those values. And our drives at the bottom are used to get us there.

Values

Reason

Drives

Desires are like the gas in a car. They are what fuel us, but they should always be subordinate to reason. Reason is the steering wheel that coordinates the aimless and often conflicting sea of drives in a strategic and coherent direction, but reason must always be subordinate to our values. We have to use reason to set rational goals, but those goals have to be guided by our emotional values to be worthy ends. Our values are the compass, or perhaps the GPS coordinates for our direction. Our ideals determine the ideal direction, and our rational mind and desires work together to get us there.

Mixing up any of these relationships can be catastrophic. Values are great for deciding what is important, but they won't take you there. You can spend a life dreaming about your ideals without ever moving closer to embodying them. Similarly, attempting to use pure reason to determine your aims or motivate you to achieve them is like sitting in a parked car turning the steering wheel. You would remain motivationally impotent and perfectly static in your life, just like Elliot.

And we can all see that flooring the gas pedal without using the steering wheel will only guide you into the nearest lamppost. Using our drives as a guide to our direction in life, or to determine the most effective strategy for getting there, is a recipe for a life full of impulsive mistakes.

Strong desires can be a great thing.[27] Having a car with a powerful engine is only a bad thing if you don't have the skill and control to wield that power without wrecking.

Although we all look to our emotions to determine desirable goals and evaluations, making decisions with your emotions and without reasoning is known as the **affect heuristic**, and results in some of the most profound mistakes humans make.[28] Some people will argue that there are some decisions you should make with your head and others you should make with your heart. But this dichotomy is problematic. All decisions must be made with your head *and* your "heart," but each has a very specific place.[29] Contrary to what your Enneagram test may have told you, there aren't really rational people and emotional people. There are people who are better at thinking clearly and coordinating their desires in the direction of their values, and those who are worse at it.

Our goals are informed by both our values and cognitive rationality. We determine the best ends in our lives by introspecting and consulting our values.

And we determine the best means by developing the most accurate views about the world possible and using reason to strategize. These two capacities come together to form wisdom. Meaning if you harbor biases distorting either your rational understanding or introspective inquiry, your goals will be distorted as well. This makes the process of eliminating arbitrary goals and constructing wise ones in their place a complex but crucial psychitectural pursuit.

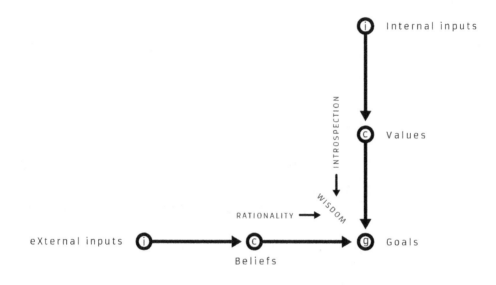

There are only a few who control themselves and their affairs by a guiding purpose; the rest do not proceed; they are merely swept along, like objects afloat in a river.

- **Seneca**, *Letters from a Stoic*

When you reflect on your life, **ask yourself if you really chose it**. If you are living it because it truly allows you to reach your ideals, or because the housing industry wanted you to think it does. If you really want to pursue that prestigious career as a notary, or if your parents just convinced you that you do. If your life is genuinely the product of a top-down goal strategy in which your decisions are directed toward your ideals, you'll get no criticism here. But if you look around you and see a life that looks like a cookie cutter - one that would seem to the Hamar community like blind conformity to arbitrary "success" milestones, it may be time to pause, reflect, and make use of wisdom.

> The demarcation between a positive and a negative desire or action is not whether it gives you an immediate feeling of satisfaction but whether it ultimately results in positive or negative consequences.
>
> - **Dalai Lama XIV**, The Art of Happiness

Wisdom allows you to understand that investing in your education is probably a better means to becoming a billionaire than investing in lottery tickets. But even more crucially, wisdom allows you to question whether becoming a billionaire is a worthy end in the first place. The heart of the pursuit of wisdom is that you can be easily deceived about your own well-being.

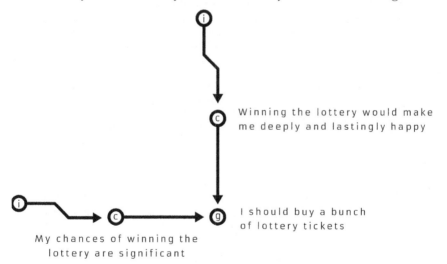

Wisdom is all about having a coherent hierarchical tree of reasons for all of your actions, not a fragmented set of rules. Most people have been taught that there are things which are right and things that are wrong, independent of context. That these moral concerns represent a separate consideration from practical ones. But the truth is that moral rules are like training wheels for people who haven't yet developed adequate wisdom.[30]

If you have cultivated wisdom, you may refrain from lying, not because it's "wrong," but because you have learned that telling a lie almost always results in more complications, damaged relationships, and worse outcomes.[31] You try not to hurt others, not because that would be "wrong," but because you have made the introspective observation that these actions make you feel worse about yourself.

When you take any action, you must carefully observe the satisfaction it brings and how long it lasts. Just as the feeling of cognitive confusion should raise a red flag in your mind, the dissonance between your expected emotional consequences and actual ones should grab your attention. If you expect that your new Segway will result in powerfully and enduringly increased satisfaction but it only excites you for a few days and then makes you regret selling your car and losing friends, you must notice and reflect. **You have to recall this unexpected experience the next time you contemplate a major purchase.**

Maybe the desire for revenge leads you to react to an act of aggression with vengeance, and it only causes you guilt. Maybe a passionate affair doesn't leave you feeling more satisfied with your life after it has run its course. **What makes wise people wise is that they notice this, and they change their goals in the future.** You cannot keep living your life without adjusting the algorithms which led you to faulty decisions. You must revise your beliefs about your own well-being to prevent yourself from making the same mistakes indefinitely.[32]

The wise have carefully observed and learned of the pitfalls of emotional prediction. They have developed an understanding of their own well-being trajectory. They have learned, from their own experience, that of others, or reflection, that the thing which seems like the best idea can be illusory. They are perceptive into their own well-being, and are not only able to observe these intuitions, but able to synthesize them into "rules" to guide their behavior when similar patterns emerge in the future. They have identified counter-intuitive practical truths, and crucially, make the decision to listen to them rather than making the same mistakes when they know better.

As you adjust and refine your cognitive algorithms, you elevate your degree of cognitive self-mastery. You free yourself from the confused life which culture prescribes for you, and you set your course for a truly fulfilling and intrinsically rewarding life in alignment with the vision of your ideal self.

Key Takeaways

• Wisdom is the capacity for judging rightly in matters relating to life and conduct; soundness of judgment in the choice of means and ends.

• Wisdom is practical insight - knowing what is good for you - strategic self-interest.

• Our culture is highly goal-oriented, but it places much less emphasis on ensuring that one is setting the right goals.

• We naturally acquire beliefs about which goals are worth striving for from our culture's "success" narratives.

• Many components of these narratives are "tourist traps" that are glorified by companies and industries.

• You must have coherent reasons behind your goals to avoid falling into these traps.

• Goal construction is like breathing - it happens automatically by default, but can also be done reflectively and coherently.

• Desires don't point to happiness, and their gratification is no more likely to result in it than their denial, but we are built not to notice this fact.

• Desires are inherently unsatisfiable, and the Buddha referred to this fact as "**dukkha.**"

• **Hedonic adaptation** causes us to adapt to present circumstances and continually want more, regardless of how high we climb.

• In order to attain genuine fulfillment, we have to learn to quit trusting our wants as valid indicators of what will genuinely satisfy us.

• There has been a long-standing debate on the relationship between reason and the passions and whether we should make decisions with our heads or our hearts.

• The key to setting and pursuing good, **defined goals** is to use our values to determine our ends, reason to determine the best means to getting there, and desires to fuel us toward them.

• It is easy to confuse values and desires, which are both emotional in nature, but desires are the screams you can't ignore, and values are the whispers it is often hard to notice.

• Mixing up the relationships between values, reason, and desire can be catastrophic.

• A wise and coherent life is the product of a top-down goal strategy in which your decisions are directed toward your ideals.

• When you take any action, you must carefully observe the satisfaction it brings and how long it lasts, and you have to recall your observations when you make similar decisions in the future.

• The wise have carefully observed and learned of the pitfalls of emotional prediction. They have developed an understanding of their own well-being trajectory, and learned, from their own experience, that of others, or reflection, that the thing which seems like the best idea can be illusory.

• As you adjust and refine your cognitive algorithms, you elevate your degree of cognitive self-mastery. You free yourself from the confused life which culture prescribes for you, and you set your course for a truly fulfilling and intrinsically rewarding life in alignment with the vision of your ideal self.

5

Emotional Algorithms and the Art of Restructuring

Controlling Your Feelings

Men are disturbed not by things, but by the views which they take of things.

- **Epictetus**, *Enchiridion*

The second realm of psychitecture is emotional. This chapter bridges the gap between the cognitive and the emotional by showing the relationship between the two. Emotional self-mastery is just what it sounds like: **the ability to control one's own emotional experience.**

For some people, emotional self-mastery will sound like fiction. The idea that we cannot control our emotions has become quite fashionable in popular culture. Music tells us you can't help how you feel. Folk psychology and self-help tell us that attempting to control your emotions is the same as running from them. Popular self-help author Mark Manson says "People who believe that emotions are the be-all-end-all of life often seek ways to 'control' their emotions. You can't. You can only react to them."[1]

The argument typically goes that emotions are meant to teach us something. Yes, every ice cream-binging self-pity session you have is trying to guide you someplace very special in your life. Apparently, trying not to feel a certain emotion you were "meant" to feel is like running away from destiny and blinding yourself to all of the valuable lessons in store for you. And if you would prefer to learn your lessons in life without the accompanying anxiety, anger, and despair, well you must be a coward.

The arguments are all very mature and reasonable. There is just one problem with them. **They're dead wrong.** The fact that you can control your emotions is well-established psychological fact.[2] You don't just learn how to deal with, channel, or react to your emotions. You change, modulate, and control them. If you had failed to learn how to control your emotions at all from childhood to adulthood, you would most certainly have a severe developmental disorder.[3]

There are a few things we can grant to those who oppose this view. First, it is true that our natural emotions can sometimes, even often serve our goals. Trying to socialize and form relationships, for example, without the help of our emotions would be utterly impossible.[4] But because our emotions were developed to benefit our genes, not us, in the world of our ancestors, not the world we live in, there is no guarantee they are always best for us.[5] **Emotions often lead us in the opposite direction of our highest goals, cause us to act in ways we later regret, and force us to suffer when there is absolutely no benefit to doing so.** That is why we not only *can* learn to control our emotions, if we want to live a great life, we *must*.

> The problem with the emotions is not that they are untamed forces or vestiges of our animal past; it is that they were designed to propagate copies of the genes that built them rather than to promote happiness, wisdom, or moral values.
>
> - **Steven Pinker**, *How the Mind Works*

Critics would also be correct in stating that suppression, the brute force "willing away" of emotion, is ineffective and often backfires.[6] I also would not recommend denying your bad feelings or attempting to hide them from others at all times. But these are far from the only methods to this expansive art. For those who disagree, the science of emotional self-regulation would like a word.

> Emotion Regulation refers to shaping which emotions one has, when one has them, and how one experiences or expresses these emotions.

> - **James Gross**, *Handbook of Emotion Regulation*

According to James Gross, one of the leading researchers in emotion regulation, there are five ways that people effectively control their feelings. The first three are quite obvious: we can choose the situations we enter (**situation selection**), change those situations once we are in them (**situation modification**), or choose only to pay attention to the things which make us feel the way we want to feel (**attentional deployment**). The fifth one is pretty straightforward as well: We can try to change our emotional response by listening to some music, getting drunk, or just getting some much needed sleep (**response modulation**). The fourth method, and the one we are most interested in here, is called **cognitive change**. In other words, we can make changes in our minds, perfectly healthy changes I might add, which allow us to determine our emotional experience from within.[7]

Practicing this art will allow you to gradually stop being upset by setbacks. Mastering it will put your emotional experience completely in your hands. If you take it on, you should expect to start hearing about how composed you remain in difficult situations. But this interpretation doesn't quite do justice to the psychitectural habits you will develop. You will learn how to rewire your emotions in real time, and the speed at which you can neutralize or reverse negative emotions will increase.

No, you will never have perfect, one-hundred percent control over your emotions.[8] But you can develop a truly surprising and increasing amount of control by mastering a few powerful psychotechnologies. This is not some esoteric, dark art that takes a lifetime to learn, nor is there anything fundamentally mystical or spiritual about it. **You can learn how to make the changes in your mind which will allow you to take control of your emotions and feel the way you would like to feel more and more of the time.**

The Principle of Cognitive Mediation

> I saw that all the things I feared, and which feared me had nothing good or bad in them save insofar as the mind was affected by them.

> - **Baruch Spinoza**, *Ethics*

Let us look at the emotional algorithm. We may be tempted to present it as a simple "if x then y" like, "If I get cut off in traffic, then experience anger."

input

Given this representation, the default approach to dealing with emotions makes perfect sense. How else could we possibly control our emotional state besides trying to change our external circumstances? As you study the inner workings of your mind, and the wisdom of some of the greatest psychitectural visionaries, I think you will find that the actual structure of emotional algorithms is not quite so simple.

As mentioned above, our attention plays a major role in our emotional responses. There are some cases in which the best route to getting rid of a negative emotion is to simply stop thinking about an issue and divert our attention to another activity. Engaging in a hobby or talking to a friend can be quick ways to short-circuit a rumination spiral before it takes control of your mood.[9]

One of the most highly touted benefits of mindfulness is its ability to pull a person out of undesirable emotions. A person who has cultivated a high degree of mindfulness can focus deeply on the sensations that constitute emotional experiences, taking away much of their impact.[10] But though useful, mindfulness is not the most thorough solution to unwanted emotions. When you circumvent an emotion through mindfulness, the original emotional algorithm remains unchanged, and similar situations will continue to trigger it. In order to understand how to change these algorithms for good, we have to go deeper.

When we detect a stick that looks like a snake, it may cause us to jump out of fear before we even know why. This is because it was advantageous for the brain to build a direct neural route from our visual cortex, which processes visual stimuli, to our amygdala, which activates emotional responses like fear.[11] But for nearly all of the harmful emotions that challenge us today, our perception of events goes through our rational prefrontal cortex before reaching the emotional limbic system.[12] The cognitive interpretation the mind forms of this stimulus is called an **appraisal**, and our appraisal of a situation determines our emotional response.[13]

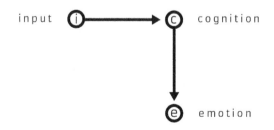

Emotional algorithms can actually be illustrated by building onto cognitive algorithms. Emotions arise from a discrepancy between a desired goal and our perceptions of our current status in relation to it. We suffer when we perceive reality to move away from our desired reality, and we experience positive emotion when reality nears our desired reality.[14] An understanding of this model will illuminate two major leverage points for controlling our emotions: **Changing our perceptions and changing our desires**. This chapter's focus is on changing our perceptions.

The ancient Greek philosophy of Stoicism was founded by Zeno of Citium in the 3rd-century BCE, and its ideas were further developed by later philosophers including the Greek slave Epictetus, Seneca the Younger, and Roman emperor Marcus Aurelius.[15] Stoicism advocated for seeking satisfaction in life, not through the satisfaction of one's appetites, but through their relinquishment. Unlike the Epicureans, the Stoics rejected pleasure altogether, and thought that emotions and desires were pathological. The school of thought placed strong emphasis on the sharp distinction between circumstances which are in the control of the individual and those which are beyond it.[16]

> Of all existing things some are in our power, and others are not in our power. In our power are thought, impulse, will to get and will to avoid, and, in a word, everything which is our own doing. Things not in our power include the body, property, reputation, office, and in a word, everything which is not our own doing. Things in our power are by nature free, unhindered, untrammeled; things not in our power are weak, servile, subject to hindrance, dependent on others.
>
> - **Epictetus**, *Enchiridion*

The ideal Stoic would refrain from any qualitative judgment of an event or circumstance and view it with total objectivity. Everything from good fortune, to insult, to our closest relationships should all be viewed with indifference.[17] Though seemingly harsh, there are some aspects of the Stoic philosophy which have proven to be powerful antidotes to suffering, and which have even influenced modern therapy.[18] The Stoics were some of the first to point out that our environmental stimuli seem not to have direct control over our emotional experience, and that **our thoughts must be complicit in any emotional reaction.** Epictetus said,

> Remember, it is not enough to be hit or insulted to be harmed, you must believe that you are being harmed. If someone succeeds in provoking you, realize that your mind is complicit in the provocation.

> - **Epictetus**, *Enchiridion*

This perspective was reexamined in the late 20th-century and has come to represent a core principle of our current psychological understanding. The idea that our cognitions mediate our emotions is critical for explaining the variation of emotional responses we observe among individuals. This cognitive model is the foundational premise underlying the most effective therapeutic method ever devised, cognitive behavioral therapy (CBT).[19]

Aaron Beck is known as the father of cognitive therapy, which in conjunction with Albert Ellis's rational emotive behavior therapy, led to the development of modern CBT. Beck observed that all of the main psychotherapeutic methods of his day, from the psychoanalytic to the behavioral, shared the assumption that neuroses arise through impenetrable forces outside of the individual's awareness or control. Whether these forces were of chemical or historical origin, they required a trained healer to resolve. Beck proposed an idea which was not at all new, but was foreign to psychotherapy at the time:

Let us conjecture, for the moment, that a person's consciousness contains elements that are responsible for the emotional upsets and blurred thinking that lead him to seek help. Moreover, let us suppose that the patient has at his disposal various rational techniques he can use, with proper instruction, to deal with these disturbing elements in his consciousness.

- **Aaron Beck**, *Cognitive Therapy and the Emotional Disorders*

It is very likely that you experience certain negative emotions habitually in response to the events in your life. But as you introspect, you will find that these repetitive feelings are always preceded or accompanied by thoughts. A thought which interprets an event to be good will result in a positive emotion, and one that interprets it to be bad will result in a negative one. In other words, when our cognitions (accurate or not) conflict with our desires, we become unhappy, and vice versa.

Depending on whether someone appraises a stimulus as beneficial or detrimental to his personal domain, he experiences a 'positive' or 'negative' reaction.

- **Aaron Beck**, *Cognitive Therapy and the Emotional Disorders*

What you may not realize is just **how much power you have to choose the interpretation of these events.** Cognitive therapy says that the cognitive catalysts for our emotional reactions are called negative automatic thoughts.[20] These cognitions are habitual interpretations of patterns in our experience. Does this description remind you of anything? These automatic thoughts, just like the biases from the previous section, are the harmful algorithms which get in the way of our goals. In this case, our happiness.

Cognitions may be triggered by real world events, but they are ultimately the product of our beliefs and desires. The emotional algorithm is triggered by the cognitive habits which may or may not be accurate representations of reality. And very often, Beck found, **they are not accurate at all.**

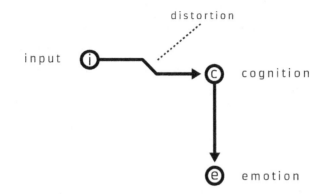

Beck observed that each person in his studies with depression and anxiety experienced predictable cognitive distortions. Mildly neurotic people had subtle misperceptions; severely neurotic people had massively warped worldviews. All of these errors can be corrected, regardless of severity.

Today, CBT is used to treat depression, several forms of anxiety, OCD, PTSD, and just about every other emotional disorder. Furthermore, **CBT is the most empirically effective therapeutic method ever devised,** beating out even the best antidepressant medications for some disorders. And even more impressively, studies have found that simply assigning patients to read *Feeling Good*, a self-help book by David Burns which distills the concepts of CBT, is just as effective in treating depression as a full course of anti-depressant medication.[21] One study found that after simply reading *Feeling Good* and completing some of its exercises, **seventy-five percent of the depressed patients studied no longer qualified for the disorder.**[22]

Our research reveals the unexpected: Depression is not an emotional disorder at all! The sudden change in the way you feel is of no more causal relevance than a runny nose is when you have a cold. Every bad feeling you have is the result of your distorted negative thinking. Illogical pessimistic attitudes play the central role in the development and continuation of all your symptoms. Intense negative thinking always accompanies a depressive episode, or any painful emotion for that matter.

- **David Burns**, *Feeling Good*

Though not all cases of depression may fit this simplistic template, Dr. Burns is right in pointing out the central role distorted thinking generally plays in the disorder. The biggest problem I see with CBT is the T: Therapy. The vast majority of people do not consider themselves to be in need of therapy. Though some of these people are prevented from going to therapy by pride or fear, many of them are right in thinking they are relatively healthy, normal individuals.

But we saw in previous chapters that healthy, normal individuals suffer from countless biases. Some of these biases are bound to manifest in one's emotional life in the form of negative automatic thoughts. This explains why the belief that we cannot control our emotions is so prevalent. We don't learn the methods for overcoming our lack of emotional control because **the inability to control one's emotions is considered normal.**

No clear line separates healing from upgrading. Medicine almost always begins by saving people from falling below the norm, but the same tools and know-how can then be used to surpass the norm.

- **Yuval Noah Harari**, *Homo Deus*

You may think that because you haven't been diagnosed with depression, the methods found in a therapeutic method would be irrelevant to you. But let me ask you this: When was the last time you experienced an unwanted emotion, if you're honest? In the last week? The last day? The last hour? Chances are, you experience emotions you would rather not experience regularly. **What if you could identify the roots of these emotions and unplug them for good?** Cognitive therapy offers a basic toolkit for dealing with emotions to people who lack it. But it is entirely possible to take these methods to an advanced level and master them.

Emotional Alchemy

Indeed, in humans the cognitive apparatus can greatly shorten, prolong, or otherwise modify the more 'hardwired' emotional tendencies we share with the other animals.

- **Jaak Panksepp**, *Affective Neuroscience*

Immediately after an emotional response, our rational mind has the opportunity to reflect and reinterpret the information before it feeds back into our emotions. **Reappraisal**, also called reframing, is the act of reinterpreting the meaning of an emotional stimulus, altering the resulting emotional trajectory. In other words, **every time we experience a negative emotion, we are given the gift of reinterpretation**, and this reinterpretation is a key leverage point to controlling our emotions.[23]

Reappraisal has been found by both self reports and functional imaging studies to reliably increase positive emotion and decrease negative emotion, though it can also be used to do the opposite if desired.[24] Its use is also correlated with enhanced memory, closer interpersonal relationships, and overall mental health. It must be stressed that reappraisal is not the same thing as the positive thinking which is so popular in today's self-help section. Thinking positive thoughts will not force the negative ones away, nor will the brute force suppression discussed earlier, which has been shown to increase painful emotion and depressive symptoms.[25]

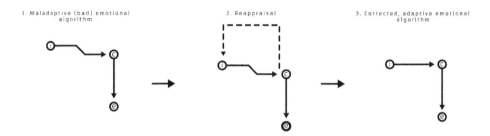

Reappraisal is an active process of replacing old pathways of reasoning with new, more accurate ones. Reframing is often quickly glossed over as an antidote to emotional pain, but the skill of reappraisal can be developed to an expert level. I have found that as you practice this skill, you get quicker and quicker at finding adaptive interpretations of situations.

You can actually become so quick at reappraising a situation that **you bypass the negative emotion altogether.**[26] You pause and remind yourself that the person who cut you off in traffic was not, in fact, trying to make you wreck, and is just doing their best. That the loss of your job does not make you a total failure, and may ultimately lead to a better outcome for you. You can gradually eliminate entire emotional categories, such as jealousy[27] or self-blame,[28] preventing them from ever afflicting you.

Reappraisal is an in-the-moment strategy we can use any time we are dealing with an undesired emotion. But in order to build a truly better mind, we are going to have to go a bit deeper to the core of emotional psychitecture. We don't simply want to become aware of our harmful emotional reactions or change them as we are dealing with them. We want to remove them on a systematic level. **We want to reprogram the cognitive algorithms which gave rise to them.**

Restructuring Your Emotions

My students and I have found that truly happy individuals construe life events and daily situations in ways that seem to maintain their happiness, while unhappy individuals construe experiences in ways that seem to reinforce unhappiness.

- **Sonja Lyubomirsky**[29]

Wouldn't it be nice if we automatically chose the adaptive interpretation of events as soon as they happened? In order to reprogram bad emotional algorithms, we have to examine the beliefs at their root, identify the distortions, and practice their rational rebuttal until it has been internalized. This method for obliterating bad emotional algorithms and replacing them with adaptive ones is known as **cognitive restructuring**.

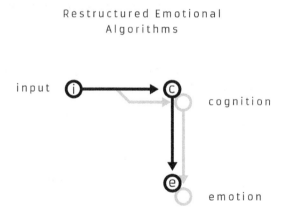

Restructured Emotional
Algorithms

input ⓘ ⟶ © cognition

ⓔ emotion

Cognitive restructuring is the fundamental tool of emotional psychitecture, and psychological research has found it to be highly effective for eliminating negative emotional responses.[30] The first step is to keep a log in the form of a notepad or a smartphone app.[31] Try to take a note of every undesirable emotion you notice - anything from minor annoyance to severe anxiety. The simple act of keeping a log should cause you to notice many more of these emotions than you normally would. Every time you log an emotion, take a note of the situation which triggered it, and if possible, the chain of thoughts which immediately preceded it.

Over time, you will begin to notice patterns and trends. You will find that certain lines of reasoning dominate your emotional experience. You may find that a certain kind of mistaken reasoning is responsible for a huge percentage of your daily struggles. **By correcting the mistaken reasoning, you can permanently reprogram the algorithm and eliminate the undesired emotion.**

Just like in the cognitive section, in order to reprogram the faulty algorithms, you must memorize the most common problematic ones. Here are the top ten found in cognitive therapy patients:

1. **All-or-Nothing Thinking:** The tendency to think in extremes like "always" and "never" without considering nuanced degrees between.

"My boyfriend broke up with me; I always ruin my relationships."

2. **Overgeneralization:** The tendency to make broad assumptions based on limited specifics.

"If one person thinks I'm stupid, everyone will."

3. **Mental Filter:** The tendency to focus on small negative details to the exclusion of the big picture.

"My A+ average doesn't matter; I got a C on an assignment."

4. **Disqualifying the Positive:** The tendency to dismiss positive aspects of an experience for irrational reasons.

"If my friend compliments me, she is probably just saying it out of pity."

5. **Jumping to Conclusions:** The tendency to make unfounded, negative assumptions, often in the form of attempted mind reading or fortune telling.

"If my romantic interest doesn't text me today, he must not be interested."

6. **Catastrophizing:** The tendency to magnify or minimize certain details of an experience, painting it as worse or more severe than it is.

"If my wife leaves me, then I will never be able to recover from my misery."

7. **Emotional Reasoning:** The tendency to take one's emotions as evidence of objective truth.

"If I feel offended by someone else's remark, then he must have wronged me."

8. **Should Statements:** The tendency to apply rigid rules to how one "should" or "must" behave.

"My friend criticized my attitude, and that is something that friends should never do."

9. **Labeling:** The tendency to describe oneself in the form of absolute labels.

"If I make a calculation error, it makes me a total idiot."

10. **Personalization:** The tendency to attribute negative outcomes to oneself without evidence.

"If my wife is in a bad mood, then I must have done something to upset her."[32]

Try to identify which of these patterns characterizes a particular cognition, and add it to your log. The next step is to use the method called Socratic questioning to challenge these distorted cognitions. Positive psychology researcher Courtney Ackerman offers some basic questions to ask:

Is this thought realistic?
Am I basing my thoughts on facts or on feelings?
What is the evidence for this thought?
Could I be misinterpreting the evidence?
Am I viewing a complicated situation as black and white?
Am I having this thought out of habit, or do facts support it?[33]

Examine the evidence supporting or challenging the automatic thought, and decide whether your automatic thought is rational or not. For example, imagine you become sad and anxious because you have the thought "I'm totally incompetent," triggered by a failure to remember an appointment you had scheduled. Look for evidence supporting the claim that you are totally incompetent and look for conflicting evidence showing that you are competent.

You may be tempted to argue that you never really believed the thought in the first place. **But the fact that the thought even made it far enough to enter your consciousness is a sign that some part of you was not convinced of its irrationality.**[34]

Let's look at an example. Let's say you land an interview for your dream job. You pour countless hours into preparation, nail the interview, and begin fantasizing about your new role as assistant to the regional manager at your local video rental store (it's a weird dream job, but I'm not here to judge). Days and then weeks pass before you get an email saying the position was given to someone else.

At this point, there are two different ways you might respond. You could 1) spend weeks sulking, speculating about why you didn't get the job, castigating yourself for your failings, and convincing yourself that you will never get a good job and are fundamentally inadequate. Or you could 2) ask your interviewers for feedback, work to make the necessary improvements to your interview skills or portfolio, and move on to the next job without wasting a moment to suffer.

We would all rather be the person who takes option 2, but not everyone does, or even readily can. We may tend to think that acting in the right way is simply a matter of being mature and responsible. But the difference between taking option 1 and option 2 fundamentally boils down to complex chains of psychological algorithms, and these chains must be understood before they can be reprogrammed.

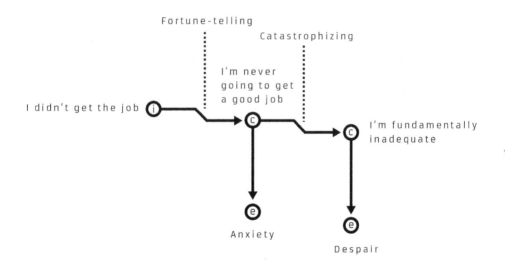

So you accurately conclude that you did not get the job after reading your rejection letter. You then come to the distorted conclusion that this one rejection is indicative of a much greater and permanent problem. If I'm rejected for this position, then I'm never going to get a good job. After confronting this fact, you have the thought that you are fundamentally inadequate as a person, triggering a wave of despair. When you see it written out, the absurdity of the inference becomes obvious. But these thoughts often find their way into our belief systems without our full awareness.

So let's go through some of the methods of self-regulation. You could have used situation selection and never applied for a job to eliminate the risk of rejection. You could put down the letter, divert your attention away from the rejection, and try never to think about it again. I would not recommend either of these strategies in this scenario. Alternatively, you could practice mindfulness to hit pause on the negative emotions and observe them for what they are, or you could engage in cognitive restructuring (better yet, combine the two).

Once you understand that your painful emotion is the result of a distorted thought, you can begin to restructure the algorithm. In this case, you could identify the distortion known as catastrophizing leading you to believe you will never get a good job, or that this would mean that you are fundamentally inadequate. You restructure the core belief that x means y, and once you have done this, your brain will learn that similar lines of reasoning are invalid the next time a similar situation arises.

By learning to quickly recognize and refute this bias, you can build the habit of short-circuiting this tendency automatically, programming it out for good. After identifying and reappraising your distorted cognition, you will have eliminated the negative emotion and can now focus your efforts on setting new goals and taking action.

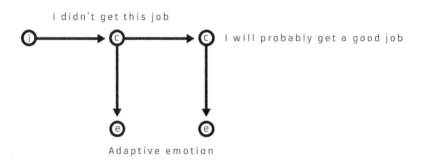

As you practice the art of restructuring, you begin to call your brain out on the nonsense it throws at you. Discipline with this practice will gradually train your brain not to think these thoughts in the first place. I want to assure you that the art of cognitive restructuring can be mastered. Whether you have a relentless inner monologue or merely an occasionally annoying one, you can develop a firm grip on the ongoing narrative of your life, proactively designing your own experience rather than simply being along for the ride.

You may wonder why the brain thinks such ridiculous thoughts in the first place. You would likely never think someone else was incompetent for forgetting a single appointment. Why do we commit these absurd errors with ourselves? Whether or not we are fully conscious of it, **we choose irrational interpretations.** And counterintuitively, **we do it because it feels good.**[35]

We are not just victim to our painful emotions. We indulge them. We choose to catastrophize because, perverse as it may seem, self-pity gives us a kind of short-term high, even if it habitually locks us into deeper lows. When we allow the mind to get away with thinking distorted and self-critical thoughts, our reward system trains it to do it more.[36] In order to choose long-term well-being, **we have to resist the urge to indulge in our own pain.**

> It is in our power to have no opinion about a thing, and not to be disturbed in our soul. For things themselves have no natural power to form our judgments.
>
> - **Marcus Aurelius**, *Meditations*

Imagine how much fun it would be to be physically invincible. To enter a sword-fight unarmed and to exit without a scratch, leaving your opponent frustrated and exhausted. When you become emotionally invincible, your opponent may be another person shelling out insults, your own inner critic, or simply the unexpected blows life deals to us all.

These petty attempts to break you will begin to amuse you more than they dishearten you once you learn their game. When a drunk man hits the wall of a castle with a stick, you don't call it an attack, you call it entertainment! When a person insults you, they embed a narrative in your mind. Whether you are forced to accept this suggestion or are able to resist it is a matter of how developed your cognitive toolkit is.

With enough practice, you can learn to instantly identify the irrational thoughts that will cause you to suffer. You can develop the knowledge and discipline to take control of the ongoing story your brain is spinning. But in order to do it, you have to build the habits of noticing every distortion that enters your awareness, resisting the urge to indulge it, and shooting down each one before it takes your emotional trajectory down with it.

Key Takeaways

• The second realm of psychitecture is emotional, and it's principle goal of emotional self-mastery is the ability to control your own emotional experience.

• Despite the popular notion that emotions are all-knowing guides for our lives, emotions do not exist for our long-term benefit, and were not built to deal with modern life.

• Emotions often lead us in the opposite direction of our highest goals, cause us to act in ways we later regret, and force us to suffer when there is absolutely no benefit to doing so.

• The similarly popular idea that it is impossible to control our emotions is also flawed, as there is strong evidence for the efficacy of emotional self-regulation.

• We can design our emotions through at least five methods, known as situation selection, situation modification, attentional deployment, cognitive change, and response modulation.

• Cognitive change is one of the most effective of these methods, and is the most relevant to emotional psychitecture.

• You may never have perfect control over your emotions, but you can develop a truly surprising and increasing amount of control by mastering a few powerful psychotechnologies.

• A key truth about emotions which was emphasized by the philosophy of Stoicism is that they are rarely triggered directly by events in our lives, and are almost always reactions to our cognitive interpretation of these events.

- The most common emotional algorithm consists of an external input, a cognition, and an emotional reaction.
- Cognitive behavioral therapy is based on the fact that we can intervene with these interpretations, or **appraisals**, by altering our beliefs about the world and ourselves.
- Though not everyone believes they are in need of psychotherapy, everyone can benefit from learning principles of CBT to take their emotional control beyond the norm.
- **Reappraisal**, also called reframing, is the act of reinterpreting the meaning of an emotional stimulus, altering the resulting emotional trajectory.
- Reappraisal is an active process of replacing old pathways of reasoning with new, more accurate ones, and you can actually become so quick at reappraising a situation that you bypass certain negative emotions altogether.
- **Cognitive restructuring** takes reappraisal to a deeper level by permanently altering beliefs that repeatedly cause us to suffer.
- To practice it, keep a log in the form of a notepad or a smartphone app, and try to take a note of every undesirable emotion you notice, the situation which triggered it, and the chain of thoughts which immediately preceded it.
- Much like the cognitive biases of chapter 2, you can memorize the most common distortions that affect our emotions.
- Label the thoughts you logged with the fitting distortion, and then use Socratic questioning to challenge these distorted cognitions.
- If getting rejected by a job opportunity sends you into a spiral of anxiety and despair, you can map out the chain of thoughts and feelings responsible. The rejection may have led to the painful emotions by triggering the thought that you are never going to get a good job (fortune-telling distortion), and that this makes you fundamentally inadequate as a person (catastrophizing distortion).
- By correcting the mistaken reasoning, you can permanently reprogram the algorithm and eliminate the undesired emotions.
- With enough practice, you can learn to instantly identify the irrational thoughts that will cause you to suffer.
- You have to build the habits of noticing every distortion that enters your awareness, resisting the urge to indulge them, and shooting down each one before it takes your emotional trajectory down with it.

6

Desires and the Keys to Modulating Them

Always Get What You Want

If thou wilt make a man happy, add not unto his riches but take away from his desires.

- **Epicurus**, *Principal Doctrines*

As we have seen, living to serve and gratify our desires is far from the key to enduring well-being. But our desires do more than serve as the red herrings of happiness: they actively cause us to suffer. Because desires cause us pain and frustration when they are not satisfied, **every desire we harbor is a potential threat to our contentment and stability.**[1]

Forming defined goals does not get rid of our desires. Even after we refuse the seductive offer of our desires to set our goals for us, they are still present, either serving to pull us toward our goals or away from them. The desires that pull us away from our goals are called temptations. The desires that push us toward our goals are fuel, and we will deal with all of these in later chapters. Some desires can be highly beneficial, and we will strive to keep them in place - even amplify and stack them.

But this tendency of our desires to propel us toward our goals becomes problematic when we fail to achieve our goals and the desires for nonexistent realities continue to writhe and cause us to suffer.[2] In these cases, previously advantageous desires become disadvantageous, as suffering is rarely conducive to our goals.

Popular wisdom offers a solution: don't fail. Try your best to succeed at achieving your goals, and maybe you won't suffer so much. However, an alternate approach has been suggested by a few wise thinkers throughout history. These thinkers indicate that it might be possible to control our desires directly rather than simply trying to control our circumstances. They argued that the negative emotions our desires cause can be hijacked. By learning to modulate our desires, we can not only reduce the temptations and increase the fuel propelling us toward our goals, **we can eliminate a major source of suffering**.

In the previous chapter, we looked at how we can modify our perceptions to change our emotions. But if our unwanted emotions are not caused by cognitive distortion, we need to pursue a different path to controlling our emotions. The algorithm which outputs emotions takes in the inputs of cognitions and desires. And if our perceptions are not the problem, we will have to change our desires.

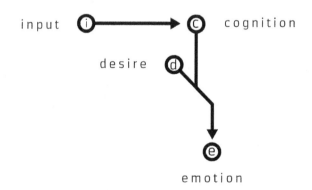

Although there seems to be a scarcity of research on the act of changing one's emotions through desire modulation, this practice has been initiated and used successfully for millennia. It has been a major focal point of almost every practical philosophy to date.

Most people are familiar with Buddhism's solution to the problem of craving. According to the prevalent interpretation of Siddhārtha Gautama's teachings, liberation from the vicious cycle of craving could be achieved through a combination of mindfulness, ethical living, and wisdom.[3] If followed properly, this path could result in a psychological state potent enough to popularize grunge music for nearly half a decade. **Nirvana** was a transcendent state characterized by the extinguishment of the fire of craving and desire. A total detachment from preference and outcome.[4]

Another wise thinker who weighed in on desire was Epicurus, who argued that we need very little to be happy and should strive to reduce our desires as much as possible. He thought we should satisfy our natural and necessary desires like food and water. But we should not strive to satisfy those which are unnatural or unnecessary, like extravagant foods, sex, power, or Instagram followers (his words, not mine).[5] It is less extreme than the Buddha's suggestion, and may strike us as more realistic, and we see this minimalistic approach to desire in countless other thinkers.

The sage desires to have few desires.

- **Lao Tzu**, *Tao Te Ching*

[I] try always to master myself rather than fortune, and to change my desires rather than the order of the world.

- **René Descartes**, *Discourse on Method*

Freedom is not achieved by satisfying desire, but by eliminating it.

- **Epictetus**, Discourses

The Stoic notion that we should not desire what we cannot control is also relevant here. Situations we have no control over are obvious examples of times you shouldn't want things to be different because these desires cause unnecessary suffering. We often long for other things which are out of our reach even though they are not, at least at the present moment, within our control. These misplaced longings often result from confusion over how much control we have.[6] No adult suffers over the fact that he cannot simply spread his arms and fly, as this is unambiguously out of reach.

There is a condition known as locked-in syndrome in which a patient is fully aware but completely paralyzed, unable to speak, and forced to communicate simple yes or no answers using a computer. Most people will claim they would rather die than have to live this way. The curious finding is that not only is the average quality of life found in these patients very high, but their brains learn to stop struggling with their condition very quickly, often within hours. They cease all desire and strain because the impossibility of controlling the external world quickly becomes unambiguously apparent.[7]

> The faculty of desire purports to aim at securing what you want...If you fail in your desire, you are unfortunate, if you experience what you would rather avoid you are unhappy... For desire, suspend it completely for now. Because if you desire something outside your control, you are bound to be disappointed; and even things we do control, which under other circumstances would be deserving of our desire, are not yet within our power to attain. Restrict yourself to choice and refusal; and exercise them carefully, within discipline and detachment.

> - **Epictetus**, *Enchiridion*

So Buddhism's solution is to eliminate all desire, Epicureanism's solution is to reduce one's desires to the absolute essentials, and Stoicism's solution is not to desire what we can't control. We will see that each of these perspectives holds keys to the mastery of desire.

It is possible for us to regulate our desires such that we cut off our suffering when the situation calls for it. But furthermore, it is entirely possible to do this and still use them to powerfully motivate us toward rational goals. **We don't need to renounce desire altogether; we just need to become proficient desire manipulators.**[8]

If we can tame our desires and develop agility at modulating them so we want the right things at any given time, we can leverage them to fuel us toward our goals as effectively as possible. Later chapters will focus on using our desires to fuel us. But before this can be done, we need to learn and practice the methods these thinkers devised for using desire to promote our own emotional peace.

The Modulation of Desire

Though they may have viewed the goal differently, a number of great psychitectural thinkers have conceived exercises for strengthening the desire modulation muscle so our wants can be bent to suit our circumstances. Many of these exercises have since been validated by modern research. Each one of these exercises is a counter algorithm which can be internalized to quash desire-based emotional friction.

Modulation

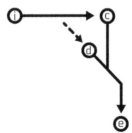

The first and most basic skill we must practice is the ability to **up-regulate**, or increase, and **down-regulate**, or decrease the strength of a particular desire. As the previous chapter described, our cognitions are deeply involved in emotion, and they are intertwined with our desires as well. Strong feelings of desire are typically accompanied or preceded by cognitive simulations and fantasies.[9]

> ...desire-related processing can be subject to a vicious circle
> of reprocessing and rumination that, in turn, increases the
> feeling of wanting and the motivational power of desire.

> *- The Psychology of Desire*

Participants of experiments who are given cognitively demanding tasks to complete are less likely to respond to stimulus with desire.[10] In other words, if our minds are preoccupied or focused on something else, they are unable to initiate the thought cycles that heighten desire. So the key to basic desire regulation has to do with our mental closeness or distance from the stimulus.

This understanding provides us with the opportunity to raise or lower the dials of desire as it serves us. To up-regulate a desire, focus purely on the desired stimulus and all of its most positive aspects and delicious details. This can be done to increase the intensity of a desire for a school lecture, a long drive, or a veggie burger.

We can also down-regulate a desire. To do this, distract yourself from the desired stimulus, focus on it in a purely objective, even alienating way, and cultivate a non-attached awareness of the feelings associated with the desire.

Marcus Aurelius offers some examples of down-regulation:

When we have meat before us and other food, we must say
to ourselves: 'This is the dead body of a fish, and this is the
dead body of a bird or of a pig, and again, this Falernian
[wine] is only a little grape juice, and this purple robe some
sheep's wool died with the blood of a shellfish'...This is how
we should act throughout life: where there are things that
seem worthy of great estimation, we ought to lay them bare
and look at their worthlessness and strip them of all the
words by which they are exalted. For the outward show [of
things] is a wonderful perverter of reason, and when we are
certain the things we are dealing with are worth the trouble,
that is when it cheats us most.

- **Marcus Aurelius**, *Meditations*

Buddhism offers a similar exercise for those under the spell of unwanted sexual desire, in which one meditates on the more repulsive aspects of the
human body such as organs, tissues, and fluids in order to "...extinguish the fire
of lust by removing its fuel."[11] The Buddhist practice of mindfulness meditation
in general can be a useful method for taking the subjectivity and passion out
of our perceptions and viewing the objects of our desire with dispassionate acceptance.

Do not indulge in dreams of having what you have not, but
reckon up the chief of the blessings you do possess, and then
thankfully remember how you would crave for them if they
were not yours.

- **Marcus Aurelius**, *Meditations*

There are many methods for regulating desires in bulk. Take the incredibly simple practice of gratitude. Our minds are wired to acclimate to our circumstances and magnify the negative to completely fill our field of view. This tendency may be biologically useful by driving us to continually push for more, but it can destroy our contentment and make life seem like one big series of hindrances and hardships.

Gratitude can be used as a method for up-regulating all desires for what you already have while down-regulating desires for what you lack. It is an excellent strategy for countering the disappointment of failure by shifting emotional investment away from new gains and toward things that you already have, such as loved ones, achievements, or fortunate living conditions. Often the greatest barrier to serenity is too many desires for what we don't possess and too few for what we do.

Numerous studies have found that people who consistently experience gratitude are more satisfied with their lives and experience more frequent positive emotions. They are also less depressed, anxious, lonely, and neurotic.[12] Gratitude is likely so effective because it causes people to savor their positive life experiences, reinterpret negative ones, build stronger interpersonal bonds, and avoid constant envy and craving.[13]

Gratitude

Desires for what you have   Desires for what you don't have

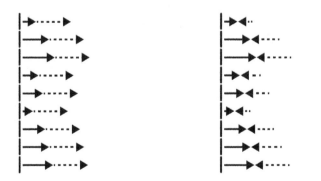

The Stoics had a related practice which has been called negative visualization, or premortem. It is closely related to the Buddhist reflection on impermanence, and the Dalai Lama has termed it "pain insurance." When you initiate this practice, you reflect on the possibility of losing the things you have. You consider the possibility that all of your plans may fail, all of your possessions may be lost, and all those you care about, including yourself, can, and eventually will die.

Desires to have in the present   Desires to keep permanently

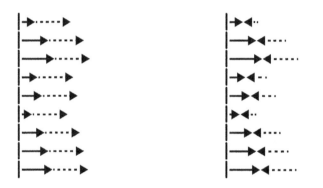

It may seem depressing, but this practice actually goes hand-in-hand with gratitude. When we down-regulate our desire to possess and keep something permanently, we up-regulate our desire and appreciation for what we have in the present moment. This visualization technique can inoculate us against loss and reduce or eliminate the blow to our emotions we have to bear if things don't go according to plan.

This act of anticipating unpleasant events has actually been proven to minimize their emotional impact. In one study, participants were delivered a series of electric shocks of varying intensity. Those who knew the intensity of the shocks in advance experienced less pain and fear than those who received less intense shocks of unpredictable intensity.[14] We can apply this insight by calibrating our expectations so we are never caught off guard by unanticipated shocks.

The Buddhist belief called anatta, or **nonself**, states that the concept of the self is entirely an illusion, and that the person you think you are today is a different entity from what you were ten years ago, or even ten seconds ago. You are an ongoing and constantly evolving process - an aggregation of uncontrolled perceptions and cognitions. Nonself serves as a reminder that we are not unified egos, but parts of an ongoing and constantly evolving process – an aggregation of uncontrolled perceptions and cognitions. We are not discrete beings detached from all others, but inextricably tied to the collective of all sentient beings.

Much of the pain we experience is caused not by events we wish to avoid, but by the identity we wish to have. The desires which cause us to suffer when we are hit with a painful insult are the desires to be a competent, lovable, and valued individual. But by contemplating nonself, we can down-regulate all identity-based desires by reminding ourselves of the flaws with the entire self-construct when circumstances clash with these desires to be liked or respected.

There is evidence that reflecting less on our personal life narratives and more on the expanded self improves well-being. A decrease in narrative-self thoughts has been found to result in greater well-being by decreasing negative and mixed negative–positive emotions.[15] This decrease in attention on the self is often achieved and studied through the practice of mindfulness meditation.[16] Mindfulness is thought by some to have this effect by decreasing activity in the brain structures collectively known as the default mode network, which are associated with rumination about the narrative-self.[17]

Identity-based desires

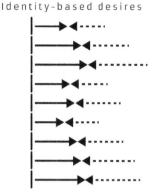

The Stoics also made use of a method known as the **view from above**, which consists of contemplating the vastness of the cosmos, and the contrasting smallness of all of one's petty concerns. This method can be used to down-regulate all of your desires in bulk when you are overly invested in general, particularly when life becomes volatile.

> To see them from above: the thousands of animal herds, the rituals, the voyages on calm or stormy seas, the different ways we come into the world, share it with one another, and leave it. Consider the lives led once by others, long ago, the lives to be led by others after you, the lives led even now, in foreign lands. How many people don't even know your name. How many will soon have forgotten it. How many offer you praise now-and tomorrow, perhaps contempt.

> - **Marcus Aurelius**, *Meditations*

It is hard to even read this quotation without feeling a humble relief over the ultimate triviality of our concerns. The Stoics thought the primary reason we suffer is because we are unable to comprehend and love nature in its entirety. When we understand that everything that happens is causally determined, we free ourselves from the blame and resentment of ourselves and others and from the anxiety of trying to control fate. When we come to see that what we naturally view as bad is derived from our limited perspective, we can put a limit to our sadness. And when we understand that the permanence of our possessions, relationships, and souls for which we long is unattainable, we can learn to love what is permanent.

View from Above

All desires

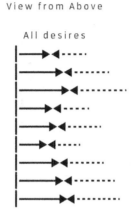

Viktor Frankl, a 20th-century psychiatrist famous for his analysis of his own experiences as a prisoner in Nazi death camps during the holocaust, notes the utility of the distancing tactic:

> All that oppressed me at that moment became objective, seen and described from the remote viewpoint of science. By this method I succeeded somehow in rising above the situation, above the sufferings of the moment and I observed them as if they were already of the past. Both I and my troubles became the interesting object of psychoscientific study taken on by myself.[18]

> - **Viktor Frankl**, *Man's Search for Meaning*

In his book, *The Philosophy of Cognitive Behavioural Therapy*, Donald Robertson points out that this thought experiment has its place in modern therapy as well.[19] Aaron Beck refers to the tendency of depressed patients to magnify their issues and take the "worm's eye view" of their situations. To counter this, patients are encouraged to take an "enlarged perspective," in which they distance themselves from their current circumstances, view them with greater objectivity, and contemplate them from a greater scale and timespan.[20]

Let's return to our video rental rejection example from the previous chapter. Let's say you have mastered the art of cognitive restructuring, and have no distortions in reasoning around this rejection. But somehow, the rejection still causes you to suffer.

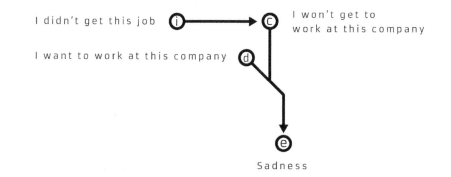

The conflict between this reality and your desire for the job results in sadness. You know this job is already out of the question for you. But a rogue desire within you is causing you to experience emotions that aren't serving you. It would be much better if your desires were fully adapted to this reality so they could start fueling you toward a better outcome instead of causing needless pain.

So let's get rid of that useless desire. You can use desire modulation to adjust the dials of desire and calibrate them to reality. You could engage in gratitude to up-regulate your desire for all the great things you have, even if this particular job isn't one of them. You also might down-regulate the specific desire causing your suffering by reminding yourself of the hour-and-a-half-long commute, or that movie rental is probably not a great industry to build a career in right now, or that you have a master's in data science. Honestly, I have no idea what you saw in that job in the first place, Sarah.

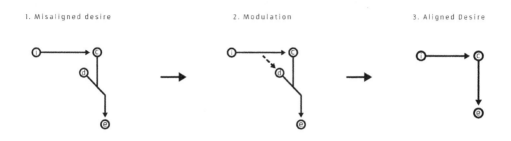

Once you learn and strengthen your ability to use these tactics, you will be able to adjust your desires at will, largely eliminating the tendency to suffer over ungratified longings.

The Counteraction of Desire

> Greed and aversion surface in the form of thoughts, and thus can be eroded by a process of 'thought substitution,' by replacing them with the thoughts opposed to them.
>
> - **Bhikkhu Bodhi**, *The Noble Eightfold Path*

A powerful tactic which uses and builds upon the basic skills of up and down-regulation is a method I call counteraction. **Counteraction**, which was briefly touched on in chapter 2, entails balancing out a desire by up or down-regulating an equal and opposing desire so they "cancel" one another out.

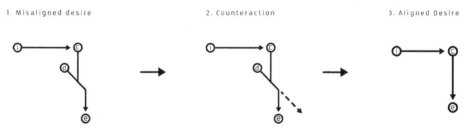

Have you ever sat at a red light full of anger that it is taking too long to change? Of course you have. Have you ever been frustrated that a red light changed to green too quickly - perhaps because it interrupted your attempt to eat a sandwich or shave your legs on your commute? In this conflict, there is an opportunity. Next time you are sitting at a red light impatiently, try cultivating the desire for the light to stay red as long as possible. Use the up-regulation techniques listed above to desire the opposite of whatever is nagging at you.

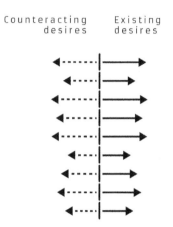

By generating conflicting desires, you hedge your bets against unwanted outcomes and turn every outcome into a wanted one. The moment one outcome actualizes, you can drop the counteracting desire. If you can develop the ability to neutralize all of your desires, you can then up-regulate and down-regulate them precisely in order to achieve the goals which align with your ideals. You can carefully increase a desire and decrease the conflicting desire like increasing the gas in a car. Eventually, you will start to enact counteraction techniques automatically and internally. **You start to immediately notice friction in your mind and generate the counteracting desire automatically.**

As we will explore in the behavioral section, desires operate algorithmically too, meaning they are based on habits and can be programmed or deprogrammed.[21] Eating ice cream after every meal will cause you to strongly desire dessert after every meal. Watching television every day after work will cause you to need to watch television every day after work. And struggling with every setback in your life, desiring reality to be otherwise, will cause you to continue to struggle.

Some of our desires are not for isolated objects, but represent ongoing dependencies from which we may aspire to free ourselves. Because we are creatures of habit, our behaviors have a strong influence on what we become. This is why, even though there is no biological reason for pieces of green paper and numbers in our bank account to capture our desires, we can be trained to crave money. Weird as it may seem, we often learn about ourselves by observing our own behaviors, so if all of our behaviors suggest to us that money, for example, is the highest good, we very well may start to believe it.[22]

One of the lesser known and more fascinating of the ancient Greek philosophers was a man known as Diogenes of Sinope. He is thought to have lived partially naked in a wine barrel in Athens, and to have frequently relieved and pleasured himself in public. According to one revealing story, Alexander the Great became dismayed that Diogenes had not come to visit him, as many others had come to lavish him in praise. So Alexander decided to pay Diogenes a visit accompanied by a large crowd and trumpets announcing his arrival. Alexander greeted and praised Diogenes, and said "Ask any favor you choose of me." After leaning up a bit and seeing the crowd of people, Diogenes told the leader of the civilized world only to "Stand a little out of my sun."[23]

Diogenes may sound like a senile homeless man, but he was actually a highly respected philosopher and founder of the school of Cynicism. He was admired for his wit and radical non-conformity. And though eccentric, he had surprisingly coherent reasons for his behaviors. He engaged in inappropriate acts in public because he believed anything natural and acceptable to do in private should be regarded as acceptable in public. He chose to live in poverty and rejected praise and favors because he held wealth, social status, and all cultural values in contempt.[24]

He was a precursor to the modern-day minimalist, rejecting anything unnecessary. His shamelessness was meant to serve as a demonstration that nature and reason were superior to convention, and that in many ways, the simple lives of animals were better than the overcomplicated lives civilized society demands. He preached the virtues of self-control and self-sufficiency and claimed that virtue of character was all anyone needed to live a good life. He once threw away his only possession, a wooden bowl, after seeing a boy cupping his hands to drink from the river, announcing, "A child has beaten me in plainness of living."[25]

Diogenes is probably not someone you will want to model your life after, and the fact that he was a great philosopher does not make the case for disregarding hygiene or social courtesy. But his life is a reminder that many of the things you may consider essential for a happy life can be discarded without losing your sense of peace or purpose. By banishing all unnecessary forms of gratification from his life, he reduced the number of things he needed to have in order to be content, and the number of things he could lose that would ruin his day.

If we find that certain desire-based dependencies are maladaptive or cause us to act against our values, we can use the practice of **asceticism**, or voluntary discomfort, to intentionally deprive ourselves of some desired and attainable object. The practice has been used by some to serve as self-punishment, which has led some to quickly write it off.

But the useful purpose of asceticism is to down-regulate a perpetual desire for anything extrinsic. By utilizing this practice, you can break dependencies and make yourself more emotionally robust. Simply choose something on which you feel you are overly reliant, and intentionally limit or sacrifice the gratification of the associated desire. Though it may feel like self-punishment, minor and temporary acts of self-denial can be fully grounded in self-compassion.[26]

If you find yourself unable to endure basic economy flights, enjoy camping trips, or are unhappy whenever the thermostat is not set to the perfect temperature, you have become overly-reliant on comfort. **This dependency will limit your ability to be content in all but the rare perfect scenario.** In this case, you can periodically force yourself to endure pain or discomfort to down-regulate the desire for comfort. Counter your dependency by sleeping on the floor for a night or walking barefoot on a gravel road.[27] Taking this to it's extreme and hiking the Appalachian Trail will completely rewire your relationship with comfort.

If it is pleasure you crave, you can temporarily deprive yourself of food (fasting), sex, or a drug to down-regulate the desire. Minor acts of social sacrifice, such as neglecting an opportunity to signal something positive about yourself, can decrease your desire for status, approval, and validation. And giving away all but the most necessary possessions in the spirit of minimalism can down-regulate the innate desire to accumulate and horde. You can even take this ascetic spirit to an extreme by completely renouncing some forms of desire. You can refuse to accumulate new toys. Reject all social media platforms. Commit to give away all excess money beyond what is needed for a sustainable lifestyle. For every type of perpetual desire you are able to renounce, you remove complication from your life.[28]

Frequent practice of moderate asceticism is a way of embedding into your mind the fact that your desires are not good indicators of worthwhile choices. When you act against those desires, your mind will learn from your behaviors and conclude that these things are not so desirable after all. Would anyone who thought pleasure was the ultimate good deliberately put herself in an uncomfortable position? Would anyone who thought social status were the highest good neglect his social media accounts? Would anyone who thought money were the highest good turn down, or even give away, a large sum of money? You teach yourself what is important to you through your behaviors, so behave wisely.

Learning the ways of your desires and strengthening the skill of modulating them will require patience, but once you have done this, you will be able to use this craft in real time. When an obstacle stands in your way, you will instantly arrange your desires to avoid the emotional friction and focus your attention on responding to the obstacle.

Principles of Modulation

On a broader level, there are principles we can follow for relating to our desires and working with them more effectively to avoid unnecessary pain. You need to detect when you want something very strongly - when there are few alternates to a particular object or outcome. Ask yourself - "What would cause me to suffer if I failed to achieve it or lost it?" Maybe failing out of college would crush you, or perhaps the loss of a favorite pet. Though we may not be eager to plan for these misfortunes, doing so can prevent us from being blindsided if and when they occur.

Let's look back at the goal hierarchy from before. We saw that defined goals are the keys to actualizing your values, but they are also the key to reducing suffering. When we aim for the intrinsic, we will be much less likely to suffer because nothing can take out our final goals.[29] Modern Stoic William Irvine illustrates this by looking at the goals of a tennis player:

> Thus, his goal in playing tennis will not be to win a match (something external, over which he has only partial control) but to play to the best of his ability in the match (something internal, over which he has complete control). By choosing this goal, he will spare himself frustration or disappointment should he lose the match: Since it was not his goal to win the match, he will not have failed to attain his goal, as long as he played his best. His tranquility will not be disrupted."[30]

- **William Irvine**, *A Guide to the Good Life*

Intrinsic goals do not result in negative emotion because it is impossible to fail at them, and building a life full of intrinsic goals is a great way to prevent constant emotional pain. But even when our highest goals and ultimate aims are intrinsic, we will inevitably have certain extrinsic sub-goals that will result in pain when they are unmet. And in order to prevent this pain, we need to structure these goals properly. Which of these structures would you rather be inside of in a tornado?

The structure on the left is incredibly vulnerable. A small breeze would be enough to destroy it. In our case, the small breeze would be the everyday occurrence of a situation not going according to plan. As soon as one link in the chain fails, the entire structure topples, which results in emotional self-destruction. The structure on the right, however, is highly robust, and a person with a goal structure like this will be far more emotionally robust. As soon as one goal fails, he can pivot over to another, and the more quickly this can be done, the less time has to be spent suffering, and the sooner he can get back to pursuing his ends.

This is why you need to develop alternates for your goals. **Carve out as many alternate paths to your higher goals as you can.**

▲ Achieve sustainable existence

▲ Make money

▲ Get this job

▲ Land this interview

If you desperately want a particular job at a particular time, you will be crushed if you fail to land it. Try to discover other companies and timelines as paths toward a fulfilling job. On a higher level, add the alternate goal of starting a business as a path toward income. Why not take it to the extreme? Develop the alternate goal of living in a monastery as a path toward a sustainable existence. Reflect on the possibility of building a new life with new opportunities for growth after a major loss.

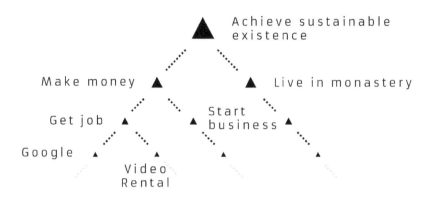

Our desires are essentially emotional investments, and many of the principles of good financial investing apply to good desire allocation. **Diversification** is the act of increasing the variety of investments to avoid being overly reliant on any particular one.[31] Just as being fully invested in one stock makes you incredibly vulnerable to its fluctuations, being fully invested in any specific goal or outcome makes you emotionally vulnerable. Whether you find yourself attached to a belief, an idea at work, a way to spend your Saturday, or a person to spend the rest of your life with, failing to cultivate positive alternatives will leave you crushed when things don't go according to plan. You should set up your desires such that you benefit from every possible outcome.[32] **Design a dense minefield of success for yourself such that it is impossible to take a step without winning.**

Use the tactics discussed earlier to up-regulate or down-regulate desires until all outcomes are appropriately balanced. "Invest" desire toward the goals with the highest and most probable emotional return. When it seems likely that a certain goal will not pan out and its outcome is out of your control, down-regulate your desire for that outcome or counteract it with an opposing desire. When you suspect that a person in your life has an overall negative effect on you, decrease your investment and increase it in other, more constructive relationships. Furthermore, if you feel you are overly invested in relationships altogether, or have a condition like autism that makes relationships more difficult, it may be a good idea to shift significant emotional investment toward other things, such as creative pursuits.

The investment principle of **liquidity** is also highly relevant to desire design. You need to be able to quickly move funds from one form of investment to another so you can respond to new circumstances with agility.[33] And you need to be able to modulate your desires quickly so you aren't stuck wanting something which has already left the realm of possibility. By exercising the muscle of desire regulation, even when it seems unnecessary, you increase your emotional agility. Try to take a relatively weak desire and ramp it up to a strong craving. Try to take a desperate longing and reduce it to indifference.

Lastly, extinguish desire for anything out of the realm of possibility as quickly as possible. It wouldn't make sense to invest in the stock of a company we knew was going out of business, and it doesn't make sense to invest emotionally in a dead end. The Stoic contrast between circumstances we can control and those we cannot becomes highly relevant here, and the most common of such outcomes, one we can absolutely never control, is one that has happened in the past.

As you get quicker and quicker at desire regulation, you increase what we might call your **refresh rate**, or the speed at which you can accept and adapt to circumstances. You gain the ability to adjust the dials of desire as it aids you in your goals, whether those goals are behavioral or emotional. Much like the reappraisal methods of the last chapter, this can become an instantaneous process. You can adapt to new circumstances as soon as they arise and skip the negative emotions altogether.

You will know you have mastered desire when you are capable of desiring whatever comes your way. Your car's battery dying becomes an unexpected adventure in an otherwise boring day. A difficult transition in life becomes an opportunity to learn and grow. Some people like to point out that without desire, we would all be apathetic and passive observers of reality, never finding motivation to achieve our goals. This is true, and that is why rather than eliminating desire, we need to design our desire structures carefully. With practice, **you can learn to desire for the present to be exactly as it is while desiring for the future to be different.**

It is no accident that we are covering how to use desire modulation for tranquility before we learn to use it for effective motivation. If you lack the ability to stabilize your emotions and feel at peace in the face of difficult circumstances, those emotions will hijack your plans to achieve bigger things. The founders of other practical philosophies have lifted emotional control and stability to the level of the highest human goal. For us, the ability to remain tranquil and content in spite of our circumstances is not the highest goal in life, but an essential instrument for aligning with our values and living a great life.[34]

Key Takeaways

• The other primary tool for altering our emotions is through altering our desires.

• Because desires cause us pain and frustration when they are not satisfied, every desire we harbor is a potential threat to our contentment and stability.

• Popular wisdom's solution to the suffering caused by desire is to try your best to succeed at achieving your goals, and maybe you won't suffer so much.

• The alternate approach suggested by wise thinkers throughout history is to control our desires directly rather than simply trying to control our circumstances.

• By learning to modulate our desires, we can not only reduce the temptations and increase the fuel propelling us toward our goals, we can eliminate a major source of suffering.

• Buddhism, Epicureanism, and Stoicism all offered different but interrelated solutions to the problems caused by desire.

• The psychitect's goal is not to eliminate all desire, but to become a proficient desire manipulator - if we can tame our desires and develop agility at modulating them so we want the right things at any given time, we can leverage them to fuel us toward our goals as effectively as possible.

- The first and most basic skill we must practice is the ability to **up-regulate**, or increase, and **down-regulate**, or decrease a particular desire.
- To up-regulate a desire, focus purely on the desired stimulus and all of its most positive aspects and delicious details.
- To down-regulate a desire, distract yourself from the desired stimulus, focus on it in a purely objective way, and cultivate a non-attached awareness of the feelings associated with the desire.
- **Gratitude** can be used as a method for up-regulating all desires for what you already have while down-regulating desires for what you lack.
- The related practice of **negative visualization** entails reflecting on the possibility of losing what you have, which down-regulates our desire to possess and keep something permanently and up-regulates our desire and appreciation for what we have in the present moment to inoculate ourselves against loss.
- The Buddhist contemplation of **nonself** states that the concept of the self is entirely an illusion, which can down-regulate all identity-based desires by reminding ourselves of the flaws with the entire self-construct when circumstances clash with these desires to be liked or respected.
- The **view from above**, which consists of contemplating the vastness of the cosmos, and the contrasting smallness of all of one's petty concerns, can be used to down-regulate all of your desires in bulk when you are overly invested in general.
- To deal with the same job rejection from the previous chapter, you could engage in gratitude to up-regulate your desire for all the great things you have, or you could down-regulate the desire causing your suffering by reminding yourself of it's negative qualities.
- Once you learn and strengthen your ability to use these tactics, you will be able to adjust your desires at will, largely eliminating the tendency to suffer over ungratified longings.
- **Counteraction** entails balancing out a desire by up or down-regulating an equal and opposing desire so they "cancel" one another out.
- You can become so skilled at counteraction techniques that you automatically notice friction in your mind and generate the counteracting desire automatically.

- Our desires are habitual, so the longings we indulge train us to want more.
- You can use **asceticism** to intentionally deprive yourself of some desired and attainable object so as to down-regulate perpetual desires, break dependencies, and make yourself more emotionally robust.
- Pursuing intrinsic goals, like playing tennis to the best of your ability rather than winning the match, is an excellent way of eliminating the suffering of failure.
- Diversify your goals and carve out as many alternate paths to your higher goals as you can so failing at any single goal will not crush you.
- Increase the speed at which you accept reality to stop longing for things which are in the past or already out of the realm of possibility.
- You can learn to desire for the present to be exactly as it is while desiring for the future to be different.

7

Emotional Self-Mastery and Equanimity

On the Pathologies of Philosophers

> Anybody can become angry - that is easy, but to be angry
> with the right person and to the right degree and at the right
> time and for the right purpose, and in the right way - that is
> not within everybody's power and is not easy.

> - **Aristotle**, *Nicomachean Ethics*

We have now learned to restructure our perceptions and to modulate our desires. Now, just as rationality and introspection came together as the building blocks for cognitive self-mastery, these tools come together to form the building blocks for emotional self-mastery. This type of mastery represents the peak of emotion regulation skills, and tends to be characterized by a state of deep tranquility. It has been lauded throughout the ages by many different philosophies, some claiming it to be the highest good in life.[1]

One might think that this type of tranquility would be universally praised, but there are always those who seem to idealize suffering. Though 19th century philosopher Friedrich Nietzsche offers crucial guidance for emotional self-mastery, he also provides examples of some of the most self-limiting perspectives on emotion.

> Here the ways of men divide. If you wish to strive for peace of soul and happiness, then believe; if you wish to be a disciple of truth, then inquire.

> - **Friedrich Nietzsche**, letter to his sister, Elizabeth

Though this quote is an inspiring call to intellectual courage, it makes the unfortunate mistake of conflating psychological well-being with dogmatism. The implication is that the truth must be painful, and those who accurately perceive it must be unhappy. It fits with our stereotypes of the pessimistic truth-seeker, and the happy-go-lucky dogmatist living an unexamined life. But here is what these stereotypes actually represent: people with one type of self-mastery but deficient in another, in this case, people with cognitive self-mastery and a lack of emotional self-mastery, and vice versa.

There is no reason we cannot have our cake and understand it too. An individual with well-rounded self-mastery would be capable of accepting seemingly harsh truths and being happy in spite of them, or better yet, because of them.[2] I have personally known people (though admittedly few) who prove that incisive beliefs need not entail cynical attitudes. If you force yourself to confront the bitter truths of this world and then go through life full of pain and pessimism, have the courage to call it what it really is: **strength in one area and weakness in another**. We must strive to cultivate intellectual maturity and emotional maturity simultaneously.

Though we only have one word for them, there are two very different meanings of "optimism." Cognitive optimism is a distortion of the truth. The willingness to believe a desired outcome or belief is more likely than the evidence suggests. But emotional optimism has nothing to do with specific truths or outcomes in our lives. It is the highly adaptive attitude that all will be well regardless of the outcome. **We must all aim to be cognitive realists and emotional optimists.**

Another eloquent Nietzsche excerpt demonstrates a similar error:

The discipline of suffering, of great suffering- do you not know that only this discipline has created all enhancements of man so far?

- **Friedrich Nietzsche**, *Beyond Good and Evil*

Here we see the incredibly popular assumption that behavioral self-mastery (the focus of the next few chapters) must come at the expense of emotional self-mastery. It is the age-old argument that people who are content have no reason to get off their couch, or out of their Zen monastery. But the idea that only suffering can motivate us to greatness commits the same type of error as the first. The myth of the neurotic but brilliant artist is just another stereotype which is not grounded in reality.[3] There is no reason we cannot simultaneously pursue both emotional and behavioral self-mastery. If we actually study the people who cannot motivate themselves out of bed in the morning, **the mental state we observe is not tranquility; it is depression.**[4]

Nothing about having positive emotions or life satisfaction preclude the ability to see opportunity for improvement in the world. To the contrary, **the happiest people, though not necessarily the most comfortable, are shown to be the most productive and motivated,**[5] making them far more likely to positively impact the world than their melancholy counterparts.[6] Just as in the optimism example, by conflating the two very different meanings of the word "happy," critics of contentedness argue that a happy person (emotional) must be "happy" with the way things are (behavioral), having no reason to act to change them. **Desire for the present to be different from the present incites pain, but desire for the future to be different from the present incites action.**[7]

Though Nietzsche often praised the optimistic outlook, he also claimed that great individuals are more emotionally fragile, and must suffer more than "common men." Nietzsche's philosophy claims that certain ethical systems, which he called "slave morality," originate through oppressed groups idealizing weakness to increase their power.[8] But could it be that Nietzsche created his own slave morality of suffering, idealizing it because it was the only option available to him?[9] **Could it be that even Nietzsche couldn't face the truth that his own involuntary suffering was in fact a form of weakness he learned to praise as a defense mechanism?**

Many thinkers throughout the ages have defended suffering in similar ways, but my reaction is always to say, "spoken like a true sufferer." **As you learn to exercise a high degree of control over your emotions, the arguments for unhappiness, pessimism, and emotional helplessness will become increasingly baffling to you.**

Strong people alone know how to organize their suffering so as to bear only the most necessary pain.

- **Emil Dorian**, *The Quality of Witness*

There is no doubt that our emotions play a central role in a life well-lived, and have a great impact on our pursuit of value alignment. Positive emotions often represent goals in and of themselves, though few people place suffering on their to-do list. But negative and positive emotions alike often stand in the way of our goals, even sabotaging them at times.

Aristotle had a lot to say about our emotions, but his approach is different from those found in later Greek thinkers. According to him, well-being is about experiencing the right emotions, whether positive or negative, not simply the most positive or peaceful ones.[10] Emotions can be powerful motivators, and they play a powerful role in how we see ourselves.

Aristotle proposed the notion that we should strive not to extirpate all negative emotion, but to experience appropriate emotions in appropriate proportions. The virtuous had to learn to master their emotions and experience them appropriately in the right balance. This balance was defined as a mean between two extremes, and this mean varied by circumstance. Courage was the ideal mean between cowardice and rashness, and pride between humility and vanity. In this sense, ethics could be compared to aesthetics, striving toward beauty, proportion, and harmony.[11]

Unlike Aristotle, I view the arbiter of appropriate emotion, not as a universal golden mean, but as the subjective value intuitions of the individual. So the question of which emotions we should experience becomes a question of **"what would my ideal self feel?"** Would my ideal self get angry over being disrespected, or simply laugh it off and deal with it as necessary? Would my ideal self be perfectly tranquil at her parent's funeral, or would she grieve for a period of time? Which reaction is most conducive to my defined goals? Each of these questions must be answered by the individual.

There is actually evidence that connects this Aristotelian approach to emotion with overall well-being. One cross-cultural study measured experienced emotions, desired emotions, and indicators of well-being and depressive symptoms.[12]

> Across cultures, happier people were those who more often experienced emotions they wanted to experience, whether these were pleasant (e.g., love) or unpleasant (e.g., hatred). This pattern applied even to people who wanted to feel less pleasant or more unpleasant emotions than they actually felt. Controlling for differences in experienced and desired emotions left the pattern unchanged. These findings suggest that **happiness involves experiencing emotions that feel right, whether they feel good or not.**

These findings do not support the aim of tranquility above all that we associate with Stoicism, Epicureanism, and Buddhism, but they do make a strong case for emotional self-control. Greater emotional self-mastery can allow us to ensure we experience the emotions which align with our goals and ideals more and more of the time.

I will not claim that negative emotions never align with our ideals. But I will argue throughout this chapter that the occasion in which they will is less common than you might think. The idealization of suffering by both philosophers and popular culture has done a great disservice to people by normalizing and perpetuating experiences that would be better left behind.[13] And the process of gradually leaving these problematic emotions behind is possible for anyone with the right toolkit and commitment.

Emotional Algorithms

> Man's lack of power to moderate and restrain the affects I call bondage. For the man who is subject to affects is under the control, not of himself, but of fortune, in whose power he so greatly is that often, though he sees the better for himself, he is still forced to follow the worst.

> - **Baruch Spinoza**, *Ethics*

Emotions exist for the purpose of triggering adaptive behaviors. They helped our ancestors navigate conflicts, connect with potential mates, and cooperate with allies. And they continue to compel us to run from potential threats to our lives, bond with and care for our children, and refrain from acting in ways that would alienate members of our community. All emotions exist for a reason, whether as direct adaptations, incidental byproducts of other adaptations, or occasionally useful safeguards. But the crucial contrast between genetic interests and human interests is just as relevant here as it has been in previous chapters.[14]

Human emotions exist to guide people toward gene propagation in a bygone world. They may overlap with modern, personal ends, but this is in no way guaranteed. **Our emotions should only be considered useful to us insofar as they serve our personal goals**. They are not inherently useful to us or even necessarily informative. They can guide us in positive directions and teach us valuable things, but to suggest that they always will is to misunderstand the reasons they exist. They may be counter-productive to our goals and values, which should lead us to view them as errors in these cases, just like the cognitive biases we have examined.[15]

Emotions are not always 'correct,' based as they are on probabilistic systems that have evolved to ensure our survival across a wide range of circumstances.

- Handbook of Emotion Regulation

Several philosophies have urged followers to numb or relinquish their passions wholesale. But the psychitectural perspective looks at individual emotional responses à la carte. We must decide on a case-by-case basis which emotions serve us in which situations. Few people struggle with uncontrollable joy, though even joy can be maladaptive, as in cases of mania.[16] But there are a number of emotional responses which most people share that seem to only cause problems.

For every negative emotional algorithm, there are strategies to be uncovered for deprogramming it. Certain cognitions can serve as counter algorithms for anxiety, jealousy, and anger, and the best of these have been preserved. We can codify the wise, therapeutic words of the great psychitectural thinkers. **If you can embed these precepts into your software, they will be triggered automatically by the thoughts which cause anger, envy, and sorrow, neutralizing the painful reactions on contact.**

We will take a brief look at some of the algorithms that have been proposed for dealing with particular emotions. This list of emotions is not exhaustive, and the algorithms listed for dealing with each one is one of hundreds of possibilities. All are merely suggestions, and you will have to decide for yourself which emotions are beneficial to you and when.

Anger and Hatred

Anger arises when one perceives that his strategic goals have been impeded through the fault of another. It is a social emotion which likely evolved as a mechanism to deter people from violating various boundaries, such as harming, shaming, or stealing from others. [17] Initially, this deterrence would seem to be a useful function even today. But most of the time, our anger is directed toward situations or inanimate objects. It is only after we remind ourselves that there is no conscious target of blame that our anger subsides, and it becomes clear that **our rage and hatred has caused no one pain but ourselves**.

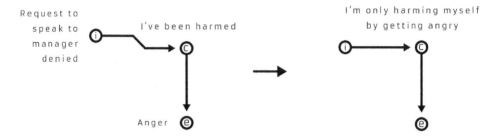

Even in circumstances in which anger is directed toward other people, it is rarely the most effective strategy for dealing with them. The Tao Te Ching reminds us that "the best fighter is never angry," and if even fighters are more effective without anger, it is hard to conceive of cases in which it benefits us. As one understands the true causes and motives of his enemy's actions, assigning blame for anything becomes less and less reasonable. Great people develop superior strategies for dealing with obstacles, threats, and aggression.[18] A person who can stand her ground while responding to aggressors with compassion, humor, and reasonable consideration will win more battles than one who goes into a rage.[19]

Stoic philosopher Seneca provides great insight into the nature of anger and how to deal with it in his writings *On Anger*. One counter-algorithm he suggests:

> The greatest remedy for anger is delay: beg anger to grant you this at the first, not in order that it may pardon the offense, but that it may form a right judgment about it - if it delays, it will come to an end. Do not attempt to quell it all at once, for its first impulses are fierce; by plucking away its parts we shall remove the whole.
>
> - **Seneca**, *On Anger*

Here he proposes a counter to anger that involves simply delaying our reactions, gradually chipping away at our impulses of rage until we can think clearly.

> In the lowest recess of the heart let it be hidden away, and let it not drive, but be driven. Moreover, let us change all its symptoms into the opposite: let the expression on our faces be relaxed, our voices gentler, our steps more measured; little by little outer features mold inner ones.
>
> - **Seneca**, On Anger

He suggests that by controlling our expressions of anger, we can keep it contained, prevent it from doing any damage, and train our inner feelings of anger to mirror our outer expressions of calmness.[20] If we can program algorithms like these to be triggered automatically by feelings of anger, we can gradually master the emotion. **Learn to view every frustration you encounter as a test of mental strength**, and you will get better and better at maintaining your patience, levity, and control.

Embarrassment and Shame

Shame is a social emotion which has to do with our social status and and observance of norms. We feel shame when we embarrass ourselves, offend other people, or feel that someone else disapproves of us. It serves the purpose of discouraging us from risking our social status or mate prospects, but it generally does more harm than good.[21] No matter how prepared we are, we cannot help being afraid of embarrassment when public speaking. No matter how inaccurate or irrelevant to our values, an insult from another person stings for days after we receive it.

We have talked about the value of allocating less emotional investment in our social status, of living for our own approval rather than that of others, and of rejecting popular and wrong ideas about how life should be lived. These can be positive ways of dealing with social shame and the need for validation. One powerful counter-algorithm which can weaken or eliminate the pain of insult is often attributed to yogi and teacher Yogi Bhajan:

> If you are willing to look at another person's behavior toward you as a reflection of the state of their relationship with themselves rather than a statement about your value as a person, then you will, over a period of time cease to react at all.

The opinions and comments of others often have more to do with their own insecurities than any meaningful statement about us.[22] In the rare case that we learn from the affronts of others, we simply need to work on changing our own behaviors, and these changes need not be accompanied by pain.

Envy and Schadenfreude

Envy is the feeling which results from comparing oneself to another and finding that they have something we want or feel we deserve. We experience envy to drive us to fight for more wealth, higher status, and more sexual partners.[23] But when we envy someone, we deprive ourselves of the satisfaction of appreciating what we have and keep ourselves on the vicious treadmill of gain which will never deliver satisfaction.[24]

Do not spoil what you have by desiring what you have not; remember that what you now have was once among the things you only hoped for.

- **Epicurus**, Principal Doctrines

Envy and comparison can prevent satisfaction from ever increasing, regardless of how high a person's or community's living standard rises.[24] In order to fight it, we have to embed what is important to us into our software, and what is important should never be relative to those around us.[25]

Don't be the best. Be the only.

- **Kevin Kelly**[26]

The best counter for envy is to shift your perspective, reminding yourself that you are competing only with yourself.[27] If you measure yourself by your unique combination of qualities and strengths instead of a one-dimensional metric, you will rarely come across people worth envying.

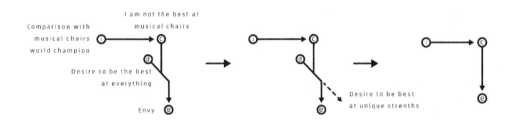

Schadenfreude is the German word for delight in the misfortune of others. Many people relish the losses of other people and feel averse to their gains - sometimes even those they care about.[28] **A good friend, and an adaptive individual, should genuinely delight in the successes of his friends.** When your own values are the benchmark of your well-being, the only person you should be envious of is one which is more you than you are. And in this event, you will know what needs to be done.

Fear, Worry, and Anxiety

Fear can serve as a helpful reaction to acute threats, but because we live in a world in which many of our decisions are made for future goals, many of us experience anxiety, a prolonged and future-oriented version of fear. Anxiety often involves rumination over the far future, but can range from worry about meeting deadlines to the intense fear of hair (Chaetophobia). Anxiety exists as a kind of alarm to let us know to avoid threats to our genes, but more often than not, it ends up resulting in useless false positives.[29]

In a conversation with Robert Wright, evolutionary psychiatrist Randolph Nesse describes a reason for this. He says that our threat detection system, like many other bodily responses, is shaped by natural selection to be hypersensitive. It errs on the side of overreaction to ensure that it goes off when it needs to. He adds,

> This is why we put up with smoke detectors. They don't warn us about a fire but once in a lifetime, but they warn us about burnt toast every week.
>
> - **Randolph Nesse**[30]

I think Dr. Nesse should probably adjust the settings on his toaster, but his smoke detector principle is nonetheless a valid explanation for much of our suffering, especially when it results from anxiety. The false positives become increasingly likely as our world resembles that of our ancestors less and less. Most of us don't need constant alarm bells in our minds in order to do what is necessary to avoid dangers and meet deadlines, making it a largely maladaptive response.

Unwanted fears can be gradually overcome through the process called extinction, which often makes use of incremental exposure methods to gradually train the brain not to associate a stimulus with danger.[31] But long-term anxiety can be more challenging.

Buddhism's focus on presence makes it particularly useful for dealing with anxiety.[32] The Buddha acknowledged that our anxieties themselves cause us far more pain than the threats they attempt to warn us about.

> Nothing can harm you as much as your own thoughts unguarded.

> - **Siddhārtha Gautama**, *Anguttara Nikaya*

Many have found it helpful to internalize a simple algorithm, articulated by the Buddhist monk Shantideva:

> If the problem can be solved why worry? If the problem cannot be solved worrying will do you no good.

> - **Shantideva**, *Guide to the Bodhisattva's Way of Life*

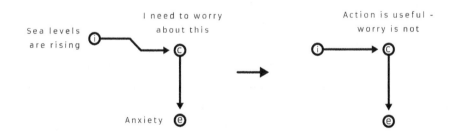

If you can program your software to remember the futility of worry as soon as it arises, you can gradually eliminate it from your emotional vocabulary. This change will free up your mental bandwidth to focus on the best course of action instead of being paralyzed by panic.

More Emotional Algorithms

Grief and Sadness

Sadness and grief are experienced when we perceive we have lost something important to us, whether that is our chances at achieving a goal, a cherished possession, or a close relationship. Though some types of sadness can help us learn to avoid bad outcomes or connect with others, much of the grief of loss we experience remains unexplained. We don't fully understand why we suffer so deeply when a loved one passes away, and some believe it to be an unfortunate byproduct of other emotional mechanisms.[33] Whatever the cause, grief is one of the most acute and common forms of suffering.

Dr. Nesse says that though he expected people who experience little grief after loss to be deeply impaired in other ways, he was surprised to find that these people seem to be just as healthy in their lives and social relationships as those who grieve deeply.[34]

The Buddha's algorithm for dealing with grief:

The world is afflicted by death and decay. But the wise do not grieve, having realized the nature of the world.

- **Siddhārtha Gautama**, *Sutta Nipata*

Buddhism encourages people to develop a different kind of relationship with their gains, possessions, and even their loved ones.[35] **When we fully understand that all things must end, we can learn to appreciate the finite amount of time we have with others and celebrate the end rather than repeatedly mourning the tragedy of impermanence.**

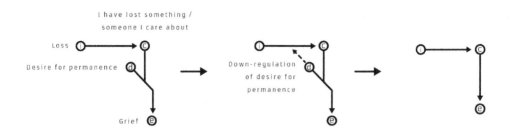

Grief is so powerful that most people should not expect to be able to eliminate it completely, and we may not want to. While some people would like to move on immediately after a loss, others find that this response does not fit their values. I have grieved over lost loved ones and almost certainly will again. But by comprehending the inevitability of death and loss, we can learn to experience grief to the right degree and duration instead of resigning to it.

Guilt and Remorse

We often experience guilt or remorse when we act in a way that violates our own values.[36] I would advise you not to eliminate this impulse completely, as it can serve a useful function by promoting your values. But we need to calibrate our conscience to activate at the right times and not the wrong ones. Say you find yourself in a difficult situation and have to make a decision. In retrospect, you realize you made the wrong one. You experience a wave of guilt and regret that lingers for months, or even years.

Though you may believe this feeling is justified, I would argue that your remorse impulse has not been properly trained. What good do painful feelings do if they are activated when you make the best decision you can given all the information available to you?

Remorse--Never give way to remorse but immediately say to yourself: that would merely mean adding a second stupidity to the first--If you have done harm, see how you can do good.

- **Friedrich Nietzsche**, *The Wanderer and His Shadow*

One of the counter-algorithms offered by Nate Soares in his book, *Replacing Guilt*, has to do with the way we talk to ourselves about our obligations:

Just stop doing things because you 'should.' As in, never let a 'should' feel like a reason to do something... When you're deliberating, your only responsibility is to figure out which action seems best given the available time and information.

- **Nate Soares**, *Replacing Guilt*

If you can't identify what you could do better, there is no use in punishing yourself for it. And as long as you make the best decisions you can at any given time, you cannot reasonably blame yourself for the outcome.[37] **Your conscience is a tool**. You want to train your remorse to activate when you knowingly act against your own values or interests. You want to incentivize yourself to align with your ideals, and carefully programmed emotional algorithms can help with this. Make the commitment never to do anything you believe is a bad decision, but never beat yourself up for doing what you believe is the best one.

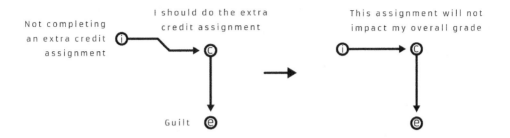

Jealousy and Possessiveness

Jealousy is contrasted with envy through its focus on something one already has but fears losing, particularly a romantic partner. It exists as a clear mechanism for preventing the loss of one's mate.[38] But like so many other negative emotions, it is a crude instrument for bringing about this outcome. Your protectiveness may keep your partner around long enough to pass on your genes, but if it is a healthy, long-term relationship you long for, you will only do damage by trying to shelter your partner from other people.[39] Your possessiveness and neediness will turn your significant other away and make your relationship fragile and weak.

There are numerous ways to weaken jealousy's hold on you. You can lower its sensitivity by restructuring your beliefs about human psychology, reminding yourself that a conversation with another person does not indicate plans to leave one's current partner for them.[40] You can remind yourself that your significant other is human, will be attracted to other people besides you, and that this is perfectly fine.[41] And you can internalize the idea that if your partner decides to part with you, it likely was not the right relationship to be in.[42] The most helpful algorithm I have come across for eliminating jealousy is a refusal to identify as another person's possessor, found in this quote attributed to Osho:

If you love a flower, don't pick it up. Because if you pick it up it dies and it ceases to be what you love. So if you love a flower, let it be. Love is not about possession. Love is about appreciation.

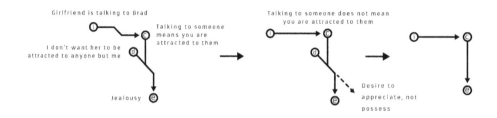

Take a radical approach of appreciating every moment you get to spend with other people, but never considering them yours. **If you love someone, you will want to promote their flourishing as an individual, not as a possession.** And this kind of selfless appreciation will only make you a more appealing partner. A relationship in which both partners can appreciate one another without compulsive attachment would encourage the growth and flourishing of both individuals.[43]

Love, Compassion, and Empathy

In addition to our competitive and aggressive tendencies, we were endowed with a number of pro-social and altruistic tendencies and emotions. We are made to care deeply about our loved ones, to feel the pain of others, and to try to help those who belong to our tribe.[44] Most people consider compassion and emotional empathy to be universally positive traits. But these emotions have a dark side too. The value of emotional empathy has been called into question by Paul Bloom in his book, *Against Empathy: The Case for Rational Compassion*.

Bloom argues that empathy is quite often counterproductive for our individualistic good, causing us unnecessary pain that does not sustainably compel us to solve problems. Some people are so compassionate that they regularly suffer pointlessly on behalf of others. But it also may hinder the good of the person with whom we are empathizing. Although many people who vent their problems to us only want someone with whom to commiserate, a caring friend would be more likely to help them solve their problems than to validate and encourage their maladaptive responses. Bloom argues that the people we typically think of as lacking empathy - psychopaths - are generally more lacking in impulse control, and that exceptional altruists are more likely to be high in self-control than in empathy.[45]

Those who praise empathy need to keep in mind that **however noble it may seem, it is still an emotion**. It does not consider facts or consequences, and if you do not maintain conscious control over your compassion, it will not serve a useful purpose.[46] The effective altruism movement encourages people to look at how much good their actions will do, rather than simply donating money or time to whichever advertisement or cause more effectively stirs up their empathy.[47] Following these principles may cause you to seem cold at times, but remember that emotions must be tamed to be used intelligently and effectively.

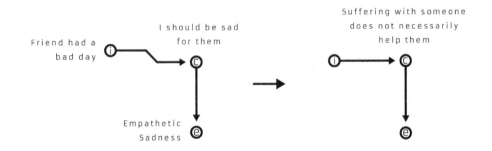

Our best hope for the future is not to get people to think of all humanity as family—that's impossible. It lies, instead, in an appreciation of the fact that, even if we don't empathize with distant strangers, their lives have the same value as the lives of those we love.

- **Paul Bloom**[48]

On the other hand, we can also hack our compassion impulses in the other direction when we determine it to be beneficial. The Buddha, Jesus, and other great teachers have encouraged people to cultivate love, compassion, and forgiveness for everyone, even our enemies,[49] and this type of universal compassion can be highly conducive to well-being and social good.[50] It can foster social connection, rid us of negative feelings of hate, and encourage us to actually act in favor of pro-social values to improve society.[51] Though most people in the Western world are not fazed by the notion of universal love, the original teachers who extolled it were considered radical at the time, and **universal compassion is actually a counterintuitive and powerful tool.**

> Love your enemies! Do good to them. Lend to them without expecting to be repaid.

> - **Jesus Christ**, Luke 6:35 NLT

Empathy was biologically intended to be felt toward family and fellow members of small tribes, but we can "misuse" it to serve our own values by extending it to members of other groups, or even those we are predisposed to dislike. We can down-regulate a number of negative emotions like anger and hate by programming the habit of experiencing love toward everyone by default. Metta, or loving-kindness meditation, is one method for cultivating this universal compassion. This practice typically consists of repeating words and thoughts wishing happiness and freedom from suffering to other people, beginning with oneself and one's loved ones, and ending with difficult people, enemies, and eventually all sentient beings.[52]

Unlocking Equanimity

There is no more reliable proof of greatness than to be in a state where nothing can happen to make you disturbed.

- **Seneca**, *On Anger*

Resilience has become a pop-psychological buzzword, and for good reason. Learning to quickly recover from inevitable setbacks is far more practical than attempting to avoid them all. Highly resilient people are better at coping with stress, have fewer depressive symptoms, live longer, and have greater physical health.[53][54] But why don't we aim higher? If emotional resilience is getting back up after getting knocked down, **emotional robustness is not getting knocked down in the first place.**

A robust mind is one with a powerful immune system - one which can bear more without bending. And we fortify our minds, not by circumventing threats, but by preparing for them. We improve ourselves by exposing ourselves to difficulties so our minds learn to deal with them effectively. We optimize our software by identifying and reprogramming the emotional algorithms likely to be triggered by the events in our lives.

Emotions are precision instruments. They can be used to achieve great things, but your conflicting passions will only undermine your efforts if you have only little or moderate control over them. Though negative emotions can occasionally serve our purposes and align with our values, people with generally stable and controlled emotions have been proven to have greater psychological health than those whose moods are constantly up and down.[55] And if your emotions are all the reactive default reflexes they were originally built to be, only luck can help you in achieving your goals.

Believing an emotion to be useful is one thing. But if you are unable to control the emotion, you are not using it. It is using you. If you are unable to keep from getting angry, you have a major weakness, no matter how hard you punched that wall. If you are unable to keep from getting jealous constantly, your partner's mind is not necessarily a problem, but yours is. And as counter-intuitive as it may seem, if you are unable to control your empathy for others, you too have a weakness, and it isn't doing anyone any favors. **You have to learn to stabilize your emotions before you can use them proficiently.**

The central idea we've covered in the last three chapters, that you can simply reprogram a negative emotional response with which you may struggle, may seem overly simplistic. But over the years, I have repeatedly proven to myself that by viewing emotional algorithms as the root of my problems, these reactions can be eliminated entirely. Each unwanted emotional response poses a unique challenge for creative problem solving. Some are more challenging than others. But I cannot emphasize enough that **resignation to negative emotions is the greatest obstacle to a tranquil mind.**

Undesirable emotions are bugs in your software. Each emotional category which causes you to feel or act against your values reveals a vulnerability in your psychological code. Culture is keen to remind people that it is okay to feel hurt and upset. This may be important for people to understand, but it's a bit like telling a programmer it is okay to have errors in his code. Sure, it's okay. Taking it personally will only create more problems. **But now it's time to debug it.** Your thoughts and emotions can be trained, whether or not you have committed to the endeavor of training them. Every problem you have is a part of your software that hasn't been optimized.

As we aim to optimize our emotions, we must attempt to cultivate the ancient ideal of equanimity. **Equanimity** is a state of undisturbed tranquility and psychological stability, with equivalent concepts in nearly every practical philosophy and religion - apatheia in Greek Stoicism, ataraxia in Epicureanism, and upekkha in Buddhism.[56] Someone with this state of mind was someone whose balance of mind could not be shaken, even in the face of great adversity. Equanimity is the pinnacle of psychological robustness and control.[57]

It is evenness of mind, unshakeable freedom of mind, a state of inner equipoise that cannot be upset by gain and loss, honor and dishonor, praise and blame, pleasure and pain.

- **Bhikkhu Bodhi**, *Toward a Threshold of Understanding*

It is easy to view this state as a spiritual aspiration achieved only by ancient sages, but you likely underestimate how attainable a state like this is for you. Think back to the problems you were dealing with five years ago. Chances are these problems are largely irrelevant to you now. Whatever circumstances were causing you anger, fear, anxiety, or sadness then have likely shifted, and they no longer cause you the suffering they once did. From where you stand now, it is easy to look at these problems and see that most of them were trivial; it may even seem laughable that the majority of them ever caused you distress. The problems likely worked themselves out, or better yet, weren't really problems in the first place. You may even be thankful for the struggles you went through.

Equanimity is about feeling the way you feel about your five-years-ago-problems right now, about your current problems. Meaning they either aren't problems, are problems that will sort themselves out, or are problems that are good to have. And this state is attained through the gradual process of identifying the emotional reactions that hold you back, using the restructuring and modulation tactics to correct them, and reprogramming each one until you are left with nearly total stability, regardless of your circumstances.

Be like a headland of rock on which the waves break incessantly; but it stands fast and around it the seething of the waters sink to rest.

- **Marcus Aurelius**, *Meditations*

Once you have learned to cultivate tranquility and keep your mind still, you will be ready to learn to masterfully maneuver it in the right direction. We will now turn to the control and mastery of our behaviors, actions, and habits.

Key Takeaways

•   Just as rationality and introspection came together as the building blocks for cognitive self-mastery, cognitive restructuring and desire modulation form the building blocks for emotional self-mastery.

•   Some people glorify perpetual suffering by associating it with other strengths.

•   Most people conflate cognitive optimism, which is a biased prediction tendency, with emotional optimism, which is a highly adaptive attitude. This leads them to associate incisive beliefs with unhappiness and vice versa.

•   Similarly, many believe that great achievers and creators must be driven by unhappiness and neuroticism, leading to another justification for suffering.

•   Do not allow your strength in one area to justify your weakness in another.

•   The psychitect takes the Aristotelian approach of trying to experience the right emotions, whether positive or negative, not simply the most positive or peaceful ones, which modern research suggests is a better indicator of deep well-being.

•   The question of which emotions we should experience becomes a question of "what would my ideal self feel?"

•   Our emotions should only be considered useful to us insofar as they serve our personal goals, and there are certain emotions which are almost always harmful to us.

•   For every negative emotional algorithm, there are strategies to be uncovered for deprogramming them. We can codify the wise, therapeutic words of the great psychitectural thinkers and embed these precepts into our software.

•   Anger often only punishes the person experiencing it and rarely serves our goals.

•   Seneca suggested that feelings of anger can be countered by delaying our responses, maintaining controlled outer expressions, and training our inner feelings of anger to mirror our outer expressions of calmness.

- Learn to view every frustration you encounter as a test of mental strength, and you will get better and better at maintaining your patience, levity, and control.
- Shame is also rarely beneficial, as it exists to preserve our social status and not our values.
- Yogi Bhajan offered a powerful counter-algorithm to shame, involving viewing other people's judgments of us as products of their own issues and insecurities rather than a reflection of us.
- Envy can lock us onto a vicious treadmill of gain which will never deliver satisfaction. In order to fight it, you can embed what is important to you into your software and remind yourself that you are competing only with yourself.
- When your own values are the benchmark of your well-being, the only person you should be envious of is one which is more you than you are, and in this event, you will know what needs to be done.
- Anxiety exists as a kind of alarm to help us avoid threats to our genes, but more often than not, it ends up resulting in useless false positives.
- Shantideva captures one of the most useful counters to anxiety - program your software to remember the futility of worry as soon as it arises, which will free up your mental bandwidth to focus on the best course of action instead of being paralyzed by panic.
- Grief is one of the most painful emotions, and some may not want to be free of it in all circumstances.
- Buddhism reminds people that all things must end, and this understanding can enable us to appreciate the finite amount of time we have with others and celebrate the end rather than repeatedly mourning the tragedy of impermanence. By comprehending the inevitability of death and loss, we can learn to experience grief to the right degree and duration instead of resigning to it.
- Guilt is not useful if it is activated when you make the best decision you can given all the information available to you.
- One counter-algorithm offered by Nate Soares is to stop doing things because you think you "should" and list out the actual reasons and consequences for certain actions.
- Make the commitment to never do anything you believe is a bad decision, but never beat yourself up for doing what you believe at the time is the best one.
- Jealousy exists to retain mates, but it can be toxic to healthy, long-term

relationships; possessiveness and neediness will make your relationship fragile and weak.

• You can take a radical approach of appreciating every moment you get to spend with other people, but never considering them yours. If you love someone, you will want to promote their flourishing as an individual, not as a possession.

• Most people consider compassion and emotional empathy to be universally positive things. But these emotions have a dark side too.

• Author Paul Bloom argues that empathy is quite often counterproductive for our individualistic good, causing us unnecessary pain that does not sustainably compel us to solve problems.

• The effective altruism movement encourages people to look at how much good their actions will do, rather than basing their actions on whatever stirs up their empathy.

• We can also hack our compassion impulses in the other direction when we determine it to be beneficial - universal compassion can be highly conducive to well-being and social good.

• Metta, or loving-kindness meditation, is one method for cultivating this universal compassion.

• If emotional resilience is getting back up after getting knocked down, emotional robustness is not getting knocked down in the first place.

• Emotions are precision instruments. They can be used to achieve great things, but your conflicting passions will only undermine your efforts if you have only little or moderate control over them.

• You have to learn to stabilize your emotions before you can use them proficiently, and resignation to negative emotions is the greatest obstacle to a tranquil mind.

• As we aim to optimize our emotions, we must attempt to cultivate the ancient ideal of **equanimity**, a state of undisturbed tranquility and psychological stability.

• Equanimity is about feeling the way you feel about your five-years-ago-problems right now, about your current problems.

• Once you have learned to cultivate tranquility and keep your mind still, you will be ready to learn to masterfully maneuver it in the right direction.

8

Self-Direction and Its Impediments

The Threat of Craving

A person who wants to be happy must evidently pursue and practice self-control.

- **Plato**, *Gorgias*

We all face countless internal conflicts every day. To read or play video games? To exercise or stay home and eat waffles? To go out to the bar or spend time with your kids? Each of these questions represents a battle between two or more drives within the mind. And the drives which perpetually win these battles determine who we will become. The behavioral realm of the self-mastery triad has been saved for last because in many ways, the other two realms are the instruments which enable us to take the best actions. Our ultimate goal of value alignment depends on our ability to reach congruence between our ideals and our behavior.

Self-control, or self-regulation, is the peak of the behavioral realm, and represents the final piece of the puzzle of self-mastery. After you have acquired the wisdom to strategically align your goals with your values and the ability to stabilize the emotional forces within you, there is only one thing left to do: **Direct your behavior toward your goals**. And to do this, you will need the ability to resist the urges to act against your defined goals, and the ability to motivate yourself toward them.

We generally talk about self-control in reference to those who lack it. The concept comes up when discussing alcoholics, violent criminals, and hyperactive kids. Books on self-control are typically about dieting and addiction. We will discuss these types of issues and temptations, but we will also look at the temptations of the easy life. We will examine the addictions which lock us into normalcy and mediocrity. We will learn to program out the behaviors which limit our character and prevent us from becoming the type of person we wish to be. When we recognize that self-control determines so much more than the ability to resist that delicious slice of pie, it becomes clear that **behavioral self-regulation deserves to be regarded among the highest of human strengths.**

> The answer to the perennial question of what facilitates individual and cultural success might be found in the concept of self-regulation. The benefits of successful self- regulation are great and its costs can be dire. Failures of self-regulation are at the root of many personal and societal ills, such as interpersonal violence, self-defeating behaviors, substance abuse, poor health, under-achievement, and obesity.
>
> - **Roy Baumeister**, *Handbook of Self-Regulation*

People high in self-control tend to have the qualities we all aspire to. They eat more healthily,[1] exercise more,[2] sleep better,[3] spend less compulsively,[4] drink and smoke less,[5] and are generally healthier both physically and mentally.[6] Poor self-control is correlated with many mental disorders, like chronic anxiety, explosive anger, depression, paranoia, psychoticism, eating disorders, and OCD,[7] as well as problematic behaviors like violence and crime.[8]

Self-control is the best predictor of college grades, beating even IQ or SAT scores.[9] Those high in it have more secure and fulfilling relationships,[10] achieve greater financial security,[11] and have greater life satisfaction.[12] They even have more fun, as people who often indulge temptations experience more negative affect and guilt.[13] If you can name a positive outcome in life, chances are it's highly correlated with self-control.[14]

Needless to say, the development of self-control is a worthy goal. And an understanding of the mechanisms behind self-control will be crucial to cultivating it and building good habits. But before we can start pulling the levers of behavior and self-control, **we must become cognizant of the potential threats which are most likely to take hold of us and take away our capacity for self-direction.**

A behavioral algorithm is known as a **habit**. But this term includes the single actions which appear to be isolated. Ultimately, all actions are habitual in the sense that they are the products of biologically ingrained and algorithmic responses. A bad habit is one which leads us away from our goals; a good habit is one which leads us toward them. The behavioral algorithm causes a specific behavioral output in response to an environmental input.[15]

input

behavior

Ultimately, desire is the driver of behavior, so in order for a behavior to be activated, the trigger must generate a desire, a term we are using interchangeably with drive or craving.[16] So bad habits arise because a trigger generates a desire which conflicts with our ideal behavior.

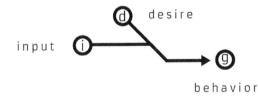

And good habits arise because the trigger generates a desire which is aligned with our ideal behavior. As in previous chapters, a straight gold line indicates that the driving desires are aligned with the behavior.

input

behavior

We need to understand the nature of our drives and cravings and why they can be so problematic in the modern world. It should be understood at this point that our ancestral, genetic programming can be a great hindrance to well-being, and these problems are often amplified in modern society. The most obvious examples are the chemicals that undeniably result in addiction. Synthetic drugs like cocaine tap directly into our brain's reward circuits, providing us with pleasures our ancestors did not have access to. These drug-induced feelings, originally built to reinforce adaptive behaviors, fail to reinforce anything besides continued use of the drug.[17]

But the things we are used to calling addictions are not the only type of modern pleasures that continually hold people back. Corporate entities craft many aspects of our world today. They are incentivized to meet every one of our desires as effectively as they can. Though there are far worse ways of organizing society, the incentives our economic systems provide can result in new addictions that harm people in the name of improving the world.[18]

Ultimately, an addiction is any maladaptive behavior which controls an individual rather than being controlled by him. Addictions often preclude adaptive behaviors, limiting people from building healthy lives and relationships and obstructing the alignment that would result in genuine satisfaction.[19] And there are many times when **good feelings can serve as bad addictions.**

We are built to crave foods high in sugar, salt, and fat because they provided our ancestors with energy, vital nutrients, and stored fat to help them get through times of food shortage. It was beneficial for them to eat as much of these as they could find because they were often scarce.[20] But the modern world has hacked the reward systems that were so beneficial in the ancient world, boosting the content of these craved compounds in the foods we eat to maximize addictiveness. Combined with the sedentary lifestyle the modern world affords, these chemicals no longer serve their original purpose, instead resulting in disease and obesity.[21]

In similar fashion, our innate desire for validation is exploited by social media companies who tailor the algorithms of their platforms to get people as hooked as possible. Randolph Nesse calls the result "social obesity."[22] We are provided with more opportunities for social approval and entertainment than our ancestors ever would have had. Digital votes of approval provide the same type of rewards that real social interaction is meant to provide.[23] Though they are ostensibly built to foster connection, these addictions can impede social connection in real life.[24]

We see the same addictive brain hacks in video games, streaming platforms, digital pornography, and online shopping. They provide us with new temptations that make it harder for us to make deliberate decisions about how we spend our time.[25] **The problem with the modern world is that it optimizes for our drives, not for our values.** If Youtube's algorithms were built to show you the videos that your ideal self would view instead of the ones you click on, it would be an entirely positive tool. But when the world around us is built to amplify our desires, it is easy to allow our lifestyle to be designed by others with ulterior motives. We become the products (literally) of the companies seeking to squeeze profits out of us.

Though you may detect a critical tone, there is not an inherent problem with any of these modern innovations. **It is no more necessary for you to delete your Facebook account than to burn the bag of sugar in your pantry for fear that you'll be tempted to shovel it into your mouth at any moment.** Technology, by definition, serves useful functions, and there is no problem with using tools for their utility as long as they aren't able to hijack your judgment.

Though the world is getting more addictive, **our best tool to counter it is still found in the cultivation of self-mastery.**[26] We must design our lifestyles intentionally, applying the process of reflecting on our values and setting goals to the way we spend our time and energy. We have to learn to develop increasing control over ourselves, and the key is not so much moderation as it is intentionality.

The next chapter will cover the fine details of self-control, but the process begins with broad strategy and awareness. And the first step to designing our behavior is to become aware of how we live currently. The quantified self movement is centered around collecting and analyzing data about our behavior and lifestyle, and this type of careful monitoring is essential to change behavior and habits.[27]

Make a list of desirable and undesirable habits, which may include how many hours you sleep, how many miles you run, or how many calories you consume, depending on the behaviors you are concerned with. It may also include behaviors like using filler words, complaining, or failing to assert yourself at restaurants. There are even ways to track your own carbon footprint.[28] For any negative behavior, keep a log of the number of times you engage in it per week. This simple act of logging is sometimes enough to break a habit.

You should also conduct a study of how you spend your weekly time. You may be surprised by how many hours per week you spend playing video games or watching Criss Angel videos. You will need to use a tool to do this monitoring, as your intuitions on the matter are likely flawed. Create a pie chart to display this weekly time allocation, followed by an ideal time allocation derived from your ideal lifestyle. Always be looking for opportunities to move closer to this ideal.

When you decide on a specific optimization, be sure to make use of **implementation intentions**, stating exactly what you intend to do ahead of time.[29] It may seem too simple to think that stating "If X then Y" would train our internal algorithms, but it seems this method can actually be highly effective. When people are trying to adopt a certain behavior, they will often say they want to smoke fewer cigarettes or start going to bed earlier, but they fail to build a specific plan, and this requires them to use more willpower in the moment.

An implementation intention consists of **stating exactly what we want to do, exactly when, and exactly where.** Instead of saying "I will write more this year," say "Every time I walk into my house after work, I will sit down at my computer and write 500 words." You wouldn't program a computer telling it to do something more often. You would tell it exactly when it needs to do what with a specific trigger and specific instructions. Your psychological software must be treated in the same way.

We all know that attempting to transform your lifestyle overnight will not result in sustained changes. Instead, focus on gradual, one-percent shifts in behavior, always nearing your ideal lifestyle more and more. This process of incremental optimization will be rewarding at many points along the way, but you may eventually wake up to find that your bad habits have been broken, positive behaviors are automatic, and one-hundred percent of your weekly time is spent constructively serving your ideals.

The Perils of Compliance

He who cannot obey himself will be commanded.

- **Friedrich Nietzsche**, *Thus Spoke Zarathustra*

Other people naturally have great influence over us. Without cognitive self-mastery, the opinions of others deeply influence and manipulate ours. They lull us into dogmatic beliefs which may or may not be accurate. And they cause us to believe certain paths in life will lead to well-being when all they lead to is monotony. Without emotional self-mastery, the words and thoughts of others cause us to suffer. We put ourselves fully into the hands of other people, unable to be content on our own. And without behavioral self-mastery, **the actions and attitudes of others compel us to conform, even when we know better.**[30]

When we are young, we hear about the dangers of peer pressure, often rolling our eyes and moving on with our lives. But though it takes on new forms, social pressure does not go away in adulthood.[31]

In an incredible psychological experiment documented in the Netflix special, *The Push*, mentalist Derren Brown led subjects to believe they were helping out in a real charity event which goes awry (spoilers ahead). In reality, they were surrounded by actors instructed to pressure the subjects to commit increasingly questionable and absurd acts. The primary subject we follow in the film is gradually led to mislabel the allergy content of foods, help hide a body, impersonate a philanthropist, and more.

It all leads up to a moment in which the subject is led to believe that the only way to avoid his own imprisonment is to push an innocent man off the roof of a building to his death. The actors are trained to use high pressure tactics to prompt the subject to commit the act. But the reasoning they give for why the push was necessary is deeply flawed, and a few moments of clear thinking would have made this obvious.

This particular subject refuses to push the man off of the roof, though he was previously convinced to push an ostensibly dead body down a flight of stairs to make it appear that he had died from the fall. But amazingly, all three of the other unfortunate subjects were successfully convinced to push the man off the building (which luckily had a net secretly positioned below it). They were then informed that the whole thing had been staged and would be turned into a hit Netflix special. At the end, Brown says:

> The point is we are all profoundly susceptible to this kind of influence. But by understanding this, understanding how we can be manipulated, we can be stronger. We can say no. We can push back.[32]

We often have strong and positive ideas about our own character, and view ourselves as simply good people independent of our circumstances. **But our behavior varies widely depending on the social forces at play around us.** Had the experiment above been real, the people who pushed the man off the building would have been guilty of murder. But even when the consequences are less obvious, they are not unimportant.

As we all know, we are deeply motivated by the desire to belong and be accepted. This is not problematic in itself, but it can be one of the easiest methods for others to abuse us and cause us to act against our own will. **Social compliance** refers to the effect of the words and actions of others on our own decisions. Though it is not always conscious, our friends and family members often attempt to subtly influence us to make certain decisions.[33]

We are most easily influenced to comply with the pressures of groups who are close to us, similar to us, powerful, and great in number. [34] [35] If you are asked by a coworker, a salesman, or an organization to complete a small task, followed by a series of successively larger commitments, they may be using the **foot-in-the-door technique**, which is often highly effective at convincing people to do things they would never agree to normally.[36] On the other hand, the **door-in-the-face technique** involves asking for a large request which will be rejected, followed by a much smaller request.[37]

Ingratiation refers to the use of flattery to compel someone to accept or complete a certain behavior.[38] A common form of ingratiation is to try to convince someone that an idea was originally theirs so as to make them more likely to favor it.

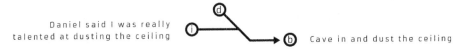

The **norm of reciprocity** is applied by doing a favor for someone before asking something in return. This method preys on an innate sense of reciprocity which helped our ancestors remain in good social standing.[39]

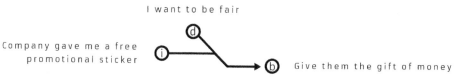

You can also be convinced to make certain decisions through **identification**, or the suggestion that a decision is characteristic of "people like you" or like you would like to be.[40] Advertisers take advantage of our desire to conform with respected and admired people by using social proof to give credibility to products. Celebrity endorsements and claims about the popularity of certain products have a strong impact on our perceptions of value. Good marketers understand that many purchases are driven by the desire to fit in with certain groups, and this can be used to compel us to make bad decisions.[41]

Advertisers frequently manufacture **urgency** or **scarcity** by creating limited time or quantity offers which causes customers to make impulsive decisions. Discounts and deals tap into our tendency of **anchoring** prices to known values, believing we are getting a good deal when an Amazon Prime day offer is ninety percent less than the original price, even when it is still not a good product. And due to the **contrast effect**, the presence of a ridiculously overpriced dish on the menu at a restaurant makes us more likely to buy the second most expensive dish.[42]

Can you think of a time when one of these tactics was used to convince you to take a certain action? What about in the decision to purchase this very book? Before you demand a refund, note that choosing not to make a purchase or decision out of objection to persuasion tactics still represents a kind of manipulation. The phenomenon of **reactance** is the tendency to do the opposite of what someone who is attempting to influence you wants.[43] It still consists in making a decision for reasons other than your own judgment of its merit, and hence is still a bias.

Not every decision that others want us to make is a bad one. What is important is that we make our decisions on our own. By developing resistance to manipulation tactics, we free ourselves to make decisions based on their benefit to us independent of the wishes of others. Much like the case of cognitive biases, **you can program immunity to persuasion and manipulation into your operating system**. As always, this process begins with familiarization. Study manipulation tactics, not to use them against others, but to defend yourself against them, and so you can apply the methods we will cover in the next chapter to reprogram our vulnerabilities.[44]

When we allow ourselves to be compelled to act against our own wishes, goals, and ideals, we place our well-being in the hands of others who have far less vested interest in it. When we let the fear of standing out prevent us from defending our values, we step away from our ideals. When we let our jealous friends talk us out of our ambitions, we step away from our ideals. And when we let the desire to be liked by others cause us to be less liked by ourselves, we step away from our ideals.

> The individual has always had to struggle to keep from being overwhelmed by the tribe. If you try it, you will be lonely often, and sometimes frightened. But no price is too high to pay for the privilege of owning yourself.
>
> - **Rudyard Kipling**, interview with Arthur Gordon

The Dangers of Comfort

> The three most harmful addictions are heroin, carbohydrates, and a monthly salary.
>
> - **Nassim Nicholas Taleb**, *The Bed of Procrustes*

We are all tempted by comfort the moment we are able to achieve it, and while comfort is not problematic in itself, a comfortable life is by no means synonymous with a good life. **Comfort can be a powerful sedative which breeds complacency and makes it difficult to do the things we know we should.**

From the literal moment we are born, we are jerked out of a warm asylum and into a confusing, chaotic struggle. This struggle pervades early life; childhood can be seen as a series of abrupt removals from one's comfort zone. Going to school for the first time, spending a night away from parents, joining a sports team, first dates, first jobs... Every year, young people are uprooted from their routines. From the people they have grown accustomed to. From the identities they thought were theirs.

Change is inherently painful. We do not tend to choose it if we are given a choice.[45] We gravitate toward homeostasis, and when we break out of it, it often feels like some terrible mistake has been made. But so often in this phase of life, we are given no apparent choice but to dive straight in. The pressures to grow and adapt are too strong to resist, and the few who are unwilling or unable to adapt are regarded as immature or impaired.[46] After making one of these shifts, we go through a distressing transitional period, often lasting months. Our old sources of reinforcement are gone, and new ones haven't had time to come in and take their place.

But with the conclusion of this transition comes a golden period. We start to acclimate to this new life. There is an air of novelty and opportunity without the alien feeling we had at first. The new people who seemed so distant at first are exciting now. Spontaneity takes the place of routine, and we start to see ourselves in a new light too. The interactions between our personalities and new stimuli let us see sides of ourselves we forgot, or didn't know, were there. We discover our own ideals and new paths to aligning with them. And this is what we call growth.[47]

The cycle is reliable for quite a while, and while some attempt to fight it every time, some learn to love it. Whether leaving for college, moving to a new city, or starting a new job, we plunge into the unknown with a kind of confidence that it will all work out. And maybe sometimes it doesn't. But it seems that **overwhelmingly, the decision to let go of comfort and embrace the unknown is met with generous reward.**

Nature loves courage. You make the commitment and nature will respond to that commitment by removing impossible obstacles... This is how magic is done. By hurling yourself into the abyss and discovering it's a feather bed.

- **Terence McKenna**, *Unfolding the Stone*

But something strange often happens once one has reached adulthood. Life stops pushing. The rapids that once left you with no choice now leave you in a pool of all the choice you ever wanted. Sure, occasionally your life gets shaken up unexpectedly. But for the most part, your precious balance remains undisturbed. Even stranger, it starts to feel like you are being pushed in the opposite direction. The pressures, social and biological, that once forced you to change and adapt have abruptly decided it's time to settle down.[48] It's time to meet someone - the last someone. It's time to settle into a good city, job, and home. Now the people insisting on change and growth are the stunted ones. It's time to commit.

Eventually, it becomes clear that your comfort zone isn't really supposed to be expanding anymore. So you cave in, and it's not so bad. You meet someone you enjoy being around and start planning your life together. You get a nice house and a job that you don't hate. And you've made it. You have achieved the life everyone wants. The life adolescence wouldn't let you have. A life that never forces you to change. That keeps you in that warm asylum of your comfort zone and never throws you into chaos.

We love comfort. We love state-of-the-art practice facilities, oak-paneled corner offices, spotless locker rooms, and fluffy towels. Which is a shame, because luxury is a motivational narcotic: It signals our unconscious minds to give less effort. It whispers, Relax, you've made it.

- **Daniel Coyle**, *The Little Book of Talent*

The evolution that you will undergo when you've achieved this kind of stability is a much more subtle kind. It's so gradual as to be nearly imperceptible. The fun and challenge and excitement slowly die down a little bit. And again in a few more years. Everything becomes a watered-down version of itself - especially you. You forget much of your personality. You forget your potential. And you forget that you've forgotten. **And this is what we call decay.**

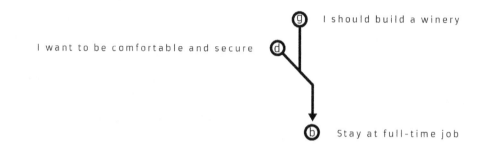

Nietzsche may be biased in his view that suffering is the key to greatness, but if we substitute "suffering" for "discomfort," things start to make far more sense. In his book, *Hiking with Nietzsche*, John Kaag points out that Nietzsche's philosophy is sometimes critiqued as immature and best suited for adolescence. But Kaag claims that many of Nietzsche's ideas are not only appropriate for those in the midst of adulthood, but may even be "lost on the young."[49]

> I had no idea how dull the world could sometimes be. How
> easy it would be to remain in the valleys, to be satisfied with
> mediocrity. Or how difficult it would be to stay alert to life...
> Being a responsible adult is, among other things, often to
> resign oneself to a life that falls radically short of the expec
> tations and potentialities that one had or, indeed, still has.
>
> - **John Kaag**, *Hiking with Nietzsche*

Though it is true that many of Nietzsche's ideas are grandiose and dramatic, they can also be powerful reminders that one has a choice to bear the discomfort needed to do great things. He argued that the great life was the life of the individual who overcomes resistance - who overcomes one's own desire for pleasure and comfort. By developing self-control and integration of the parts of the psyche, she could develop autonomy over her own actions and direct them toward her highest goals. **She could be a creative force and live in a way that affirmed her own nature and promoted her growth.** [50]

It is time for man to fix his goal. It is time for man to plant the seed of his highest hope. His soil is still rich enough for it. But this soil will one day be poor and weak; no longer will a high tree be able to grow from it... I tell you: one must have chaos in one, to give birth to a dancing star.

- **Friedrich Nietzsche**, *Thus Spoke Zarathustra*

There is a popular belief that most of the personal evolution and growth you undergo in life will be wrapping up by the time you're thirty. But this is a self-fulfilling prophecy. By the time most people reach thirty, they've carved themselves into a life that leaves them no room for growth and accepted that this is simply the norm. This kind of stagnation is not inevitable, but **you must build the habit of continually breaking out and expanding your comfort zone to prevent it.**[51]

A life limited to your comfort zone will almost certainly hold you back from your potential. You cannot build a robust mind by sheltering yourself from reality. We have seen in previous chapters that avoiding uncomfortable surroundings will make you vulnerable when things don't go according to plan.[52] Avoiding uncomfortable feedback will keep you from developing your ideas and developing into the person you are capable of being. Avoiding uncomfortable beliefs will shield you from the truth. And avoiding uncomfortable situations will create barriers which may keep you from ever knowing who you were capable of being.[53] **You must learn to do what scares you.**

That which does not kill us, makes us stronger.

- **Kelly Clarkson** - Just kidding, that one's Nietzsche too.[54]

Another strong supporter of choosing growth over fear was Abraham Maslow. But he is also responsible for popularizing one of the greatest obstacles to this choice: needs. Maslow's hierarchy of needs taught people that they have certain psychological needs, and if these needs are not met, they are incomplete or deficient as people. Securing these needs is challenging, but losing them is easy. Many choose not to take risks in their lives for fear of losing the people and circumstances that meet their needs. But the truth is that you don't have mandatory needs. You are not deficient if all of your longings are not met - in fact, it would be impossible to have all of your longings met. Maslow said:

One can choose to go back toward safety or forward toward growth. Growth must be chosen again and again; fear must be overcome again and again.

- **Abraham Maslow**, *The Psychology of Science*

You must understand that your mind is not a delicate machine to be protected from variability and stress. **The mind can be made better through stress and discomfort.**[55] When you force yourself out of your comfort zone, you gain reference experiences that teach you the things you feared aren't so bad. You defend yourself against the threats to your comfort, expanding your comfort zone until everything is comfortable, and all barriers to value alignment have been demolished.

The older you get, the more resolve it requires to choose change and growth, and the harder it becomes to sacrifice security and comfort and order.

Choosing anything other than growth is a sure path to regret. And allowing your craving for comfort to stand in the way of your unique potential is one of the most common barriers to living the greatest life possible and aligning with your ideals.

Do not confuse a life of comfort and ease for the good life. The good life is one of pushing your boundaries, incrementally overcoming yourself, striving for greatness - whatever that means for you. The happiness that results from the absence of discomfort is the happiness of mediocrity. Live your life, not as if you were trying to hoard a precious treasure, but as if you were crafting your own autobiography with every decision - **because you are.**

The Risk of Corruption

Do not act as if you were going to live ten thousand years.
Death hangs over you. While you live, while it is in your
power, be good.

- **Marcus Aurelius**, *Meditations*

Marcus Aurelius is known as the last of the Five Good Emperors of Rome, and he was a great Stoic philosopher as well. Every quote of his that we have referenced comes from his book, *Meditations,* which is one of the most powerful sources of philosophical wisdom available, but not because of its innovative ideas or clever arguments. What makes this book so incredible is found in the fact that it was the Roman emperor's personal journal. It was never intended to be published. It was written by the most powerful man in the world at the time for the sole purpose of helping himself to live a better life through daily reminders of Stoic wisdom and principles.[56]

The reason we find this type of work so incredible is that most of us realize how easy it would be for someone with immense power to quit trying to live with integrity. We expect the powerful to be corrupt. We expect politicians to betray their promises when they get the chance. We assume companies will sell out after they have grown large enough. We have all seen friends compromise their principles after an increase in social status. And many of us have personally had the experience of slowly slipping away from our values as soon as we were no longer held externally accountable for them.

Negative habits of character can slowly creep in if we are not vigilant. We may develop the habit of putting down the people in our lives if they allow it. We may be drawn in to talk negatively about others behind their backs. We find ways to justify our own behavior even when we know we would find it repulsive in someone else.

Corruption of character is a very real phenomenon, and although Marcus Aurelius is testament to the fact that absolute power does not always "corrupt absolutely," it is all too easy to allow one's behavior to degrade.[57]

> Nothing discloses real character like the use of power. It is easy for the weak to be gentle. Most people can bear adversity. But if you wish to know what a man really is, give him power. This is the supreme test.

> - **Robert Ingersoll**, *The Works of Robert G. Ingersoll*

You, like everyone else, have had impulses to do terrible things before, things which may have violated not only the law, but more importantly, your own personal values. The reason you merely thought about these acts instead of committing them ultimately must be explained by your behavioral self-regulation skills - the ability to direct your own drives instead of having them directed beneath your awareness.[58]

Who hasn't been tempted to violate a significant other's trust or drive while intoxicated, risking multiple potential lives? Most people have not only been tempted, but have caved into such temptations. It isn't my place to tell you which actions you should engage in or avoid; that is the role of your values. But as soon as the drive is present and the risks of getting caught or punished disappear, **our default behavior will be to do whatever it is we crave without regard for our values.**

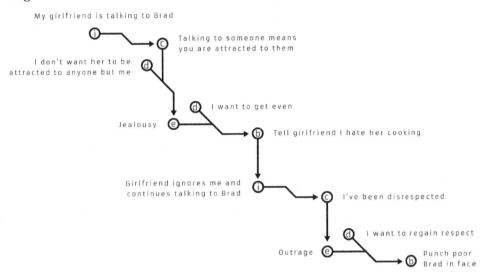

One of the least discussed keys to overcoming one's default behaviors comes down to identity. Humans are built to try to preserve a positive view of themselves.[59] Though this tendency can result in distorted self-perceptions and narcissism, it is also the key to some of the greatest human capacities. In many ways, **our sense of identity shapes the actions we take and the habits we build.**[60] There is a major difference between someone who believes she is trying to learn to play the guitar and someone who believes she is a musician, or someone who believes he is trying to stop drinking and someone who believes he is not a drinker.

In his excellent book, *Atomic Habits*, author James Clear illustrates the link between our identity and our behavior, claiming that "every action you take is a vote for the type of person you wish to become."

Becoming the best version of yourself requires you to continuously edit your beliefs, and to upgrade and expand your identity.

- **James Clear**, *Atomic Habits*

But the relationship between identity and behavior is a two way street. **Not only does your identity shape your behavior, your behavior shapes your identity as well.**[60] Despite the perception many of us share that we know ourselves deeply, we largely learn about ourselves the same way others do: by observing our behavior.[61] Self-signaling refers to our tendency to signal certain traits to ourselves to shape our own self-perceptions. We signal our character to ourselves through the actions we perform repeatedly.And the implications for our pursuit to align with our ideals are tremendous. Though we can deceive ourselves on some level, we are always monitoring our own behavior and evaluating ourselves based on it, even when we are not conscious of this process.[62]

We can see how this effect relates to well-being in psychotherapy as well. The reason for the "behavioral" part of cognitive behavioral therapy is that it is often not enough to simply tell ourselves that something is true or untrue of us. We have to prove it. People who are depressed often have incredibly low self-regard, along with a difficult time completing even the simplest tasks like getting out of bed. One of the most common exercises for these patients is a daily activity schedule, in which the patient commits to a list of activities like taking a shower or going for a walk. Over time, the difficulty level of the tasks is increased until it is possible to live a normal life and maintain a healthy self-image. The fact that this behavioral method is often highly effective in treating depression demonstrates that our well-being is deeply tied to our behavior.[63]

Our habits serve as evidence of the type of person we are to ourselves, which in turn adds fuel to the habits themselves. If we do nothing, we have no evidence of the type of person we are. And if we consistently do all the things our ideal self would, we have all the evidence we need. This perspective brings us back to Aristotle's view of character as the sum of one's habits. Our behaviors are the constant neuroplastic reinforcement that program our software, and this software is the source of our habits. **So unless we take an active role in this programming, who we are and how closely we align with our ideals will be purely a consequence of chance.**

We have to be careful when crafting our identity, as there is risk in centering your identity around certain traits, even positive traits. For example, when you are naturally gifted in a certain skill, you will quickly recognize it as a strength, and it will almost inevitably become a part of your identity. Your self-worth will become dependent on this trait, whether it is attractiveness, intelligence, or humor. You will invest more in it and less in other qualities, potentially leading to underdevelopment in those areas. If the traits you identify with are unearned or uncontrollable, they will not be able to shape your character in positive directions. And as soon as these strengths fail you or fade, your entire self-image will be broken.[64]

> The effect of one-off experiences tends to fade away while the effect of habits gets reinforced with time, which means your habits contribute most of the evidence that shapes your identity. In this way, the process of building habits is actually the process of becoming yourself.
>
> - **James Clear**, *Atomic Habits*

An increasingly common concern voiced today is that humans have no reason to be accountable for their actions without the commands of objective morality. If you don't believe you are always being watched by an omniscient judge or audited by a karmic cycle of rebirth, why do the right thing? Why not simply follow your every desire? What is integrity besides the dogmatic acceptance of rules with no consequences?

But from the perspective of value alignment, it becomes clear that the consequences are entirely real and acute. **The reason to act in accordance with your values, even when no one is watching, is that you are always being watched by the most important person: yourself.** You are constantly measuring yourself by your behaviors, and even though you may consciously deceive yourself into believing you measure up to your standards, you cannot trick yourself on every level.[65] To achieve this alignment, the correspondence between your actions and your ideals must be genuine.

> Whenever you do a thing, though it can be known but to yourself, ask yourself how you would act were all the world looking at you, and act accordingly. Encourage all your virtuous dispositions, and exercise them whenever an opportunity arises; being assured that they will gain strength by exercise, as a limb of the body does, and that exercise will make them habitual.

> - **Thomas Jefferson**, Letter to Peter Carr

Concepts like virtue, integrity, and character, seem dry and dated to the modern ear because they have come to be associated with antiquated and overbearing doctrines. But these ideas have more to offer than categorical demands. The state of being a person you yourself don't approve of is the worst form of prison in this life. Being a person you truly love and respect, not merely someone with an inflated self-esteem, is the highest hallmark of the good life. If you value your own values - which by definition, you do - you have the most powerful reason to live according to them that could possibly be given. **You are both the protagonist and the audience of your own life, and how greatly you appeal to this audience of one is the measure of well-being you will realize.**

Key Takeaways

- Behavioral self-mastery is the ability to direct your behaviors toward your goals effectively, and behavioral self-regulation, or self-control is one of the highest of human strengths.
- But before we can start pulling the levers of behavior and self-control, we must become cognizant of the potential threats which are most likely to take

hold of us and take away our capacity for self-direction.

- A behavioral algorithm is known as a **habit**, but this term includes single actions which appear to be isolated.
- Behaviors are activated when external triggers cause a desire, or drive, to be generated.
- Our cravings can lead us away from our ideals, and the modern world amplifies these cravings, making it more difficult than ever to resist them.
- The modern world has hacked our reward systems by maximizing the addictiveness of foods and chemicals and making them readily available.
- Social media platforms hijack our desire for social validation, resulting in "social obesity."
- Video games, streaming platforms, digital pornography, and online shopping all provide us with new temptations that make it harder for us to make deliberate decisions about how we spend our time.
- The problem with the modern world is that it optimizes for our drives, not for our values.
- Though the world is getting more addictive, our best tool to counter it is still found in the cultivation of self-mastery.
- The first step to designing our behavior is to become aware of how we live currently. Create lists of desirable and undesirable habits, and keep count of how often you engage in them.
- Make use of **implementation intentions** by stating exactly what you want to do, exactly when, and exactly where.
- Design your ideal lifestyle, including a breakdown of the percentages of your time you want to spend on certain things, and constantly try to get one percent closer to this lifestyle.
- The actions and attitudes of others can compel us to conform, even when we know better.
- **Social compliance** refers to the effect of the words and actions of others on our own decisions. Though it is not always conscious, our friends and family members often attempt to subtly influence us to make certain decisions.
- Manipulation tactics like the **foot-in-the-door technique**, the **door-in-the-face technique**, **ingratiation**, and the **norm of reciprocity** can be used by

others to get you to do things that don't align with your goals.

• You can develop resistance to manipulation tactics by studying them and identifying when they are being used against you.

• Comfort can be a powerful sedative which breeds complacency and makes it difficult to do the things we know we should, and the decision to let go of comfort and embrace the unknown is often met with generous reward.

• Nietzsche believed that by developing self-control and integration of the parts of the psyche, a person could develop autonomy over her own actions and direct them toward her highest goals. She could be a creative force and live in a way that affirmed her own nature and promoted her growth.

• To avoid stagnation, you must build the habit of continually breaking out and expanding your comfort zone. You must learn to do what scares you.

• Live your life, not as if you were trying to hoard a precious treasure, but as if you were crafting your own autobiography with every decision - because you are.

• Negative habits can slowly creep in and corrupt our character if we are not vigilant.

• Our sense of identity shapes the actions we take and the habits we build, but the relationship between identity and behavior is a two way street, as your behavior shapes your identity as well.

• The reason to act in accordance with your values even when no one is watching is that you are always being watched by the most important person: yourself.

• You are both the protagonist and the audience of your own life, and how greatly you appeal to this audience of one is the measure of well-being you will realize.

9

Behavioral Algorithms and Self-Control

Behavior, Self-Control, and Willpower

Men's natures are alike; it is their habits that separate them.

- **Confucius**, *Analects*

Now that we have covered the greatest obstacles to living a self-directed life, we can dive into the nuts and bolts of behavioral psychitecture. Some people have the capacity to overcome their impulses a remarkable amount of the time. They seem to exert superhuman control over their impulses, consistently following through on their goals throughout their lives. But these people are not merely endowed with abnormal levels of willpower. They make use of strategies that can be learned by anyone, and their secrets may surprise you.[1]

We all know that it is possible to overcome negative behaviors, break bad habits, and act according to our goals. But you also may believe that for many of your highest goals, you simply don't have the willpower to make them happen. You want to break the habits which clash with your ideals, find the motivation to work toward them, and do the things you know you should. But sometimes, you just can't. You can't muster the strength.

Since the Medieval era, the key to self-control has been thought to lie in the special strength of willpower.[2] This mysterious energy of effortful restraint inside us allows us to resist our strongest urges and work toward what really matters. Willpower, we are often told, is like a muscle. It depletes in the moment as we use it. The more we demand of it, the stronger it gets in the long run. But this notion of willpower has fallen in light of modern thought and research.[3]

As it turns out, the willpower muscle may amount to the percentage of glucose in one's blood. Yes, like a muscle, glucose can be depleted, and one's ability to resist urges along with it. It can also be temporarily replenished by sipping a sugary drink, though this will come at the expense of longer-term self-control. But unlike a muscle, it seems that increased exertion of willpower does not necessarily increase capacity for it, though a healthy diet and proper sleep do seem to increase its capacity.[4] But the greatest problem with the notion of willpower as the key to self-control is this: **the people with the highest self-control aren't even using willpower.**[5]

We have all heard the inspiring sentiment that we must overcome our desires and do what is rational. What we don't realize when we say these things is that the idea of overcoming desire is a bit delusional. We don't actually resist our drives. No matter what we do, we always succumb to our strongest desires. This does not mean we are helpless to control ourselves. But it does mean that if we want to harness the power of self-control, we will have to change the way we think about it.

Nietzsche believed that all beings could be viewed as the sum of a multitude of drives - competing, conflicting, and struggling for power. He denied that an individual possessed a unified will which could overcome these drives, arguing instead that the most powerful drives always win out and determine our actions. The key to self-mastery, he suggested, was not found in using reason or willpower to conquer our drives, but in the coordination of those drives toward organizing ideals. The ideal state was one in which the individual had organized his passions and directed them toward his highest goals.[6]

Nietzsche's view on drives has aged well. It seems that taking the right actions and avoiding the wrong ones is once again a creative design process, not a white-knuckled battle of will. Some of our drives long to align with our ideals and achieve our goals. They are just not the most powerful drives by default. If we want these drives to win out, we have to domesticate the stronger desires, canceling out the noise so the whispers of our values can be heard. **The secrets to self-control and good habits lie in the management and training of these desires.**

The initial trigger is one major leverage point for reprogramming behaviors.[7] In order for a trigger to generate a drive, one must not only encounter the trigger, but must pay attention to it, and must interpret it to be desirable. Our behaviors are mediated by our cognitions and emotions. So we can use our environmental inputs, our thoughts, or our emotions to reprogram habits.[8]

The immediate result of a certain behavior also plays a major role in habit formation and can be designed to alter habits. The strength of a drive is conditioned by the strength of the immediate reward resulting from our response to the trigger. We see the bag of candy in our pantry, and the craving we feel compels us to grab a piece. The strength of the immediate reward reinforces the link between input and output. This reward, or lack thereof, is called the consequence.[9]

And in many cases, the reassessment and restructuring of goals can make it so that desires which would be working against us can work for us instead.[10] This leaves us with several promising opportunities for reprogramming our behaviors - all found in modulating, activating, and using our desires.

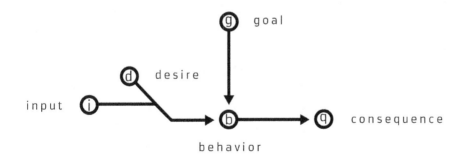

The ability to use these levers to manipulate our drives is the key to self-control. By using smarter strategies and modulating the strength of existing desires and emotions, we can ensure that our goals are completed not only effectively, but effortlessly.[11] We can gradually become proficient at using our drives to fuel us in the right directions and at keeping them from leading us astray. We have seen that our drives are not to be trusted as guides to the good life. We have seen that emotional tranquility depends on the ability to modulate these drives to keep them from causing us needless pain. **Now it is time to learn to harness them.**

Design Your Inputs

> We design our world, while our world acts back on us and
> designs us.
>
> - **Anne-Marie Willis**, "Ontological Designing"

Soon enough, virtual reality environments may overtake our physical world as the primary locus of our experience, which means every aspect of our environment will have been designed by someone.[12] Even today, it is hard to go anywhere that has not been deliberately shaped by human design. The concept of ontological design posits that in the act of designing our environments, we actually design ourselves, as the human mind is shaped greatly by its experiences. Hence there is a continual cycle of shaping between the individual and his environment.[13]

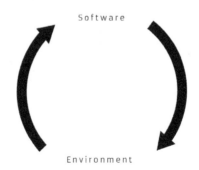

Software

Environment

The earliest opportunity we have to shape our own behavioral algorithms is through the active structuring of our environments. This process allows us to avoid the inputs which trigger unwanted behaviors or ensure that we encounter those that trigger desired behavior. However, the purpose of environmental design does not just lie in avoiding negative cues, but in using cues to condition habits, making us invulnerable to threats when they inevitably come along. It may seem obvious that we can influence our own behavior by choosing the situations we enter. An alcoholic can choose not to enter a bar in the first place. An unhealthy eater can choose not to purchase the jumbo jar of Nutella, or at least not to put it on his bedside table.[14]

The Stoics may have considered environmental conditions to be irrelevant and worthy only of our indifference.[15] But when you neglect the role of your environment, you do so at your own detriment. Though the internal world may be our focus, the external world is certainly not irrelevant. The world around us shapes us in powerful ways. We can make ourselves resistant to the manipulation of others, but we can't eliminate all influence our environment has on us. For us, **the environment is a powerful tool for shaping our software.**

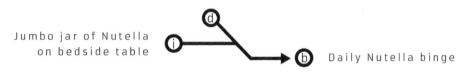

If you want to change your software, it is important to ask if there is an environmental change which would do the work for you. If your goal is to get more focused work done, design your workspace to be free from distractions. If you want to start meditating, going to a meditation retreat will lock you into an environment that will build stronger habits than you will alone in your room. In many ways, **the process of designing your environment is the process of designing yourself.**

You shape the garden of your mind by planting specific things from your environment, such as the books you read, experiences you have, and people you surround yourself with.

- **Benjamin Hardy**, *Willpower Doesn't Work*

One crucial way to design yourself through your environment is by surrounding yourself with people who have priorities, traits, or practices you would like to cultivate in yourself. Statistically, the more overweight people in your social circles, the more likely you are to become overweight.[16] So if you want to become more fit, you'll be swimming against the current if you haven't embedded yourself in active environments or built connections with people who prioritize fitness. The character traits of the people around you will rub off on you as well, so people who are honest, narcissistic, altruistic, or manipulative will gradually shape you in the direction of those traits.[17]

Look around at how your living space is arranged. What behaviors does it promote and what does it neglect or discourage? Would you say the physical space you spend your time in is representative of the person you would like to be? Your digital environments shape you as well. The websites you visit regularly, the podcasts you subscribe to, and the apps you keep on your phone will shape you. If you want to be less distracted, disable the notifications and unsubscribe from the email newsletters that you don't feel push you in the direction of your ideals, and consider subscribing to those that do.

The second opportunity for changing behaviors is through our attention and thoughts. Just as we established in the emotional section, our external experiences are generally filtered through our thoughts before they trigger behaviors. This means **our thoughts and focus play a powerful role in the actions we take**.

Most people are familiar with the marshmallow test - Stanford psychologist Walter Mischel's classic experiment which linked self-control and delayed gratification to nearly every important metric of the good life. It asked children to resist the urge to eat a marshmallow for as long as they could. They did not have the option of changing their environment because they were asked to sit right in front of the marshmallow.

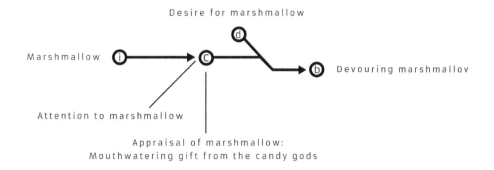

But the kids who did this successfully were not gritting their teeth and fighting back their urges, suppressing their cravings, or trying to power through them. The kids who used those methods didn't make it long. The successful kids were making use of cognitive strategies which decreased their desire for the marshmallow, bypassing the need to exert the willpower "muscle."[18] And there are a number of ways you can design your habitual behavior by designing its inputs.

Input Design

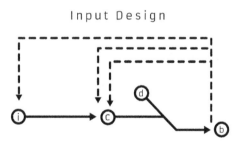

One of these strategies is **attentional deployment** - in this case, simple self-distraction. Numerous studies have shown that the ability, and the automatic habit of distracting oneself from tempting stimuli can be a highly effective method for keeping from caving in.[19] Children who chose to play with toys or pretend to do so could resist the marshmallow longer. If you can realize you are being tempted by something, remind yourself of your defined goals, look away if the temptation is physical, and engage your mind in another activity. It is important to note that distraction can also be a great hindrance to self-control if it is done while engaging in a tempting activity. People who are distracted while they eat don't remember how much they've eaten and consume far more than those who eat consciously.[20]

Another use of our attention is to practice **mindfulness**. People who were trained in mindfulness strategies were able to develop an awareness of the physical feelings of craving and observe them from a non-attached and non-identified perspective until they subsided.[21] Once again, mindfulness operates within the gaps of algorithms to weaken the connection between our cravings and our behaviors, giving us a greater degree of choice in the decisions we make.

Another powerful method is **cognitive reappraisal**, which we have discussed in regard to emotion. Just as we can reinterpret the meaning of an emotionally salient stimulus, we can reinterpret a tempting stimulus to weaken its hold on us. Kids who thought of the marshmallows as mouth-watering treats were more likely to lose control and eat them quickly. Kids who pretended the marshmallows weren't real or compared them to fluffy clouds were able to cool their desire more effectively.[22] Similarly, we can reframe tempting foods as artery clogging fat, addictive media platforms as psychologically toxic noise, and drugs or alcohol as poison.

Marshmallow ⓘ ⟶ ⓒ ⟶ ⓑ Resisting Marshmallow

Appraisal of marshmallow:
Intestinal glue made of connective
tissue and air

We can also reappraise beneficial activities to make them more desirable. Instead of thinking of exercise as painful and exhausting, we can imagine each lap or rep making us stronger. We can envision the nutrients from healthy foods permeating our bodies and minds and energizing us. And we can think of every dollar we don't spend as a unit of freedom.

The third input we can change to alter our behaviors is emotion. Sometimes people adopt certain behaviors as coping mechanisms to deal with difficult emotions.[23] Binge drinking, compulsive sex, and online shopping can all be used as temporary numbing agents for emotional pain without solving any problems systemically. Sometimes these coping behaviors are as trivial as occasionally skipping an appointment or ordering a Cheesy Gordita Crunch from Taco Bell. But they can also be far more severe - even life-threatening.

Dialectical behavior therapy (DBT), a therapeutic practice which originally emerged from CBT, often focuses on treating harmful behaviors such as addiction, self-harm, and even suicidal ideation and attempts. One of the core exercises is known as behavioral chain analysis, in which a patient investigates what led to the target behavior and which leverage points exist for preventing it in the future.[24] Here is a heavy and complex example adapted from a patient's experience documented in Shireen Rizvi's *Chain Analysis in Dialectical Behavior Therapy*.

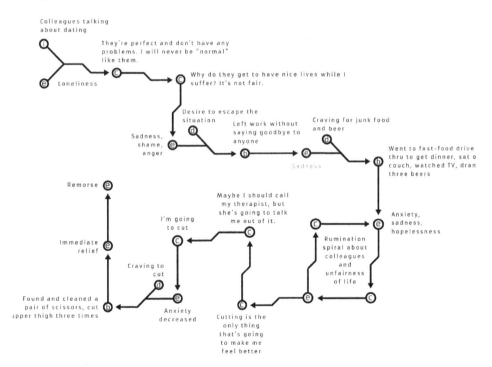

All previously covered methods for modifying emotions can be used instrumentally for changing behaviors. This patient's cognitive evaluations are highly distorted, and one promising path to changing the problematic behavior would be the cognitive restructuring methods covered in chapter 5. But it is also worth noting that not everyone dealing with feelings of loneliness and anxiety resorts to extreme behaviors like self-harm.

Because a habit is essentially a behavior that has become linked to an input, one of the best methods for changing a habit is to replace the problem behavior with another response to the same input.[25] Imagine how much less tragic the example above would be if cutting were replaced with exercise. If you are able to notice that your Nutella problem is triggered by the feeling of boredom, your problem is halfway solved. You can then explore opportunities for changing the behavior, such as replacing Nutella with a similar but healthier snack like yogurt. You can reroute the paths leading from your emotions to your behaviors and direct them to a healthier place - ideally one that doesn't reinforce the negative emotion that triggered it.

Design Your Consequences

We can also shape our behavior by altering the consequences of our actions. The strength of the desire connecting an environmental input with a behavioral output is determined by the resulting reward.[26] If we win money after gambling at a slot machine, this reward will condition and strengthen the connection between the cue of casino bells and the act of sitting down and trying the slots. This will increase our craving next time and make the behavior more habitual. Unfortunately, going home feeling terrible after having lost lots of money will have less conditioning power than a small win because more immediate rewards have more power. The feeling of satisfaction we get from running a marathon has less power than the immediate pleasure of a Baby Bottle Pop®.

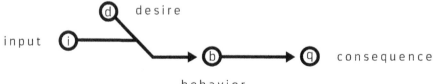

Fortunately, there are ways we can take advantage of this programming power by designing the consequences of our behaviors. Through the method known as **pre-commitment**, you can set up certain rewards and sanctions for your behaviors prior to facing the temptation to cave in or slack off.[27]

You can leverage your drive for financial accumulation by making the commitment to give money to a friend for every day that you fail to practice an instrument you want to learn. Simply make a deposit to a trusted friend that you can only get back if you meet your specific behavioral goal. You can also construct an allowance system in which you "pay yourself" spendable money for every time you complete a desired action. Just make sure it isn't set up so that good behavior will deplete your savings. By making these commitments, you set up meaningful consequences for behaviors that wouldn't normally result in them.[28]

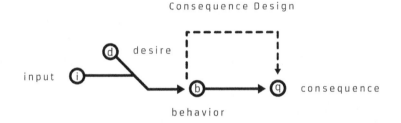

Consequence Design

There are many ways to leverage your social drives to make your defined goals more rewarding or failing them more punishing. By publicly announcing the behavioral changes you intend to make, you can raise the stakes of failure. This will effectively stack your aversion to social disapproval onto the desired action.[29] By getting a personal trainer or workout partner, you can add accountability to your habits and make it so failing to go to the gym will cause you to disappoint others. We can also ask people close to us to deliver praise when we successfully perform a predefined action.[30]

It has even been shown that creating a physical contract stating exactly what we intend to do and signing it will make us more likely to go through with it. We have a natural aversion to breaking our commitments, and **the more formal the commitment, the more strongly we will feel the violation.**[31]

As I write this, I'm using an online tool called Focusmate which calls itself a virtual coworking tool.[32] It sets up roughly hour-long video sessions between strangers trying to accomplish their own goals and asks each person to work silently, only sharing their goal at the beginning and how well they did at the end. It's a surprisingly powerful productivity tool, and it works because it reroutes our desires to follow through on our goals and to gain social approval toward the end of efficiently achieving our personal goals.

There are other technologies which can help us create immediate rewards or punishments for our behaviors. Though rewards tend to work better than punishments, wearables such as Pavlok will deliver electric shocks for failing to get up when your alarm goes off, smoking a cigarette, or going to a fast food restaurant you have sworn off, which may train you not to crave these things.[33] Some evidence has shown that the simple act of smiling can serve as a reward, so you may be able to condition positive behaviors by smiling immediately after completing them.[34]

A method known as **temptation bundling** allows us to stack enjoyable activities onto our defined goals. Whether you love fantasy football, bubble baths, or dressing up like a pirate, you can structure your plans such that you only allow yourself to do these things after completing a particular disciplined activity. This will slowly cause you to associate the positive behavior with the indulgence until you begin to crave the positive activity itself.[35]

One of the most interesting ways to take advantage of your reward system is through the construction of a **token economy**. Create some kind of token, be it a poker chip, a paper clip, or a check mark in your notebook. Assign a particular value to the token, and give yourself one immediately every time you perform a predetermined action. You can say that a token equals a coffee, a concert, or one episode of your favorite streaming show. **Over time, the token will become so closely associated with the reward that it will serve as a powerful reward itself.**[36]

A **forcing function** is a self-imposed circumstance which "forces" you to execute behaviors which would otherwise be difficult or impossible. When you pre-commit to a certain situation, you lock yourself into a positive spiral which is very difficult to escape. Although there are plenty of free, online resources for learning the skill of programming, using these to develop the level of proficiency that you would get in a university education would be incredibly difficult, simply because free courses don't serve as a significant forcing function. In school courses, you have a financial investment, the respect of your peers and professors, grades, and degrees on the line, and **these motives will pull you up far more effectively and efficiently than your own brute willpower.**

If you can name a craving or a guilty pleasure, chances are there is a way to stack it onto a beneficial behavior or habit to reinforce it. Can you find a way to make use of your drive for sugar to fuel you toward your goals? What about your desire for relaxation? Your sex drive? Don't limit yourself - every drive you have is a tool for effortlessly propelling yourself toward your ideals. Find a way to rotate your existing drives so that they stack onto the weaker drives for good behavior. If you can strengthen your motivations to complete defined goals, the behavior will become automatic, and the need to use willpower will be eliminated.

There are times when the best way to build a habit is to leverage existing drives so that the behavior seems to happen automatically. We can directly regulate our drives, strengthening or weakening the connection between cues and cravings, and many of the modulation tactics we used to dial up or down our emotions in chapter 6 can be used for the purpose of directing behavior as well. Asceticism can be used to weaken a desire's hold on us and break the soft addictions that lock us into bad habits. Seneca speaks of fasting as a method for making one less addicted to regular meals:

> I am so firmly determined, however, to test the constancy of your mind that, drawing from the teachings of great men, I shall give you also a lesson: Set aside a certain number of days, during which you shall be content with the scantiest and cheapest fare, with coarse and rough dress, saying to yourself the while: 'Is this the condition that I feared?'

> - **Seneca**, *Letters from a Stoic*

Nietzsche named specific methods for gaining greater self-control as well. One was the same method of fasting and asceticism that Seneca referenced. But another was to schedule specific times to indulge in certain cravings, strictly refraining from doing so outside of the schedule. This could help ensure that acceptable moderation does not get out of hand.

An interesting suggestion he offers is that we may associate a painful or unpleasant idea (or conversely, a very enjoyable idea) with a particular action such that over time, the behavior and the idea become intertwined and our desires push us accordingly. If certain emotions become associated with a behavior, they can help to promote or discourage that behavior.[37] Which emotions fuel you the most?

You can use the frustration you feel when other people doubt your potential to fuel you. Just make sure you can keep this anger contained and prevent it from leading you to make impulsive mistakes. You can use pride to lock yourself into positive habits. When you practice playing an instrument, imagine performing for the people you would most like to impress. The sense of pride you get from a nonexistent audience is still real, and it still results in motivation. When you finish reading a book, add it to either a physical bookshelf or a profile on a platform like Goodreads. Seeing your accomplishments add up will boost your motivation, and sharing them with others will lock you into positive habits.[38]

Your primary reason for giving to charity may be to impress friends with your generosity. But if you are aware of this fact, there is no reason you can't use this social drive to motivate the actions which align with your values. Use social drives to help lock you into your own personal goals which you have determined are consistent with your values. Build an imaginary council of people who collectively embody your values, and consult this group in your head when you need to make a decision.

Design Your Goals

Our subjects no longer strive in the ordinary sense, but rather develop. They attempt to grow to perfection and to develop more and more fully in their own style. The motivation of ordinary men is a striving for the basic need gratifications that they lack.

- **Abraham Maslow**, *Motivation and Personality*

A major source of motivation comes from choosing goals we truly find rewarding and authentic. Though we have talked about the importance of setting up rewards for positive behaviors, rewards can have a dark side when it comes to motivation for thoughtful and creative activities. According to Maslow's observations, one of the most prominent qualities of more highly developed and fulfilled individuals was a tendency to be motivated by intrinsically rewarding processes, such as growth, inquiry, and creativity, rather than by "flattery, applause, popularity, status, prestige, money, honors..."[39]

Today, we have even more evidence for this fact. Numerous studies have shown that intrinsic motivation, which consists of doing things we find enjoyable and engaging, can be more powerful than extrinsic rewards.[40] It can be far more effective to choose goals we already have strong desires pushing us toward than to reward ourselves for going against our desires. But counterintuitively, the overwhelming evidence suggests that **extrinsic rewards can not only be weakly motivating, but can actually hurt our motivation and yield inferior work than intrinsic drive.**[41]

One study found that the less evidence of extrinsic motivation in school, the more likely students were to be successful twenty years later. Amazingly, **a lack of interest in external rewards appears to be positively correlated with attaining those external rewards.** These art students who were more intrinsically motivated were more likely to have created work which received positive recognition and superior evaluation.[42]

Daniel Pink, author of *Drive: The Surprising Truth About What Motivates Us*, lists seven problems with extrinsic, carrot-and-stick motivations:

1. They can extinguish intrinsic motivation.
2. They can diminish performance.
3. They can crush creativity.
4. They can crowd out good behavior.
5. They can encourage cheating and unethical behavior.
6. They can become addictive.
7. They can foster short-term thinking.[43]

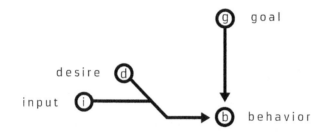

More and more of the world is adapting to this counterintuitive truth. As automation takes over more mundane work, carrot-and-stick incentives are being used less to ensure that work is done. More platforms like Wikipedia, which work only because of the intrinsic motivation of their contributors, are being built. Although many aspire to retire and stop working, the truth is that humans are not wired to be without work. They are simply wired to crave creative, challenging, and meaningful work. As the promise of artificial intelligence looms, so does the possibility that all work will be done for intrinsically rewarding purposes.

Pink points out three properties of intrinsically motivating activities: autonomy, mastery, and purpose. If an activity provides us with a creative challenge that contributes to a meaningful cause, it can fuel us more than activities for which we are extrinsically rewarded. It should be noted that repetitive tasks lacking in creativity are still enhanced by extrinsic rewards.[44] And because many of the behaviors and habits we wish to cultivate are important but mundane tasks, it is crucial to make use of rewards for these activities. But for the important work which provides us with a sense of autonomy, mastery, and purpose, we should be wary of extrinsic rewards and strive to cultivate innate motivation to fuel us. **An individual with a high degree of self-mastery will strategically design rewards in key places, and let intrinsic drive push them forward in others.**

These mastery motives can remove the effortful strain we typically associate with hard work and major accomplishments. Struggling to motivate ourselves toward our goals is often a product of choosing goals that do not align with our personal passions and values. We also may struggle with motivation if the goals we have set do not fit into our "Goldilocks zone" of challenge. They must not be too lofty or unrealistic, but they also must not be too easy to be challenging.[45]

Whether you are exercising, playing an instrument, or starting a business, **you must be able to see and measure progress in order to stay motivated.**[46] The minute you plateau in your exercise goals and are no longer progressing, exercise will become a chore. The moment you stop challenging yourself musically, the more effort it will take to maintain your skills. And as soon as your business ceases to improve in whatever metrics constitute success for you, it will become an obligation. The will to build is fundamental to intrinsic motivation, so if you are wondering why you can't get into a job, a hobby, or a project, ask yourself if you feel like you are building something. If you aren't overcoming resistance, facing new challenges, and noticeably progressing, **don't be surprised when your motivation fails you.**

If you want to be highly driven, you have to find a way to connect your goals with your innate fascinations.

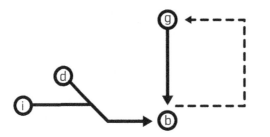

If all of the goals you set for yourself run counter to your own passions, it is probably time to return to chapter 5 and question the goals you have set in the first place. Satisfaction is not found in the achievement of goals, but in their pursuit, so many of the steps along the way to your goals should be enjoyable.[47] The most proficient and prolific artists, authors, and architects all achieved what they did because they found a way to capitalize on what they already loved. Set goals that fit who you are, what you enjoy, and what you value.

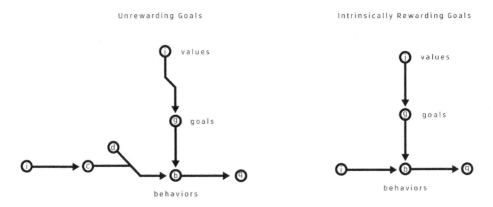

If you want to get in shape but hate jogging, start playing tennis, which will demand just as much from you physically but will provide the fun and engaging challenges of the sport. If your goal is to start a business, connect it to a cause you genuinely care about instead of using it to chase extrinsic rewards. The feeling of working hard when your drives have been aligned with your goals is no different from the feeling of play or deeply engaged flow. **What you**

aim for is not an absence of desire, but a frictionless experience with desire. You want your desires to carry you to where you want to be in a way that is seemingly effortless. When your life compass points in a consistent direction that you can align your drives toward, everything else falls into place.

Key Takeaways

• Most people think the reason they lose their internal battles of self-control is because they lack the willpower, but the people with the highest self-control aren't even using willpower.

• Taking the right actions and avoiding the wrong ones is not a white-knuckled battle of will, but a creative design process. The secrets to self-control and good habits lie in the management and training of our desires.

• In order for a behavior to be activated, we must encounter a trigger, or **input**, pay attention to it, and interpret it to be desirable.

• The strength of a drive is conditioned by the immediate reward of a behavior, or lack thereof, called the **consequence**.

• This leaves us with several promising opportunities for reprogramming our behaviors - all found in modulating, activating, and using our desires.

• By using smarter strategies and modulating the strength of existing desires and emotions, we can ensure that our goals are completed not only effectively, but effortlessly.

• Our environment can be a powerful tool for shaping our software.

• You can design your physical and digital environments, as well as the people you surround yourself with, to help design your own software.

• Our external experiences are generally filtered through our thoughts before they trigger behaviors, so our thoughts and focus play a powerful role in the actions we take.

• Methods like **attentional deployment** and **mindfulness** can be used to alter desires through paying greater or lesser attention to them.

• **Reappraisal** can be used to increase or decrease the power of a desire by changing the way we interpret the objects of desire.

• People adopt certain behaviors as coping mechanisms to deal with difficult emotions.

- Sometimes the best solution to a problematic behavior is to use the methods from chapters 5-7 to reduce or eliminate the problematic emotions at their source.

- Other times, you can change a habit by replacing the problem behavior with another response to the same input.

- We can also design the consequences of certain behaviors, as it is these consequences that program our desires.

- Through the method known as **pre-commitment**, you can set up certain rewards and sanctions for your behaviors prior to facing the temptation to cave in or slack off.

- You can leverage your social drive to make your defined goals more rewarding, or failing them more punishing, by publicly announcing the behavioral changes you intend to make, getting a personal trainer or accountability buddy, or asking people close to you to deliver praise when you successfully perform a predefined action.

- **Temptation bundling** allows us to stack enjoyable activities onto our defined goals.

- You can create a **token economy** to assign a value to a poker chip, a paper clip, or a check mark and give yourself one immediately every time you perform a predetermined action. Over time, the token will become so closely associated with the reward that it will serve as a powerful reward itself.

- A **forcing function** is a self-imposed circumstance which "forces" one to execute behaviors which would otherwise be difficult or impossible.

- There are times when the best way to build a habit is to leverage existing drives so that the behavior seems to happen automatically, and many of the modulation tactics we used to dial up or down our emotions in chapter 6 can be used for the purpose of directing behavior as well.

- You can use feelings like frustration and pride to fuel you toward your goals.

- Though rewards can be useful in certain cases, in others, extrinsic rewards can not only be weakly motivating, but can actually hurt our motivation and yield inferior work than intrinsic drive.

- When it comes to creative tasks, intrinsic motivations that provide people with a sense of autonomy, mastery, and purpose are more effective than extrinsic rewards.

- An individual with a high degree of self-mastery will strategically design rewards in key places, and let intrinsic drive push them forward in others.

• To remain motivated, we must be challenged, but not too challenged, by our goals. We also must be able to see and measure progress and feel like we are building something.

• If you want to be highly driven, you have to find a way to connect your goals with your innate fascinations.

• The feeling of working hard when your drives have been aligned with your goals is no different from the feeling of play or deeply engaged flow. What you aim for is not an absence of desire, but a frictionless experience with desire.

10

Self-Mastery

The Self-Mastery Triad

To compose our character is our duty, not to compose books, and to win, not battles and provinces, but order and tranquility in our conduct. Our great and glorious masterpiece is to live appropriately. All other things, ruling, hoarding, building, are only little appendages and props, at most.

- **Michel de Montaigne**, *The Complete Essays*

Now we have reached the final fragment of the self-mastery triad. When we combine the behavioral realm with the cognitive and emotional realms, the full picture of self-mastery comes into view. These domains represent the ability to become the self of your highest vision. To resist the many forces which would lead you away from it.

Self-mastery represents the degree to which you are capable of aligning with your own ideals. In other words, it is your ability to become a great individual and live a great life - by your own standards. The capacities found in the various forms of self-mastery like wisdom, equanimity, and self-control are not merely important virtues. **They are the prerequisite, second-order virtues that enable all other strengths to emerge.**[1]

Despite many differences, all of our psychitectural guides come together to sing the praises of self-mastery:

Though one may conquer a thousand times a thousand men in battle, yet he indeed is the noblest victor who conquers himself.

- **Siddhārtha Gautama**, Dhammapada

You have power over your mind — not outside events. Realize this, and you will find strength.

- **Marcus Aurelius**, *Meditations*

What the superior man seeks, is in himself; what the ordinary man seeks, is in others.

- **Confucius**, *Analects*

The chief use of wisdom lies in its teaching us to be masters of our passions and to control them with such skill that the evils which they cause are quite bearable, and even become a source of joy.

- **René Descartes**, *The Passions of the Soul*

Stop honoring externals, quit turning yourself into the tool of mere matter, or of people who can supply you or deny you those material things... It is enough if I hold the right idea about poverty, illness and removal from office: all such challenges will only serve my turn. No more, then, should I look for bad, and good, in external conditions.

- **Epictetus**, Discourses

Conquering others takes force.
Conquering yourself is true strength.

- **Lao Tzu**, *Tao Te Ching*

The most intelligent men, like the strongest, find their happiness where others would find only disaster: in the labyrinth... their delight is in self-mastery... They regard a difficult task as a privilege; it is to them a recreation to play with burdens that would crush all others.

- **Friedrich Nietzsche**, *Antichrist*

What makes the philosophies behind these words unique is that they reject the fundamental assumption we form early in our lives - that the best measure of success in life, and the best means for attaining it, is through our life circumstances and achievements. These ancient thinkers may have had slightly different ideas about how to get there, but they agreed that the best state of being is achieved, not through external measures, but through the individual mind. They aimed to overcome themselves rather than overcome the world. In psychitectural language, **they were software optimizers**. People who subscribe to these philosophies don't strive primarily to meet their deficiencies through the world, but **live to fortify and master the vehicle through which they traverse it.**

We have all heard the ancient cliche that "true happiness comes from within," but this truism is ambiguous and sends too many people down spiritual rabbit-holes that often amount to nothing. To become useful, it needs to be combined with the rational methods for reprogramming our psychological software "from within." I have attempted to provide a start to this process, but the fundamental mindset must be understood, internalized, and committed to first.

Psychological well-being is a systemic property of the mind; it cannot be gifted to anyone, nor can it be taken away. There are too many people with great lives on paper who are still miserable at the end of the day. Many who face immense adversity who are genuinely fulfilled. You can only be as happy as your mind is programmed to be. This means that although you may feel content at any given time, that satisfaction is illusory insofar as it can be taken away. If losing all of your possessions, circumstances, social standing, and relationships would deprive you of all your happiness, **what you have cannot be called happiness in the first place.**

Your body will be declining for most of your life. Your relationships will come and go. Material success can be lost. These things must all be icing on the cake of your well-being. Nothing you gain in life is yours. **Your psychological software is your sole possession.** It is the best investment you can make - one of the few things you can start developing now and get to keep for the rest of your life. When your external world is in chaos, **you can place your focus on your internal world**. Let your mind become your sanctuary. Build a palace of clarity and peace within you that you can visit any time.

I have had too many conversations with people who have not even questioned the assumption that their external life was all that mattered - who are convinced that they are failures because their life circumstances have not met their expectations. Others are self-satisfied and complacent because they have built an impressive resume and bought a nice house.

To those who have not achieved the external life of your dreams, do not allow the popular narrative to convince you that you are a failure. The world will tell you that you are deficient if you haven't had success in all of your endeavors. It will tell you that if your financial or professional or social life is lacking, you are somehow worth less. It will try to convince you that internal self-mastery is irrelevant. And don't you dare believe it. Never envy the people with the most impressive credentials or social media accounts unless you have reason to believe their internal accomplishments match their external ones. **Only those who have achieved greatness of the mind are worthy of our deep admiration.**

If your career isn't where you had hoped it would be, your financial means are modest, or your relationships are few, you are not a failure unless you are also lacking in wisdom, integrity, and self-mastery. But be careful not to idealize external failures. Our external lives may be secondary, but they are not inconsequential. Your environment, lifestyle, and relationships will inevitably shape your mind and change you. If you romanticize or justify your life as it is, it will keep you locked in a place that may not have a positive effect on you.

To those who have achieved success in your external life, congratulations. You are winning the great mini-game of life for the time being. But be vigilant. The stories of your culture will tell you that you've made it, and complacency and corruption will creep in the minute you think your work is done. Say to yourself, "now the real work begins" as you step away from the external game, unplug, and start to optimize your mind.

I have personally been very fortunate in my circumstances - so far. It is not my goal to trivialize the struggles of those who have been dealt more difficult hands. If you have endured painful circumstances, you have my deepest condolences. But before you justify the current state of your mind, ask yourself if everyone with similar conditions has resigned to them, or if there are some who have endured equal or greater difficulties and managed to thrive.

The teachers who inspired this work have included orphans,[2] crippled slaves,[3] and concentration camp prisoners.[4] Some were plagued by illness their entire lives,[5] and some lost their own children.[6] Aleksandr Solzhenitsyn, prisoner of the Gulag Soviet labor camps and author of *The Gulag Archipelago* reminds us that "the meaning of earthly existence lies not, as we have grown used to thinking, in prospering, but... in the development of the soul."[7]

The Self-Slavery Hypothesis

But self-mastery does not merely concern your happiness. The opposite of self-mastery is not merely self-incompetence. **It is self-slavery.** When you lack self-mastery, you are captive to your own mind. Your biological pre-programming tells you what to think, how to feel, how to act, and how to direct your life. You are in the hands of your default software, and this may affect far more people than just you.

There is an ancient and still prevalent notion that destructive, anti-social behaviors are the product of evil, some enigmatic psychological inclination that causes a person to commit terrible acts. But it is no coincidence that these people also seem to be the least psychologically fulfilled, or that the happiest people exhibit the most altruistic behavior.[8] The truth is that **many, if not all, of the so-called evil people in the world are simply lacking in self-mastery**. With enough information, understanding, and the right motives, we could understand and cure murderous psychopaths, brutal dictators, school shooters, and belligerent bigots purely in reference to weaknesses in their psychological software.

We have already seen that those lacking in behavioral self-mastery are more likely to experience explosive anger and commit violent crimes. In fact, among those with the lowest self-control, **forty percent have criminal convictions by age thirty-two**.[9] These people experience the same violent urges that everyone has from time to time, but fail to constrain them, and often regret their actions soon after taking them. They are short-sighted, cave in to their immediate desires, and act in ways that violate both the law and their own values.[10]

We see a lack of emotional self-mastery in those who plot murderous tantrums in revolt against a world in which they couldn't find peace. These people often lash out and take their pain out on innocent others because they couldn't deal with their problems and desires in healthy ways. Mass murderers typically feel wounded and victimized by the world, and their plots to kill are often their attempts to play out revenge fantasies against the people they perceive hurt them.[11] Though these people have often dealt with abuse or chronic rejection, their lack of emotional resilience and equanimity makes them unable to cope with their difficulties in healthy ways.[12] **Their unregulated emotions punish them because they lack effective strategies for managing them.**[13]

> When some men fail to accomplish what they desire to do they exclaim angrily, 'May the whole world perish!' This repulsive emotion is the pinnacle of envy, whose implication is 'If I cannot have something, no one can have anything, no one is to be anything!'
>
> - **Friedrich Nietzsche**[14]

And many of the greatest catastrophes and future risks result from a lack of cognitive self-mastery. In his book, *Evil*, Roy Baumeister points out that "...many especially evil acts are performed by people who believe they are doing something supremely good." Everyone from terrorists to assassins to dictators have all committed their terrible acts in the name of higher ideals and a better future.[15]

Most acts of war, genocide, and terrorism occur because the perpetrators lack critical thinking skills and wisdom. Hitler, Stalin, and Thanos all believed they were doing what was necessary to create a better world. The reason we call them evil is that **they were very, very wrong.** And this ultimately stems from mistaken, deeply biased beliefs and tremendous overconfidence in those beliefs. These people often accept unfounded ideologies without question. They often have dogmatic and distorted value systems. They are unable to think or introspect clearly, and these limitations result in myopia, foolishness, and corruption.[15]

And what about the sadists and psychopaths? We all have some antisocial or even sadistic urges, whether or not we are able to admit this to ourselves. But this need not be the defining characteristic of evil. As we have discussed, many of our drives will not align with our values. But values, not drives, are the true indicators of good choices. Most serial killers report that though they expected their murderous acts to be deeply satisfying, they found the actual act to be disappointing.[16] They continue to commit these acts despite continually finding disappointment, which is the hallmark of a lack of wisdom. It is the decision to cave in to our misaligned desires, not the mere presence of those desires, which represents a lack of wisdom or self-control.

The core trait of psychopaths has always been thought to be a lack of empathy. But psychopaths who are prompted to feel another person's pain show they are capable of "turning on" their empathy at will, much as many people are able to turn down their empathy when needed.[17] Research has found that self-control is a much better indicator of antisocial behavior than empathy.[18] And despite the stereotypes of psychopaths being brilliant and calculating, antisocial personality disorder, the formal diagnosis associated with psychopathy, has been found to be associated with impulsive behavior, short-term thinking, and emotion dysregulation.[19] [20] [21] In other words, psychopaths are often lacking in all three forms of self-mastery.

I am open to the possibility that there exist human beings who can think incisively, introspect clearly, set goals wisely, control their emotions and behavior effectively, and who still choose to commit destructive and antisocial acts. **But I have yet to find compelling evidence of such a person**. All of the cases of so called evil I have studied demonstrate extreme weakness and self-slavery in at least one realm of their software. And most importantly, for each of these cases, that software could theoretically be restructured. We need to shift our attention and conversations from surface-level events and actions to their psychitectural underpinnings. We need to drill down to the algorithmic patterns behind the best and worst of human nature.

Aristotle argued that a person's upbringing, wealth, and personal strengths play an important role in living a good life.[22] This has been misinterpreted as a claim that there are hard barriers preventing poor, unlucky, or unattractive people from living a happy, moral life. But there is a much better interpretation of his claim. Our genes, upbringing, natural strengths, and early life experiences exclusively shape our psychological software until we develop the autonomy to examine and shape it ourselves. These factors represent our default settings. Our psychitectural starting point.

The software of an individual who is naturally neurotic or violent, had a difficult childhood, or has dealt with serious trauma will have further to go than others to build a mind which aligns with his ideals. Trauma, loss, and abuse can embed and habitualize whole networks of algorithms which may pose great challenges for the psychitect. And these challenges may be too great for some. **But the only truly insurmountable barrier to psychitecture is the failure to take on the project at all.**

Software Optimization

> Your entire life runs on the software in your head—why wouldn't you obsess over optimizing it? ...And yet, not only do most of us not obsess over our own software—most of us don't even understand our own software, how it works, or why it works that way.

> - Tim Urban[23]

This book has offered a new model for psychological algorithms which can illuminate many of the relationships between mental phenomena of which few people are cognizant. But this model is better viewed as a kind of functional interface than a theory. Though this structure is based on lots of psychological research, it is not the final word on the structure of psychological software. In truth, psychological algorithms are far too complex to be represented by a functional model.

The value of this model is to give form to the software framework, and to convert you to thinking about psychological problems algorithmically. Think about how your cognitions, desires, emotions, and behaviors interconnect and how they relate to their external inputs. Understand that these different variables influence each other and chain together to form worldviews, behavioral patterns, and mood disorders. But also understand that it is possible to form networks made up of adaptive traits, character strengths, and wisdom.

Understand that there are indisputable leverage points for reprogramming these negative patterns and turning them into positive ones.

Every design process, from construction architecture to software architecture, attempts to develop a blueprint for a system or artifact which bridges the gap between what is and a vision of what could be, guided by our shared values and principles. And anyone who has engaged in this creative process knows the immense satisfaction of looking at your own creation as it nears this more ideal state.

Psychitecture is no exception. As you near your ideals, you can look down on your software with both the satisfaction of seeing how far it has come and excitement at how far it still has to go. Who is your ideal self? What are the highest values and principles that this person embodies? What does this person's psychological software look like? And most importantly, what is the difference between it and your current software? When you have answered these questions, you can begin taking steps toward this ideal.

A psychitect lives in a state of perpetual becoming - experimenting with his mind, reinventing himself, and gradually elevating his state of being. He makes a game out of unlocking and implementing beneficial mindsets.

The life of a true psychitect is a kind of meta-existence. She continues to live in the world as a human but comes to live above her mind in a sense as she **starts to identify as the designer of her software rather than synonymous with it**. She starts to see through the illusions presented to her by her default dispositions and the social reality presented by other people. The automatic stories constructed by her cognition begin to appear as just that: stories - rather than as reality itself. Her painful emotions become the programmed, and not yet deprogrammed reactions to these stories.

A psychitect is a collector of adaptive mental mechanisms- a craftsman of strategic psychological structures. He comes to see unwanted negative emotions as inefficiencies in his programming. Wise ideas and principles come to be viewed as snippets of open-source cognitive code. He takes responsibility for his innate human flaws and biases and for programming them out. Psychitecture is a mindset which can allow you to increasingly embrace and enjoy life. **It is about getting out of your own way and removing the obstacles to the full appreciation for this incredible world.**

Have you ever met a person who was invincible? Someone who seemed never to lose her balance regardless of what happened to her. Someone who laughed when others would break down - who seemed to have a way of turning every setback into a victory without ever compromising what matters to her. A seasoned psychitect may act as if she had somehow never had normal human suffering programmed into her - a naturally calm and easy-going person. But realistically, this type of person is most likely the product of her own rigorous endeavor to program out the uncongenial aspects of herself.

The first time you successfully reprogram a pain-point, a self-limiting belief, or a problematic behavior to which you were previously subject, it doesn't just feel like you got a little better at coping with life. **It feels like you've opened the door to a new way of being**. Each time you unlock one of these tools, you climb to a higher cliff of perspective, able to look down on the issue and laugh at the fact that it ever troubled you.

Beyond the Human Condition

> This painting—that which we humans call life and experience—has gradually become, is indeed still fully in the process of becoming, and should thus not be regarded as a fixed object...
>
> - **Friedrich Nietzsche**, *Human, All Too Human*

What if we could provide each individual with an array of powerful psychotechnologies for understanding and optimizing the functions of their own minds? What would be the cumulative effects on society if every person's highest goal was to overcome themselves and build the best possible mind? The purpose of psychitecture is not just to decrease suffering, but to pursue greatness and active flourishing. I am interested in psychological development beyond the norm - in human potential. And I believe that for reasons entirely within their control, most people today fall radically short of their own values.

There is a massive and growing gap in our culture between skill and wisdom - **a gap that is becoming increasingly dangerous.**[24] Modern culture is obsessed with the external. We appoint leaders who present thin veneers of strength and superficial accomplishment. We pay so much attention to these facades that we fail to inquire into their foundations. As a result, we live in a world whose fate increasingly falls in the hands of the least wise and most power-obsessed individuals.

When people set out to improve their lives, they look outward. They ask how they might elevate their lifestyle, their status, or their possessions. When we talk about life skills, most think of the skills needed to get jobs, attract partners, and manage finances. These are all perfectly admirable skills. But they are secondary. Every external end is a means to an internal end. And many of our deepest internal goals can be achieved directly. The primary sense in which people today need to get better at living their lives has to do with wisdom, character, and well-being. These are not skills which are taught in school.

Companies promise to make the world a better place[25] by creating devices and services which often only serve as new obstacles to well-being. I strongly believe in the promise of technology, when directed toward the right ends, to lead to a genuinely better world for all. But I would estimate that ninety-nine percent of technologies created today only create new addictions. They "improve" our lives only in the sense that they become our new baseline of expectation, ultimately creating new barriers to contentment.

There are technologies, like medicine, which truly improve life for people. But most of the technologies which can actually serve this end effectively are psychotechnologies. We need tools and methods for cultivating robust well-being and self-mastery. We need to find and provide the keys to the kind of flourishing which is less dependent on external things, not more dependent on them. If we want to truly improve the world, we need to train people to build systematically better minds - **our emphasis on "making people happy" needs to shift to "making happy people."**

I want to work toward a world of individuals who see through the illusion. Who are no longer fooled by the vanity metrics and tourist traps of life. Who can slow their judgments, call the bluff of facades and personas, and ask the questions which matter most. Who put the cultivation of a better mind at the top of their priorities, not only because it is the most important in and of itself, but because it is at the root of every other endeavor.

I have attempted to build a starting toolkit to inspire and enable people to make modifications to their own minds, but this toolkit is nowhere near complete, and this book is only the beginning. That is why it is my primary goal to ignite the flame of psychitecture in as many people as possible. That way, each individual can construct his own tools and contribute to the great collective toolkit.

> Fundamentally, there is no reason why pleasure, excitement, profound well-being and simple joy at being alive could not become the natural, default state of mind for all who desire it.

> - **Nick Bostrom**[26]

Though it is so often accompanied by descriptions of futuristic gadgets, body augmentation, and distant concerns, the Transhumanist vision provides a reminder that humanity can be far greater than it is today. The human condition is a work in progress. An early and very rough draft of what could be a masterpiece. And the evolution of society begins with the evolution of the individual mind. This evolution cannot be left to chance. It must be the result of deliberate design conducted by each person and directed toward the highest values within them. The software framework and the principles of psychitecture are basic psychotechnologies which, if provided and instilled in each individual, **could radically advance our evolution.**

The ambition of this book is not just to offer a manual. It may be based on timeless wisdom, but the manual provided here is still only an ever-evolving draft. This book exists, first and foremost, to reinvigorate the directive issued by the many psychitectural visionaries: You must be a software optimizer first and a circumstance optimizer second. Place the development of your mind above all else. Make the psychitectural pursuit your highest priority, and watch your experience, your life, and your being transform. No matter who you are or where you are starting from, know that you have the power to transform your software and attain self-mastery. **You can design your mind.**

FREE PSYCHITECT'S TOOLKIT

+

THE BOOK OF SELF MASTERY

You have reached the end of *Designing the Mind: The Principles of Psychitecture*. If this book has been valuable to you and you would like a way to contribute, **please consider writing a quick and honest review.**

In addition to this book, verified readers can join the community of psychitects and download the *Psychitect's Toolkit*, a **free, 50-page guide on psychitecture**, which includes 64 recommendations for incredible books to read next.

I will also give you a free copy of *The Book of Self Mastery: Timesless Quotes About Knowing, Changing, and Mastering Yourself.*

Just go to designingthemind.org/psychitecture to get your Psychitect's Toolkit and Book of Self Mastery.

Acknowledgements

I have never liked acknowledgment sections. Like footnotes and appendices, no one is quite sure if they are supposed to read them. Acknowledgments seem irrelevant to the reader, who doesn't know any of the people being thanked and probably doesn't care. I wanted to give readers a crisp, clean message that was designed just for them.

But at the end of the day, life, and the process of writing, are not crisp and clean - they're messy. And when it comes time to publish your book, it seems wrong not to recognize the people who helped along the way. There are more people who have helped me in some way than I will endeavor to thank here, but some played direct roles in helping make this book happen.

Katlyn, it is only because of your ongoing encouragement that I was able to finish this book, and because of our many jokes and adventures forcing me to pause that I wasn't completely consumed by it. Thank you for being a part of this journey.

To my parents, Ron and Dena, thank you for your lifelong support for my passions, for your brutally honest feedback on my first draft, and for your kind praise of my final draft.

To my friends, mentors, and beta readers, this book is orders of magnitude better because of your thoughtful guidance, feedback, and ideas. Thank you to Aaron Perkins, Alan K, Ben Rogers, Cavell H-B, Christopher Clay, Felipe Olchenski, Hamish S, Jakub Smrček, Jeff Shreve, Jo Ann Miller, Jorge Rodighiero, Justin Qubrosi, Kate Theobald, Kelsey Butts, Konstantin V, Mark Mulvey, Matt Karamazov, Nate Shenkute, Nishit Chauhan, Philip L, Thibaut Meurisse, and several incredible anonymous readers.

And special thanks to Hootie. You are my light and my muse.

Notes

Chapter 1

1. Joseph LeDoux, *The Deep History of Ourselves: The Four-Billion-Year Story of How We Got Conscious Brains*, Illustrated edition (New York City: Viking, 2019).

2. Colleen A. McClung and Eric J. Nestler, "Neuroplasticity Mediated by Altered Gene Expression," *Neuropsychopharmacology* 33, no. 1 (January 2008): 3–17, https://doi.org/10.1038/sj.npp.1301544.

3. Sibylle Delaloye and Paul E. Holtzheimer, "Deep Brain Stimulation in the Treatment of Depression," *Dialogues in Clinical Neuroscience* 16, no. 1 (March 2014): 83–91.

4. Akhlaq Farooqui, "The Effects of Diet, Exercise, and Sleep on Brain Metabolism and Function," 2014, 1–42, https://doi.org/10.1007/978-3-319-04111-7_1.

5. Jon Kabat-Zinn, "Mindfulness-Based Interventions in Context: Past, Present, and Future," *Clinical Psychology: Science and Practice* 10, no. 2 (2003): 144–56, https://doi.org/10.1093/clipsy.bpg016.

6. "13 Effects of Transcranial Direct Current Stimulation (TDCS)," *Self-Hacked* (blog), December 17, 2019, https://selfhacked.com/blog/tdcs-benefits/.

7. L-S Camilla d'Angelo, George Savulich, and Barbara J Sahakian, "Lifestyle Use of Drugs by Healthy People for Enhancing Cognition, Creativity, Motivation and Pleasure," *British Journal of Pharmacology* 174, no. 19 (October 2017): 3257–67, https://doi.org/10.1111/bph.13813.

8. Michael Pollan, *How to Change Your Mind: What the New Science of Psychedelics Teaches Us About Consciousness, Dying, Addiction, Depression, and Transcendence*, Softcover large print edition (New York: Penguin Press, 2018).

9. "What Is Transhumanism?," What is Transhumanism?, accessed November 25, 2020, https://whatistranshumanism.org/.

10. "Six Paths to the Nonsurgical Future of Brain-Machine Interfaces," accessed November 25, 2020, https://www.darpa.mil/news-events/2019-05-20.

11. "Home," Neuralink, accessed November 25, 2020, https://neuralink.com/.

12. Eberhard Fuchs and Gabriele Flügge, "Adult Neuroplasticity: More Than 40 Years of Research," *Neural Plasticity* 2014 (2014), https://doi.org/10.1155/2014/541870.

13. Norman Doidge, *The Brain That Changes Itself: Stories of Personal Triumph from the Frontiers of Brain Science*, n.d.

14. Melanie J. Zimmer-Gembeck and Ellen A. Skinner, "Review: The Development of Coping across Childhood and Adolescence: An Integrative Review and Critique of Research," *International Journal of Behavioral Development* 35, no. 1 (January 1, 2011): 1–17, https://doi.org/10.1177/0165025410384923.

15. David Whitebread and Marisol Basilio, "The Emergence and Early Development of Self-Regulation in Young Children," *Profesorado: Journal of Curriculum and Teacher Education* 16 (January 1, 2012): 15–34.

16. Malcolm Gladwell, *Outliers: The Story of Success*, n.d.

17. Carol S. Dweck, *Mindset: The New Psychology of Success*, n.d.

18. David Buss and Martie Haselton, "The Evolution of Jealousy," *Trends in Cognitive Sciences* 9 (December 1, 2005): 506–7; author reply 508, https://doi.org/10.1016/j.tics.2005.09.006.

19. Cory J. Clark et al., "Tribalism Is Human Nature," *Current Directions in Psychological Science* 28, no. 6 (December 1, 2019): 587–92, https://doi.org/10.1177/0963721419862289.

20. Tammy Saah, "The Evolutionary Origins and Significance of Drug Addiction," *Harm Reduction Journal* 2 (June 29, 2005): 8, https://doi.org/10.1186/1477-7517-2-8.

21. "Definition of ALGORITHM," accessed November 25, 2020, https://www.merriam-webster.com/dictionary/algorithm.

22. "The Thing We Fear More Than Death," Psychology Today, accessed November 25, 2020, http://www.psychologytoday.com/blog/the-real-story-risk/201211/the-thing-we-fear-more-death.

23. David L. Watson and Roland G. Tharp, *Self-Directed Behavior: Self-Modification for Personal Adjustment. Chapter 1: The Skills of Self-Direction*, 10th edition (Australia: Cengage Learning, 2013).

24. Warren Tryon, *Cognitive Neuroscience and Psychotherapy: Network Principles for a Unified Theory. Chapter 3 - Core Network Principles: The Explanatory Nucle-

us, 1st edition (London, UK ; Waltham, MA, USA: Academic Press, 2014).

25. Aaron T. Beck, *Cognitive Therapy and the Emotional Disorders. Chapter 2: Tapping the Internal Communications*, n.d.

26. "Emotional Competency - Human Nature," accessed November 25, 2020, http://www.emotionalcompetency.com/human%20nature.htm.

27. David D. Burns, *Feeling Good: The New Mood Therapy. Chapter 1*, n.d.

28. Carey K. Morewedge et al., "Debiasing Decisions: Improved Decision Making With a Single Training Intervention," *Policy Insights from the Behavioral and Brain Sciences*, August 13, 2015, https://doi.org/10.1177/2372732215600886.

29. Benjamin Gardner and Amanda L. Rebar, "Habit Formation and Behavior Change," Oxford Research Encyclopedia of Psychology, April 26, 2019, https://doi.org/10.1093/acrefore/9780190236557.013.129.

30. Aristotle, *Nicomachean Ethics*, trans. C. D. C. Reeve, n.d.

31. "A Philosophical Approach to Routines Can Illuminate Who We Really Are – Elias Anttila | Aeon Ideas," Aeon, accessed November 25, 2020, https://aeon.co/ideas/a-philosophical-approach-to-routines-can-illuminate-who-we-really-are.

32. John H. Flavell, "Metacognition and Cognitive Monitoring: A New Area of Cognitive–Developmental Inquiry," *American Psychologist* 34, no. 10 (1979): 906–11, https://doi.org/10.1037/0003-066X.34.10.906.

33. Jon Kabat-Zinn, "Mindfulness-Based Interventions in Context: Past, Present, and Future," *Clinical Psychology: Science and Practice* 10, no. 2 (2003): 144–56, https://doi.org/10.1093/clipsy.bpg016.

34. Shian-Ling Keng, Moria J. Smoski, and Clive J. Robins, "Effects of Mindfulness on Psychological Health: A Review of Empirical Studies," *Clinical Psychology Review* 31, no. 6 (August 2011): 1041–56, https://doi.org/10.1016/j.cpr.2011.04.006.

35. Sam Harris, *Waking Up: A Guide to Spirituality Without Religion. Chapter 1*, n.d.

36. "Meditation Trains Metacognition - LessWrong," accessed November 25, 2020, https://www.lesswrong.com/posts/JMgffu9AzhYpTpHFJ/meditation-trains-metacognition.

37. Peter Sedlmeier et al., "The Psychological Effects of Meditation: A Me-

ta-Analysis," *Psychological Bulletin* 138, no. 6 (November 2012): 1139–71, https://doi.org/10.1037/a0028168.

38. "A Map of Bay Area Memespace - LessWrong," accessed November 25, 2020, https://www.lesswrong.com/posts/WzPJRNYWhMXQTE-j69/a-map-of-bay-area-memespace.

39. Tim Buschmann et al., "The Relationship Between Automatic Thoughts and Irrational Beliefs Predicting Anxiety and Depression," *Journal of Rational-Emotive & Cognitive-Behavior Therapy* 36 (July 1, 2017): 1–26, https://doi.org/10.1007/s10942-017-0278-y.

40. Paradigm, "Mindfulness & Bias: Literature Review," Medium, May 8, 2017, https://medium.com/inclusion-insights/mindfulness-bias-literature-review-3e4a9993cb41.

41. Diana J. Burgess, Mary Catherine Beach, and Somnath Saha, "Mindfulness Practice: A Promising Approach to Reducing the Effects of Clinician Implicit Bias on Patients," *Patient Education and Counseling* 100, no. 2 (February 1, 2017): 372–76, https://doi.org/10.1016/j.pec.2016.09.005.

42. Richard F. Gombrich, *Theravada Buddhism: A Social History from Ancient Benares to Modern Colombo*, 2nd edition (Routledge, 2006).

43. Yair Dor-Ziderman et al., "Mindfulness-Induced Selflessness: A MEG Neurophenomenological Study," *Frontiers in Human Neuroscience* 7 (2013), https://doi.org/10.3389/fnhum.2013.00582.

Chapter 2

1. Atsuo Murata, Tomoko Nakamura, and Waldemar Karwowski, "Influence of Cognitive Biases in Distorting Decision Making and Leading to Critical Unfavorable Incidents," *Safety* 1, no. 1 (December 2015): 44–58, https://doi.org/10.3390/safety1010044.

2. Kevin N. Ochsner and James J. Gross, "The Cognitive Control of Emotion," *Trends in Cognitive Sciences* 9, no. 5 (May 2005): 242–49, https://doi.org/10.1016/j.tics.2005.03.010.

3. Hedy Kober et al., "Regulation of Craving by Cognitive Strategies in Cigarette Smokers," *Drug and Alcohol Dependence* 106, no. 1 (January 1, 2010):

52–55, https://doi.org/10.1016/j.drugalcdep.2009.07.017.

4.   Robert Alan Burton, *On Being Certain: Believing You Are Right Even When You're Not*, Reprint edition (St. Martin's Press, 2008).

5.   Alfred Korzybski, *Science and Sanity: An Introduction to Non-Aristotelian Systems and General Semantics* (International Non-Aristotelian Library Publishing Company, 1933).

6.   Henry Markovits and Guilaine Nantel, "The Belief-Bias Effect in the Production and Evaluation of Logical Conclusions," *Memory & Cognition* 17, no. 1 (January 1, 1989): 11–17, https://doi.org/10.3758/BF03199552.

7.   Steven Novella and Yale School of Medicine, *Your Deceptive Mind:A Scientific Guide to Critical Thinking Skills* (the great courses, 2012).

8.   Mark P. Mattson, "Superior Pattern Processing Is the Essence of the Evolved Human Brain," *Frontiers in Neuroscience* 8 (August 22, 2014), https://doi.org/10.3389/fnins.2014.00265.

9.   Scott D. Blain et al., "Apophenia as the Disposition to False Positives: A Unifying Framework for Openness and Psychoticism," *Journal of Abnormal Psychology* 129, no. 3 (2020): 279–92, https://doi.org/10.1037/abn0000504.

10. Alexander Alvarez, "Destructive Beliefs: Genocide and the Role of Ideology," 2008.

11. "Cognitive Bias," in *Wikipedia*, November 24, 2020, https://en.wikipedia.org/w/index.php?title=Cognitive_bias&oldid=990416478.

12. Buster Benson, "Cognitive Bias Cheat Sheet, Simplified," Medium, April 2, 2019, https://medium.com/thinking-is-hard/4-conundrums-of-intelligence-2ab78d90740f.

13. "The Illusion of Transparency: Biased Assessments of Others' Ability to Read One's Emotional States. - PsycNET," accessed November 25, 2020, https://doi.apa.org/doiLanding?doi=10.1037%2F0022-3514.75.2.332.

14. "Reducing Implicit Racial Preferences: II. Intervention Effectiveness across Time. - PsycNET," accessed November 25, 2020, https://psycnet.apa.org/doiLanding?doi=10.1037%2Fxge0000179.

15. Paradigm, "Mindfulness & Bias: Literature Review," Medium, May 8, 2017, https://medium.com/inclusion-insights/mindfulness-bias-literature-review-3e4a9993cb41.

16. Daniel Kahneman, *Thinking, Fast and Slow. Chapter 23*, 1st edition (New York: Farrar, Straus and Giroux, 2013).

17. Anne-Laure Sellier, Irene Scopelliti, and Carey K. Morewedge, "Debiasing Training Improves Decision Making in the Field:," *Psychological Science*, July 26, 2019, https://doi.org/10.1177/0956797619861429.

18. Carey K. Morewedge et al., "Debiasing Decisions: Improved Decision Making With a Single Training Intervention," *Policy Insights from the Behavioral and Brain Sciences*, August 13, 2015, https://doi.org/10.1177/2372732215600886.

19. Vasco Correia, "Contextual Debiasing and Critical Thinking: Reasons for Optimism," *Topoi* 37, no. 1 (March 1, 2018): 103–11, https://doi.org/10.1007/s11245-016-9388-x.

20. Wayne Weiten, *Psychology: Themes and Variations, Briefer Version*, n.d.

21. Thomas Mussweiler, Fritz Strack, and Tim Pfeiffer, "Overcoming the Inevitable Anchoring Effect: Considering the Opposite Compensates for Selective Accessibility," *Personality and Social Psychology Bulletin* 26, no. 9 (November 1, 2000): 1142–50, https://doi.org/10.1177/01461672002611010.

22. Martie G. Haselton, Daniel Nettle, and Paul W. Andrews, "The Evolution of Cognitive Bias," in *The Handbook of Evolutionary Psychology* (John Wiley & Sons, Ltd, 2015), 724–46, https://doi.org/10.1002/9780470939376.ch25.

23. Małgorzata Kossowska, Aneta Czernatowicz-Kukuczka, and Maciek Sekerdej, "Many Faces of Dogmatism: Prejudice as a Way of Protecting Certainty against Value Violators among Dogmatic Believers and Atheists," *British Journal of Psychology (London, England : 1953)* 108 (February 19, 2016), https://doi.org/10.1111/bjop.12186.

24. Melvin J. Lerner, "The Belief in a Just World," in *The Belief in a Just World: A Fundamental Delusion*, ed. Melvin J. Lerner, Perspectives in Social Psychology (Boston, MA: Springer US, 1980), 9–30, https://doi.org/10.1007/978-1-4899-0448-5_2.

25. Zick Rubin and Anne Peplau, "Belief in a Just World and Reactions to Another's Lot: A Study of Participants in the National Draft Lottery1," *Journal of Social Issues* 29, no. 4 (1973): 73–93, https://doi.org/10.1111/j.1540-4560.1973.tb00104.x.

26. Susan T. Fiske, "Intent and Ordinary Bias: Unintended Thought and

Social Motivation Create Casual Prejudice," *Social Justice Research* 17, no. 2 (June 1, 2004): 117–27, https://doi.org/10.1023/B:SORE.0000027405.94966.23.

27. Shelley E. Taylor and Jonathon D. Brown, "Positive Illusions and Well-Being Revisited: Separating Fact from Fiction," *Psychological Bulletin* 116, no. 1 (1994): 21–27, https://doi.org/10.1037/0033-2909.116.1.21.

28. Aaron M. Scherer, Paul D. Windschitl, and Andrew R. Smith, "Hope to Be Right: Biased Information Seeking Following Arbitrary and Informed Predictions," *Journal of Experimental Social Psychology* 49, no. 1 (January 1, 2013): 106–12, https://doi.org/10.1016/j.jesp.2012.07.012.

29. Giovanni Luca Ciampaglia US Filippo Menczer,The Conversation, "Biases Make People Vulnerable to Misinformation Spread by Social Media," Scientific American, accessed November 25, 2020, https://www.scientificamerican.com/article/biases-make-people-vulnerable-to-misinformation-spread-by-social-media/.

30. Agnes Makhene, "The Use of the Socratic Inquiry to Facilitate Critical Thinking in Nursing Education," *Health SA = SA Gesondheid* 24 (April 23, 2019), https://doi.org/10.4102/hsag.v24i0.1224.

31. Carl Sagan and Ann Druyan, *The Demon-Haunted World: Science as a Candle in the Dark. Chapter 2: Science and Hope*, n.d.

32. "Alternative Medicine Kills Cancer Patients – Science-Based Medicine," accessed November 25, 2020, https://sciencebasedmedicine.org/alternative-medicine-kills-cancer-patients/.

33. Naomi Oreskes and Erik M. Conway, *Merchants of Doubt: How a Handful of Scientists Obscured the Truth on Issues from Tobacco Smoke to Climate Change. Chapter 6: The Denial of Global Warming*, n.d.

34. Roy F. Baumeister Ph.D and Aaron Beck, *Evil: Inside Human Violence and Cruelty. Chapter 6: True Believers and Idealists* (New York: Holt Paperbacks, 1999).

35. Seán Ó hÉigeartaigh, "Technological Wild Cards: Existential Risk and a Changing Humanity," SSRN Scholarly Paper (Rochester, NY: Social Science Research Network, October 5, 2016), https://papers.ssrn.com/abstract=3446697.

36. "The Cook and the Chef: Musk's Secret Sauce," Wait But Why, November 6, 2015, https://waitbutwhy.com/2015/11/the-cook-and-the-chef-musks-secret-sauce.html.

37. J. Lambie, *How to Be Critically Open-Minded: A Psychological and Historical Analysis. Chapter 6: Effects of Open-Mindedness on Decision Making, Morality, and Well-Being*, 2014th edition (Palgrave Macmillan, 2014).

38. Maryam MALMIR, Mohammad KHANAHMADI, and Dariush FARHUD, "Dogmatism and Happiness," *Iranian Journal of Public Health* 46, no. 3 (March 2017): 326–32.

Chapter 3

1. Lauren B. Alloy and Lyn Y. Abramson, "Learned Helplessness, Depression, and the Illusion of Control," *Journal of Personality and Social Psychology* 42, no. 6 (1982): 1114–26, https://doi.org/10.1037/0022-3514.42.6.1114.

2. "Predictability: Does the Flap of a Butterfly's Wings in Brazil Set Off a Tornado in Texas? | Weather Forecasting | Weather," Scribd, accessed November 25, 2020, https://www.scribd.com/document/130949814/Predictability-Does-the-Flap-of-a-Butterfly-s-Wings-in-Brazil-Set-Off-a-Tornado-in-Texas.

3. "2.4.1 Swimming Headless Part 1 | AlanWatts.Org," accessed November 25, 2020, https://www.alanwatts.org/2-4-1-swimming-headless-part-1/.

4. Timothy Wilson and Daniel Gilbert, "The Impact Bias Is Alive and Well," *Journal of Personality and Social Psychology* 105 (November 1, 2013): 740–48, https://doi.org/10.1037/a0032662.

5. Daniel Gilbert, *Stumbling on Happiness*. Part III: Realism (New York: Vintage, 2007).

6. Daniel Gilbert, *Stumbling on Happiness*. Part IV: Presentism (New York: Vintage, 2007).

7. Daniel Gilbert, *Stumbling on Happiness*. Part V: Rationalization (New York: Vintage, 2007).

8. Tasha Eurich, *Insight: The Surprising Truth About How Others See Us, How We See Ourselves, and Why the Answers Matter More Than We Think*, Reprint edition (New York: Currency, 2018).

9. Kieran C. R. Fox et al., "Meditation Experience Predicts Introspective Accuracy," *PLOS ONE* 7, no. 9 (September 25, 2012): e45370, https://doi.org/10.1371/journal.pone.0045370.

10. Marcus Johansson, Terry Hartig, and Henk Staats, "Psychological Benefits of Walking: Moderation by Company and Outdoor Environment," *Applied Psychology: Health and Well-Being* 3, no. 3 (2011): 261–80, https://doi.org/10.1111/j.1758-0854.2011.01051.x.

11. Eugene T. Gendlin, *Focusing*, n.d.

12. Christopher R. Long and James R. Averill, "Solitude: An Exploration of Benefits of Being Alone," *Journal for the Theory of Social Behaviour* 33, no. 1 (2003): 21–44, https://doi.org/10.1111/1468-5914.00204.

13. Inge Huijsmans et al., "A Scarcity Mindset Alters Neural Processing Underlying Consumer Decision Making," *Proceedings of the National Academy of Sciences* 116, no. 24 (June 11, 2019): 11699–704, https://doi.org/10.1073/pnas.1818572116.

14. Pamela Tierney and Steven M. Farmer, "Creative Self-Efficacy Development and Creative Performance over Time.," *Journal of Applied Psychology* 96, no. 2 (2011): 277–93, https://doi.org/10.1037/a0020952.

15. Edward P. Lemay and Noah R. Wolf, "Projection of Romantic and Sexual Desire in Opposite-Sex Friendships: How Wishful Thinking Creates a Self-Fulfilling Prophecy," *Personality and Social Psychology Bulletin* 42, no. 7 (July 1, 2016): 864–78, https://doi.org/10.1177/0146167216646077.

16. Abraham H. Maslow, *Toward a Psychology of Being*. Chapter 1: Introduction: Toward a Psychology of Health *3rd Edition*, n.d.

17. David Moshman, "Cognitive Development beyond Childhood," in *Handbook of Child Psychology: Volume 2: Cognition, Perception, and Language* (Hoboken, NJ, US: John Wiley & Sons Inc, 1998), 947–78.

18. Christopher Peterson and Martin Seligman, *Character Strengths and Virtues: A Handbook and Classification*, 1st edition (Washington, DC : New York: American Psychological Association / Oxford University Press, 2004).

19. Bertrand Russell, *The Problems of Philosophy*, n.d.

20. Albert Speer, *Inside the Third Reich*, n.d.

21. Stephen J. Whitfield, "Hannah Arendt and the Banality of Evil," *The History Teacher* 14, no. 4 (1981): 469–77, https://doi.org/10.2307/493684.

22. Daniela Barni et al., "Value Transmission in the Family: Do Adolescents Accept the Values Their Parents Want to Transmit?," *Journal of Moral Educa-*

tion 40, no. 1 (March 1, 2011): 105–21, https://doi.org/10.1080/03057240.2011.5 53797.

23. Christopher Peterson and Martin Seligman, *Character Strengths and Virtues: A Handbook and Classification*, n.d.

24. Donald Robertson, *The Philosophy of Cognitive Behavioural Therapy: Stoic Philosophy as Rational and Cognitive Psychotherapy*, 1st edition (London: Routledge, 2010).

25. "5 Steps to Define Your Core Values: A Compass for Navigating Life's Decisions," *Mindful Ambition* (blog), June 8, 2017, https://mindfulambition.net/values/.

26. Carl Rogers and Peter D. Kramer M.D, *On Becoming a Person: A Therapist's View of Psychotherapy*, 2nd ed. edition (New York: Mariner Books, 1995).

Chapter 4

1. George Benson et al., "Cultural Values and Definitions of Career Success," *Human Resource Management Journal* 30 (March 1, 2020), https://doi.org/10.1111/1748-8583.12266.

2. "HAMER PEOPLE: THE ETHIOPIAN TRIBE WITH THE FAMOUS BULL JUMPING CEREMONY," *HAMER PEOPLE* (blog), accessed November 25, 2020, https://kwekudee-tripdownmemorylane.blogspot.com/2012/10/hamer-people-ethiopian-tribe-with.html.

3. Marsha L. Richins, "Social Comparison and the Idealized Images of Advertising," *Journal of Consumer Research* 18, no. 1 (June 1, 1991): 71–83, https://doi.org/10.1086/209242.

4. Monique Boekaerts, Paul R. Pintrich, and Moshe Zeidner, eds., *Handbook of Self-Regulation. Chapter 1: Self-Regulation of Action and Affect - Charles S. Carver, Michael F. Scheier*, n.d.

5. Jonathan Gutman, "Means–end chains as goal hierarchies," *Psychology & Marketing* 14, no. 6 (1997): 545–60, https://doi.org/10.1002/(SICI)1520-6793(199709)14:6<545::AID-MAR2>3.0.CO;2-7.

6. "Are Animals Stuck in Time? - PsycNET," accessed November 25, 2020, https://doi.apa.org/doiLanding?doi=10.1037%2F0033-2909.128.3.473.

7. Richard Dawkins, *The Selfish Gene: 30th Anniversary Edition--with a New Introduction by the Author. Chapter 1: Why Are People?*, n.d.

8. Ted Chu, *Human Purpose and Transhuman Potential: A Cosmic Vision of Our Future Evolution* (San Rafael, CA: Origin Press, 2014).

9. Ran R. Hassin, John A. Bargh, and Shira Zimerman, "Automatic and Flexible," *Social Cognition* 27, no. 1 (2009): 20–36.

10. Plato, *Phaedrus*, trans. Alexander Nehamas and Paul Woodruff, UK ed. edition (Indianapolis: Hackett Publishing Company, Inc., 1995).

11. W. Mischel, Y. Shoda, and M. I. Rodriguez, "Delay of Gratification in Children," *Science* 244, no. 4907 (May 26, 1989): 933–38, https://doi.org/10.1126/science.2658056.

12. David Hume, *A Treatise of Human Nature*, n.d.

13. Antonio Damasio, *Descartes' Error: Emotion, Reason, and the Human Brain*, n.d.

14. Antonio R. Damasio, "A Second Chance for Emotion," in *Cognitive Neuroscience of Emotion*, ed. Richard D. R. Lane et al. (Oxford University Press, 2000), 12–23.

15. Kevin Simler and Robin Hanson, *The Elephant in the Brain: Hidden Motives in Everyday Life. Chapter 5: Self-Deception*, n.d.

16. Claire Matson Cannon and Richard D. Palmiter, "Reward without Dopamine," *Journal of Neuroscience* 23, no. 34 (November 26, 2003): 10827–31, https://doi.org/10.1523/JNEUROSCI.23-34-10827.2003.

17. Zachary B. Bulwa et al., "Increased Consumption of Ethanol and Sugar Water in Mice Lacking the Dopamine D2 Long Receptor," *Alcohol (Fayetteville, N.Y.)* 45, no. 7 (November 2011): 631–39, https://doi.org/10.1016/j.alcohol.2011.06.004.

18. Wilhelm Hofmann and Loran F. Nordgren, eds., *The Psychology of Desire. Chapter 6: Motivation and Pleasure in the Brain - Morten L. Kringelbach, Kent C. Berridge*, n.d.

19. Daniel Gilbert and Timothy Wilson, "Miswanting: Some Problems in the Forecasting of Future Affective States.," October 11, 2012.

20. Raymond G. Miltenberger, *Behavior Modification: Principles and Procedures. Chapter 4: Reinforcement*, 6th edition (Boston, MA: Cengage Learning,

2015).

21. Rupert Gethin, *The Foundations of Buddhism. Chapter 1: The Buddha: The Story of the Awakened One*, 1st edition (Oxford: Oxford University Press, 1998).

22. Walpola Rahula, *What the Buddha Taught: Revised and Expanded Edition with Texts from Suttas and Dhammapada*, n.d.

23. Steven M. Emmanuel, ed., *A Companion to Buddhist Philosophy*, n.d.

24. Robert Wright, *Why Buddhism Is True: The Science and Philosophy of Meditation and Enlightenment. Chapter 1: Taking the Red Pill*, n.d.

25. Daniel Kahneman, Edward Diener, and Norbert Schwarz, eds., *Well-Being: Foundations of Hedonic Psychology. Chapter 16: Hedonic Adaptation*, First Paperback Edition (New York, NY: Russell Sage Foundation, 2003).

26. Abraham H. Maslow, *Toward a Psychology of Being, 3rd Edition. Chapter 1: Introduction: Toward a Psychology of Health*, 3rd edition (cNew York: Wiley, 1998).

27. Joachim C. Brunstein, "Personal Goals and Subjective Well-Being: A Longitudinal Study," *Journal of Personality and Social Psychology* 65, no. 5 (1993): 1061–70, https://doi.org/10.1037/0022-3514.65.5.1061.

28. Michael Siegrist and Bernadette Sütterlin, "Human and Nature-Caused Hazards: The Affect Heuristic Causes Biased Decisions," *Risk Analysis* 34, no. 8 (2014): 1482–94, https://doi.org/10.1111/risa.12179.

29. Antonio R. Damasio, "A Second Chance for Emotion," in *Cognitive Neuroscience of Emotion*, ed. Richard D. R. Lane et al. (Oxford University Press, 2000), 12–23.

30. Richard Garner, *Beyond Morality*, n.d.

31. Sam Harris, *Lying*, ed. Annaka Harris, n.d.

32. Igor Grossmann et al., "A Route to Well-Being: Intelligence vs. Wise Reasoning," *Journal of Experimental Psychology. General* 142, no. 3 (August 2013): 944–53, https://doi.org/10.1037/a0029560.

Chapter 5

1. Psychology, "5 Skills to Help You Develop Emotional Intelligence," Mark Manson, April 11, 2019, https://markmanson.net/emotional-intelligence.

2. James J. Gross, ed., *Handbook of Emotion Regulation, Second Edition*,

Second edition (New York, NY: The Guilford Press, 2015).

3. Ellen Leibenluft, "Severe Mood Dysregulation, Irritability, and the Diagnostic Boundaries of Bipolar Disorder in Youths," *The American Journal of Psychiatry* 168, no. 2 (February 2011): 129–42, https://doi.org/10.1176/appi.ajp.2010.10050766.

4. Jaak Panksepp, *Affective Neuroscience: The Foundations of Human and Animal Emotions. Chapter 13: Love and the Social Bond: The Sources of Nurturance and Maternal Behavior*, Illustrated edition (Oxford: Oxford University Press, 2004).

5. Randolph M. Nesse MD, *Good Reasons for Bad Feelings: Insights from the Frontier of Evolutionary Psychiatry. Chapter 4: Good Reasons for Bad Feelings*, n.d.

6. "Emotional Suppression: Physiology, Self-Report, and Expressive Behavior. - PsycNET," accessed November 25, 2020, https://psycnet.apa.org/doiLanding?doi=10.1037%2F0022-3514.64.6.970.

7. James J. Gross, ed., *Handbook of Emotion Regulation, Second Edition. Chapter 1: Emotion Regulation: Conceptual and Empirical Foundations*, n.d.

8. "Total Control vs. No Control Theory of Emotions: Can You Control Your Emotions or Not?," Psychology Today, accessed November 25, 2020, http://www.psychologytoday.com/blog/ambigamy/201006/total-control-vs-no-control-theory-emotions-can-you-control-your-emotions-or.

9. Ravi Thiruchselvam, Greg Hajcak, and James J. Gross, "Looking Inward: Shifting Attention Within Working Memory Representations Alters Emotional Responses," *Psychological Science* 23, no. 12 (December 1, 2012): 1461–66, https://doi.org/10.1177/0956797612449838.

10. James J. Gross, ed., *Handbook of Emotion Regulation, Second Edition. Chapter 32: Mindfulness Interventions and Emotion Regulation*, Second edition (New York, NY: The Guilford Press, 2015).

11. Pritha Das et al., "Pathways for Fear Perception: Modulation of Amygdala Activity by Thalamo-Cortical Systems," *NeuroImage* 26, no. 1 (May 15, 2005): 141–48, https://doi.org/10.1016/j.neuroimage.2005.01.049.

12. Matthew Dixon et al., "Emotion and the Prefrontal Cortex: An Integrative Review," *Psychological Bulletin* 143 (June 15, 2017), https://doi.org/10.1037/bul0000096.

13. Richard S. Lazarus and Susan Folkman, *Stress, Appraisal, and Coping. Chapter 2: Cognitive Appraisal Processes*, 1st edition (New York: Springer Publishing Company, 1984).

14. E. Diener and F. Fujita, "Resources, Personal Strivings, and Subjective Well-Being: A Nomothetic and Idiographic Approach," *Journal of Personality and Social Psychology* 68, no. 5 (May 1995): 926–35, https://doi.org/10.1037//0022-3514.68.5.926.

15. Keimpe Algra et al., eds., *The Cambridge History of Hellenistic Philosophy*, n.d.

16. William J. Prior, *Virtue and Knowledge: An Introduction to Ancient Greek Ethics*, n.d.

17. William B. Irvine, *A Guide to the Good Life: The Ancient Art of Stoic Joy*, 1st edition (Oxford University Press, 2008).

18. Donald Robertson, *The Philosophy of Cognitive Behavioural Therapy: Stoic Philosophy as Rational and Cognitive Psychotherapy*, 1st edition (London: Routledge, 2010).

19. Aaron T. Beck, *Cognitive Therapy and the Emotional Disorders* (New York, N.Y.: Plume, 1979).

20. Judith S. Beck, *Cognitive Behavior Therapy*, 3rd edition (The Guilford Press, 2021)

21. David D. Burns, *Feeling Good: The New Mood Therapy*, Reprint edition (New York: Harper, 2008).

22. Elizabeth V. Naylor et al., "Bibliotherapy as a Treatment for Depression in Primary Care," *Journal of Clinical Psychology in Medical Settings* 17, no. 3 (September 1, 2010): 258–71, https://doi.org/10.1007/s10880-010-9207-2.

23. James J. Gross and Oliver P. John, "Individual Differences in Two Emotion Regulation Processes: Implications for Affect, Relationships, and Well-Being," *Journal of Personality and Social Psychology* 85, no. 2 (August 2003): 348–62, https://doi.org/10.1037/0022-3514.85.2.348.

24. Tianqiang Hu et al., "Relation between Emotion Regulation and Mental Health: A Meta-Analysis Review," *Psychological Reports* 114 (April 1, 2014): 341–62, https://doi.org/10.2466/03.20.PR0.114k22w4.

25. James J. Gross, *Handbook of Emotion Regulation, Second Edition. Chapter 1:*

Emotion, 2nd edition (The Guilford Press, 2013).

26. Shengdong Chen et al., "Automatic Reappraisal-Based Implementation Intention Produces Early and Sustainable Emotion Regulation Effects: Event-Related Potential Evidence," *Frontiers in Behavioral Neuroscience* 14 (July 1, 2020): 89, https://doi.org/10.3389/fnbeh.2020.00089.

27. Justin K. Mogilski et al., "Jealousy, Consent, and Compersion Within Monogamous and Consensually Non-Monogamous Romantic Relationships," *Archives of Sexual Behavior* 48, no. 6 (August 1, 2019): 1811–28, https://doi.org/10.1007/s10508-018-1286-4.

28. Jessica L. Jenness et al., "Catastrophizing, Rumination, and Reappraisal Prospectively Predict Adolescent PTSD Symptom Onset Following a Terrorist Attack," *Depression and Anxiety* 33, no. 11 (2016): 1039–47, https://doi.org/10.1002/da.22548.

29. "Sonja Lyubomirsky," accessed November 25, 2020, http://sonjalyubomirsky.com/.

30. Debra A. Hope et al., "Automatic Thoughts and Cognitive Restructuring in Cognitive Behavioral Group Therapy for Social Anxiety Disorder," *Cognitive Therapy and Research* 34, no. 1 (February 1, 2010): 1–12, https://doi.org/10.1007/s10608-007-9147-9.

31. "Cognitive Restructuring (Guide)," Therapist Aid, accessed November 25, 2020, https://www.therapistaid.com/therapy-guide/cognitive-restructuring.

32. David D. Burns, *Feeling Good: The New Mood Therapy. Chapter 3: Understanding Your Moods: You Feel the Way You Think*, Reprint edition (New York: Harper, 2008).

33. "CBT's Cognitive Restructuring (CR) For Tackling Cognitive Distortions," PositivePsychology.com, February 12, 2018, https://positivepsychology.com/cbt-cognitive-restructuring-cognitive-distortions/.

34. Aaron T. Beck, *Cognitive Therapy and the Emotional Disorders. Chapter 2: Tapping the Internal Communications*, n.d.

35. Patrick B. Wood, "Role of Central Dopamine in Pain and Analgesia," *Expert Review of Neurotherapeutics* 8, no. 5 (May 2008): 781–97, https://doi.org/10.1586/14737175.8.5.781.

36. R. C. Lane, J. W. Hull, and L. M. Foehrenbach, "The Addiction to Negativity," *Psychoanalytic Review* 78, no. 3 (1991): 391–410.

Chapter 6

1. William B. Irvine, *On Desire: Why We Want What We Want. Chapter 7: The Biological Incentive System* (Oxford University Press, 2005).

2. Epictetus, *The Discourses of Epictetus: The Handbook, Fragments*, ed. Christopher Gill and Richard Stoneman, trans. Robin Hard, 2nd Original ed. edition (London : Rutland, Vt: Everyman Paperbacks, 1995).

3. Bhikkhu Bodhi, *The Noble Eightfold Path: Way to the End of Suffering. Chapter 1: The Way to the End of Suffering*, n.d.

4. Walpola Rahula, *What the Buddha Taught: Revised and Expanded Edition with Texts from Suttas and Dhammapada. Chapter 4: The Third Noble Truth*, n.d.

5. Epicurus, *Principal Doctrines*, n.d.

6. Epictetus, *Enchiridion*, trans. George Long, unknown edition (Mineola, NY: Dover Publications, 2004).

7. Marie-Aurélie Bruno et al., "A Survey on Self-Assessed Well-Being in a Cohort of Chronic Locked-in Syndrome Patients: Happy Majority, Miserable Minority," *BMJ Open* 1, no. 1 (January 1, 2011): e000039, https://doi.org/10.1136/bmjopen-2010-000039.

8. "Personal Strivings: An Approach to Personality and Subjective Well-Being. - PsycNET," accessed November 25, 2020, https://psycnet.apa.org/doiLanding?doi=10.1037%2F0022-3514.51.5.1058.

9. Wilhelm Hofmann and Loran F. Nordgren, eds., *The Psychology of Desire. Chapter 3 - Desire and Desire Regulation*, Reprint edition (New York, NY: The Guilford Press, 2016).

10. Lotte Dillen, Esther Papies, and Wilhelm Hofmann, "Turning a Blind Eye to Temptation: How Cognitive Load Can Facilitate Self-Regulation," *Journal of Personality and Social Psychology* 104 (December 31, 2012), https://doi.org/10.1037/a0031262.

11. Bhikkhu Bodhi, *The Noble Eightfold Path: The Way to the End of Suffering - Chapter 6: Right Mindfulness*, n.d.

12. "The Grateful Disposition: A Conceptual and Empirical Topography. - PsycNET," accessed November 25, 2020, /doiLanding?doi=10.1037% 2F0022-3514.82.1.112.

13. "Beyond Reciprocity: Gratitude and Relationships in Everyday Life. - PsycNET," accessed November 25, 2020, /doiLanding?doi=10.1037% 2F1528-3542.8.3.425.

14. Arnoud Arntz and Miranda Hopmans, "Underpredicted Pain Disrupts More than Correctly Predicted Pain, but Does Not Hurt More," *Behaviour Research and Therapy* 36, no. 12 (December 1, 1998): 1121–29, https://doi. org/10.1016/S0005-7967(98)00085-0.

15. Yair Dor-Ziderman et al., "Mindfulness-Induced Selflessness: A MEG Neurophenomenological Study," *Frontiers in Human Neuroscience* 7 (2013), https://doi.org/10.3389/fnhum.2013.00582.

16. Paul Verhaeghen, "The Self-Effacing Buddhist: No(t)-Self in Early Buddhism and Contemplative Neuroscience," *Contemporary Buddhism* 18, no. 1 (January 2, 2017): 21–36, https://doi.org/10.1080/14639947.2017.1297344.

17. M. E. Raichle et al., "A Default Mode of Brain Function," *Proceedings of the National Academy of Sciences* 98, no. 2 (January 16, 2001): 676–82, https://doi. org/10.1073/pnas.98.2.676.

18. Viktor E. Frankl, William J. Winslade, and Harold S. Kushner, *Man's Search for Meaning*, 1st edition (Boston: Beacon Press, 2006).

19. Donald Robertson, *The Philosophy of Cognitive Behavioural Therapy: Stoic Philosophy as Rational and Cognitive Psychotherapy. Chapter 13: The View from Above and Stoic Metaphysics*, n.d.

20. Aaron Beck, Gary Emery, and Ruth L. Greenberg, *Anxiety Disorders and Phobias: A Cognitive Perspective. Chapter 11: Strategies and Techniques for Cognitive Restructuring*, n.d.

21. Anna Rose Childress, A. Thomas McLELLAN, and Charles P. O'brien, "Abstinent Opiate Abusers Exhibit Conditioned Craving, Conditioned Withdrawal and Reductions in Both through Extinction," *British Journal of Addiction* 81, no. 5 (1986): 655–60, https://doi.org/10.1111/j.1360-0443.1986. tb00385.x.

22. Daryl J. Bem, "Self-Perception Theory, in *Advances in Experimen-*

tal Social Psychology, ed. Leonard Berkowitz, vol. 6 (Academic Press, 1972), 1–62, https://doi.org/10.1016/S0065-2601(08)60024-6.

23. Diogenes Laertius, *Lives of the Eminent Philosophers: By Diogenes Laertius. Book 6 - Diogenes Laertius*, ed. James Miller, trans. Pamela Mensch (New York: Oxford University Press, 2018).

24. "Diogenes of Sinope | Internet Encyclopedia of Philosophy," accessed November 25, 2020, https://iep.utm.edu/diogsino/.

25. "Diogenes," accessed November 25, 2020, https://penelope.uchicago.edu/~grout/encyclopaedia_romana/greece/hetairai/diogenes.html.

26. William B. Irvine, *A Guide to the Good Life: The Ancient Art of Stoic Joy. Chapter 7: Self-Denial*, 1st edition (Oxford University Press, 2008).

27. Cynthia King and William B. Irvine, *Musonius Rufus: Lectures and Sayings*, n.d.

28. Wilhelm Hofmann et al., "Yes, But Are They Happy? Effects of Trait Self-Control on Affective Well-Being and Life Satisfaction," *Journal of Personality* 82, no. 4 (2014): 265–77, https://doi.org/10.1111/jopy.12050.

29. Kennon M. Sheldon and Sonja Lyubomirsky, "The Challenge of Staying Happier: Testing the Hedonic Adaptation Prevention Model," *Personality and Social Psychology Bulletin* 38, no. 5 (May 1, 2012): 670–80, https://doi.org/10.1177/0146167212436400.

30. William B. Irvine, *A Guide to the Good Life: The Ancient Art of Stoic Joy. Chapter 5 - The Dichotomy of Control: On Becoming Invincible*, 1st edition (Oxford University Press, 2008).

31. Nick K. Lioudis, "The Importance Of Diversification," Investopedia, accessed November 25, 2020, https://www.investopedia.com/investing/importance-diversification/.

32. Andrew K. MacLeod, Emma Coates, and Jacquie Hetherton, "Increasing Well-Being through Teaching Goal-Setting and Planning Skills: Results of a Brief Intervention," *Journal of Happiness Studies: An Interdisciplinary Forum on Subjective Well-Being* 9, no. 2 (2008): 185–96, https://doi.org/10.1007/s10902-007-9057-2.

33. James Chen, "Liquidity," Investopedia, accessed November 25, 2020, https://www.investopedia.com/terms/l/liquidity.asp.

34. June Gruber et al., "Happiness Is Best Kept Stable: Positive Emotion Variability Is Associated With Poorer Psychological Health," *Emotion (Washington, D.C.)* 13 (November 19, 2012), https://doi.org/10.1037/a0030262.

Chapter 7

1. Tim O'Keefe, *Epicureanism. Chapter 12 - Varieties of Pleasure, Varieties of Desire*, n.d.

2. Maryam MALMIR, Mohammad KHANAHMADI, and Dariush FARHUD, "Dogmatism and Happiness," *Iranian Journal of Public Health* 46, no. 3 (March 2017): 326–32.

3. Marc Kreidler, "Stardust, Smoke, and Mirrors: The Myth of the Mad Genius | Skeptical Inquirer," September 1, 2013, https://skepticalinquirer. org/2013/09/stardust-smoke-and-mirrors-the-myth-of-the-mad-genius/.

4. Aaron T. Beck and Brad A. Alford, *Depression: Causes and Treatment, 2nd Edition. Chapter 17: Cognition and Psychopathology*, n.d.

5. Andrew J. Oswald, Eugenio Proto, and Daniel Sgroi, "Happiness and Productivity," *Journal of Labor Economics* 33, no. 4 (September 26, 2015): 789–822, https://doi.org/10.1086/681096.

6. Stephen G. Post, "Altruism, Happiness, and Health: It's Good to Be Good," *International Journal of Behavioral Medicine* 12, no. 2 (June 1, 2005): 66–77, https://doi.org/10.1207/s15327558ijbm1202_4.

7. Kai Epstude and Kai J. Jonas, "Regret and Counterfactual Thinking in the Face of Inevitability: The Case of HIV-Positive Men," *Social Psychological and Personality Science* 6, no. 2 (March 1, 2015): 157–63, https://doi. org/10.1177/1948550614546048.

8. Friedrich Nietzsche, *On the Genealogy of Morals and Ecce Homo. Essay 1: 'Good and Evil', 'Good and Bad,'* ed. Walter Kaufmann, Reissue edition (New York: Vintage, 1989).

9. D. Hemelsoet, K. Hemelsoet, and D. Devreese, "The Neurological Illness of Friedrich Nietzsche," *Acta Neurologica Belgica* 108, no. 1 (March 2008): 9–16.

10. Aristotle, *Nicomachean Ethics. Book II Chapter 6*, trans. C. D. C. Reeve (Indianapolis: Hackett Publishing Company, Inc., 2014).

11. Richard Kraut, "Aristotle's Ethics," in *The Stanford Encyclopedia of Philosophy*, ed. Edward N. Zalta, Summer 2018 (Metaphysics Research Lab, Stanford University, 2018), https://plato.stanford.edu/archives/sum2018/entries/aristotle-ethics/.

12. Maya Tamir et al., "The Secret to Happiness: Feeling Good or Feeling Right?," *Journal of Experimental Psychology: General* 146 (August 14, 2017), https://doi.org/10.1037/xge0000303.

13. Emily Rose Dunn, "Blue Is the New Black: How Popular Culture Is Romanticizing Mental Illness," December 2017, https://digital.library.txstate.edu/handle/10877/6985.

14. Randolph M. Nesse MD, *Good Reasons for Bad Feelings: Insights from the Frontier of Evolutionary Psychiatry. Chapter 4: Good Reasons for Bad Feelings*, n.d.

15. James J. Gross, ed., *Handbook of Emotion Regulation, Second Edition. Chapter 4: The Neural Basis of Emotion Dysregulation*, Second edition (New York, NY: The Guilford Press, 2015).

16. June Gruber, "Can Feeling Too Good Be Bad?: Positive Emotion Persistence (PEP) in Bipolar Disorder," *Current Directions in Psychological Science* 20, no. 4 (August 1, 2011): 217–21, https://doi.org/10.1177/0963721411414632.

17. Heather C. Lench, ed., *The Function of Emotions: When and Why Emotions Help Us. Chapter 8: Functions of Anger in the Emotion System*, 1st ed. 2018 edition (Cham, Switzerland: Springer, 2018).

18. Siew-Maan Diong and George D. Bishop, "Anger Expression, Coping Styles, and Well-Being," *Journal of Health Psychology* 4, no. 1 (January 1, 1999): 81–96, https://doi.org/10.1177/135910539900400106.

19. Craig Winston LeCroy, "Anger Management or Anger Expression," *Residential Treatment for Children & Youth* 5, no. 3 (August 9, 1988): 29–39, https://doi.org/10.1300/J007v05n03_04.

20. Seneca, *On Anger: De Ira*, trans. Aubrey Stewart (Independently published, 2017).

21. "The True Trigger of Shame: Social Devaluation Is Sufficient, Wrongdoing Is Unnecessary - ScienceDirect," accessed November 25, 2020, https://www.sciencedirect.com/science/article/abs/pii/S1090513817303872.

22. Courtland S. Hyatt et al., "The Anatomy of an Insult: Popular Deroga-

tory Terms Connote Important Individual Differences in Agreeableness/Antagonism," *Journal of Research in Personality* 78 (February 1, 2019): 61–75, https://doi.org/10.1016/j.jrp.2018.11.005.

23. Vilayanur S. Ramachandran and Baland Jalal, "The Evolutionary Psychology of Envy and Jealousy," *Frontiers in Psychology* 8 (September 19, 2017), https://doi.org/10.3389/fpsyg.2017.01619.

24. Christopher J. Boyce, Gordon D. A. Brown, and Simon C. Moore, "Money and Happiness: Rank of Income, Not Income, Affects Life Satisfaction," *Psychological Science*, February 18, 2010, https://doi.org/10.1177/0956797610362671.

25. "Emotional Competency - Envy," accessed November 25, 2020, http://www.emotionalcompetency.com/envy.htm.

26. Kevin Kelly, "68 Bits of Unsolicited Advice," *The Technium* (blog), accessed November 25, 2020, https://kk.org/thetechnium/68-bits-of-unsolicited-advice/.

27. "How to Deal with Extreme Envy," Time, accessed November 25, 2020, https://time.com/4358803/jealousy-envy-advice/.

28. Wilco W. van Dijk et al., "The Role of Self-Evaluation and Envy in Schadenfreude," *European Review of Social Psychology* 26, no. 1 (January 1, 2015): 247–82, https://doi.org/10.1080/10463283.2015.1111600.

29. Randolph M. Nesse MD, *Good Reasons for Bad Feelings: Insights from the Frontier of Evolutionary Psychiatry. Chapter 5: Anxiety and Smoke Detectors*, Illustrated edition (New York, New York: Dutton, 2019).

30. MeaningofLife.tv, *Good Reasons for Bad Feelings | Robert Wright & Randolph Nesse [The Wright Show]*, 2019, https://www.youtube.com/watch?v=17-ypeL88kQ.

31. Raymond G. Miltenberger, *Behavior Modification: Principles and Procedures. Chapter 5: Extinction*, 6th edition (Boston, MA: Cengage Learning, 2015).

32. B. Alan Wallace and Shauna L. Shapiro, "Mental Balance and Well-Being: Building Bridges between Buddhism and Western Psychology," *American Psychologist* 61, no. 7 (2006): 690–701, https://doi.org/10.1037/0003-066X.61.7.690.

33. Randolph M. Nesse MD, *Good Reasons for Bad Feelings: Insights from the Frontier of Evolutionary Psychiatry. Chapter 9: Guilt and Grief: The Price of Goodness*

and Love, n.d.

34. Michael Caserta, Rebecca Utz, and Dale Lund, "Spousal Bereavement Following Cancer Death," *Illness, Crises, and Loss* 21 (January 1, 2013): 185–202, https://doi.org/10.2190/IL.21.3.b.

35. Walpola Rahula, *What the Buddha Taught: Revised and Expanded Edition with Texts from Suttas and Dhammapada*, n.d.

36. R. M. A. Nelissen, A. J. M. Dijker, and N. K. de Vries, "Emotions and Goals: Assessing Relations between Values and Emotions," *Cognition and Emotion* 21, no. 4 (June 1, 2007): 902–11, https://doi.org/10.1080/02699930600861330.

37. Nate Soares, *Replacing Guilt: Minding Our Way* (Independently published, 2020).

38. Heather C. Lench, ed., *The Function of Emotions: When and Why Emotions Help Us. Chapter 7: The Adaptive Functions of Jealousy*, n.d.

39. Rachel Elphinston et al., "Romantic Jealousy and Relationship Satisfaction: The Costs of Rumination," *Western Journal of Communication* 77 (April 4, 2013): 293–304, https://doi.org/10.1080/10570314.2013.770161.

40. Stephen Kellett and Peter Totterdell, "Taming the Green-Eyed Monster: Temporal Responsivity to Cognitive Behavioural and Cognitive Analytic Therapy for Morbid Jealousy," *Psychology and Psychotherapy* 86, no. 1 (March 2013): 52–69, https://doi.org/10.1111/j.2044-8341.2011.02045.x.

41. Valerie Rubinsky, "Identity Gaps and Jealousy as Predictors of Satisfaction in Polyamorous Relationships," *Southern Communication Journal* 84, no. 1 (January 1, 2019): 17–29, https://doi.org/10.1080/1041794X.2018.1531916.

42. Robert L. Leahy and Dennis D. Tirch, "Cognitive Behavioral Therapy for Jealousy," *International Journal of Cognitive Therapy* 1, no. 1 (February 1, 2008): 18–32, https://doi.org/10.1521/ijct.2008.1.1.18.

43. "Attachment Styles of Predictors of Relationship Satisfaction Within Adulthood – Nevada State Undergraduate Research Journal," accessed November 25, 2020, http://nsurj.com/v4-i1-2/.

44. Richard Dawkins, *The Selfish Gene: 40th Anniversary Edition. Chapter 1: Why Are People?*, 4th edition (New York, NY: Oxford University Press, 2016).

45. Paul Bloom, *Against Empathy: The Case for Rational Compassion*, n.d.

46. Barbara Oakley et al., eds., *Pathological Altruism. Chapter 2: Empa-*

thy-Based Pathogenic Guilt, Pathological Altruism, and Psychopathology, n.d.

47. "Introduction to Effective Altruism," Effective Altruism, accessed November 25, 2020, https://www.effectivealtruism.org/articles/introduction-to-effective-altruism/.

48. Paul Bloom, "The Baby in the Well," The New Yorker, accessed November 25, 2020, https://www.newyorker.com/magazine/2013/05/20/the-baby-in-the-well.

49. Shoyu Hanayama, "Christian 'Love' and Buddhist 'Compassion,'" *Journal of Indian and Buddhist Studies (Indogaku Bukkyogaku Kenkyu)* 20, no. 1 (1971): 464–455, https://doi.org/10.4259/ibk.20.464.

50. "Open Hearts Build Lives: Positive Emotions, Induced through Loving-Kindness Meditation, Build Consequential Personal Resources. - PsycNET," accessed November 25, 2020, https://psycnet.apa.org/doiLanding?-doi=10.1037%2Fa0013262.

51. "Loving-Kindness Meditation Increases Social Connectedness. - PsycNET," accessed November 25, 2020, https://psycnet.apa.org/doiLanding?-doi=10.1037%2Fa0013237.

52. Peter Harvey, *An Introduction to Buddhism, Second Edition: Teachings, History and Practices*, n.d.

53. Michael A. Cohn et al., "Happiness Unpacked: Positive Emotions Increase Life Satisfaction by Building Resilience," *Emotion (Washington, D.C.)* 9, no. 3 (June 2009): 361–68, https://doi.org/10.1037/a0015952.

54. Arantzazu Rodríguez-Fernández, Estibaliz Ramos-Díaz, and Inge Axpe-Saez, "The Role of Resilience and Psychological Well-Being in School Engagement and Perceived Academic Performance: An Exploratory Model to Improve Academic Achievement," *Health and Academic Achievement*, September 19, 2018, https://doi.org/10.5772/intechopen.73580.

55. June Gruber et al., "Happiness Is Best Kept Stable: Positive Emotion Variability Is Associated With Poorer Psychological Health," *Emotion (Washington, D.C.)* 13 (November 19, 2012), https://doi.org/10.1037/a0030262.

56. "Similitudes: Stoicism and Buddhism," accessed November 25, 2020, https://stoicandzen.com/stoicism-and-buddhism-similarities/.

57. Marcin Fabjański and Eric Brymer, "Enhancing Health and Wellbeing

through Immersion in Nature: A Conceptual Perspective Combining the Stoic and Buddhist Traditions," *Frontiers in Psychology* 8 (September 12, 2017), https://doi.org/10.3389/fpsyg.2017.01573.

Chapter 8

1. Wilhelm Hofmann et al., "Dieting and the Self-Control of Eating in Everyday Environments: An Experience Sampling Study," *British Journal of Health Psychology* 19, no. 3 (September 2014): 523–39, https://doi.org/10.1111/bjhp.12053.

2. Marja Kinnunen et al., "Self-Control Is Associated with Physical Activity and Fitness among Young Males," *Behavioral Medicine (Washington, D.C.)* 38 (July 1, 2012): 83–89, https://doi.org/10.1080/08964289.2012.693975.

3. Larissa Barber, Matthew Grawitch, and David Munz, "Are Better Sleepers More Engaged Workers? A Self-Regulatory Approach to Sleep Hygiene and Work Engagement.," *Stress and Health : Journal of the International Society for the Investigation of Stress*, October 1, 2012, https://doi.org/10.1002/smi.2468.

4. Anja Achtziger et al., "Debt out of Control: The Links between Self-Control, Compulsive Buying, and Real Debts," *Journal of Economic Psychology* 49 (August 1, 2015): 141–49, https://doi.org/10.1016/j.joep.2015.04.003.

5. Thomas A. Wills et al., "Behavioral and Emotional Self-Control: Relations to Substance Use in Samples of Middle and High School Students," *Psychology of Addictive Behaviors: Journal of the Society of Psychologists in Addictive Behaviors* 20, no. 3 (September 2006): 265–78, https://doi.org/10.1037/0893-164X.20.3.265.

6. Adriel Boals, Michelle R. Vandellen, and Jonathan B. Banks, "The Relationship between Self-Control and Health: The Mediating Effect of Avoidant Coping," *Psychology & Health* 26, no. 8 (August 2011): 1049–62, https://doi.org/10.1080/08870446.2010.529139.

7. June P. Tangney, Roy F. Baumeister, and Angie Luzio Boone, "High Self-Control Predicts Good Adjustment, Less Pathology, Better Grades, and Interpersonal Success," *Journal of Personality* 72, no. 2 (2004): 271–324, https://doi.org/10.1111/j.0022-3506.2004.00263.x.

8. June Price Tangney et al., "Reliability, Validity, and Predic-

tive Utility of the 25-Item Criminogenic Cognitions Scale (CCS)," *Criminal Justice and Behavior* 39, no. 10 (October 1, 2012): 1340–60, https://doi.org/10.1177/0093854812451092.

9. Angela L. Duckworth and Martin E.P. Seligman, "Self-Discipline Outdoes IQ in Predicting Academic Performance of Adolescents," *Psychological Science* 16, no. 12 (December 1, 2005): 939–44, https://doi.org/10.1111/j.1467-9280.2005.01641.x.

10. Eli Finkel and W. Keith Campbell, "Self-Control and Accommodation in Close Relationships: An Interdependence Analysis," *Journal of Personality and Social Psychology* 81 (September 1, 2001): 263–77, https://doi.org/10.1037/0022-3514.81.2.263.

11. Camilla Strömbäck et al., "Does Self-Control Predict Financial Behavior and Financial Well-Being?," *Journal of Behavioral and Experimental Finance* 14 (June 1, 2017): 30–38, https://doi.org/10.1016/j.jbef.2017.04.002.

12. Wilhelm Hofmann et al., "Yes, But Are They Happy? Effects of Trait Self-Control on Affective Well-Being and Life Satisfaction," *Journal of Personality* 82, no. 4 (2014): 265–77, https://doi.org/10.1111/jopy.12050.

13. Wilhelm Hofmann, Hiroki Kotabe, and Maike Luhmann, "The Spoiled Pleasure of Giving in to Temptation," *Motivation and Emotion* 37, no. 4 (December 1, 2013): 733–42, https://doi.org/10.1007/s11031-013-9355-4.

14. T. E. Moffitt et al., "A Gradient of Childhood Self-Control Predicts Health, Wealth, and Public Safety," *Proceedings of the National Academy of Sciences* 108, no. 7 (February 15, 2011): 2693–98, https://doi.org/10.1073/pnas.1010076108.

15. David L. Watson and Roland G. Tharp, *Self-Directed Behavior: Self-Modification for Personal Adjustment. Chapter 5: Antecedents*, n.d.

16. James Clear, *Atomic Habits: An Easy & Proven Way to Build Good Habits & Break Bad Ones. Chapter 8: How to Make a Habit Irresistible*, Illustrated edition (New York: Avery, 2018).

17. George F. Koob and Eric J. Simon, "The Neurobiology of Addiction: Where We Have Been and Where We Are Going," *Journal of Drug Issues* 39, no. 1 (January 2009): 115–32.

18. David T. Courtwright, *The Age of Addiction: How Bad Habits Became Big*

Business, n.d.

19. Daniel H. Angres and Kathy Bettinardi–Angres, "The Disease of Addiction: Origins, Treatment, and Recovery," *Disease-a-Month*, The Disease of Addiction: Origins, Treatment, and Recovery, 54, no. 10 (October 1, 2008): 696–721, https://doi.org/10.1016/j.disamonth.2008.07.002.

20. Daniel Lieberman, *The Story of the Human Body: Evolution, Health, and Disease*, n.d.

21. Angela Jacques et al., "The Impact of Sugar Consumption on Stress Driven, Emotional and Addictive Behaviors," *Neuroscience & Biobehavioral Reviews* 103 (August 1, 2019): 178–99, https://doi.org/10.1016/j.neubiorev.2019.05.021.

22. MeaningofLife.tv, *Good Reasons for Bad Feelings | Robert Wright & Randolph Nesse [The Wright Show]*, 2019, https://www.youtube.com/watch?v=17-ypeL88kQ.

23. Lauren E. Sherman et al., "What the Brain 'Likes': Neural Correlates of Providing Feedback on Social Media," *Social Cognitive and Affective Neuroscience* 13, no. 7 (September 4, 2018): 699–707, https://doi.org/10.1093/scan/nsy051.

24. Russell Clayton, Alexander Nagurney, and Jessica Smith, "Cheating, Breakup, and Divorce: Is Facebook Use to Blame?," *Cyberpsychology, Behavior, and Social Networking* 16 (October 22, 2013): 717–20, https://doi.org/10.1089/cyber.2012.0424.

25. Mark Griffiths, Halley Pontes, and Daria Kuss, "The Clinical Psychology of Internet Addiction: A Review of Its Conceptualization, Prevalence, Neuronal Processes, and Implications for Treatment.," *Neurosciences and Neureconomics* 4 (January 1, 2015).

26. Ahmet AKIN et al., "Self-Control/Management And Internet Addiction," *International Online Journal of Educational Sciences* 7 (August 11, 2015): 95–100, https://doi.org/10.15345/iojes.2015.03.016.

27. Kashmir Hill, "Adventures in Self-Surveillance, Aka The Quantified Self, Aka Extreme Navel-Gazing," Forbes, accessed November 25, 2020, https://www.forbes.com/sites/kashmirhill/2011/04/07/adventures-in-self-surveillance-aka-the-quantified-self-aka-extreme-navel-gazing/.

28. "Carbonfootprint.Com - Carbon Footprint Calculator," accessed November 25, 2020, https://www.carbonfootprint.com/calculator.aspx.

29. Peter M. Gollwitzer and Veronika Brandstätter, "Implementation Intentions and Effective Goal Pursuit," *Journal of Personality and Social Psychology* 73, no. 1 (1997): 186–99, https://doi.org/10.1037/0022-3514.73.1.186.

30. Elliot Aronson and Joshua Aronson, *The Social Animal. Chapter 4: Conformity*, n.d.

31. S. E. Asch, "Effects of Group Pressure upon the Modification and Distortion of Judgments," in *Groups, Leadership and Men; Research in Human Relations* (Oxford, England: Carnegie Press, 1951), 177–90.

32. Netflix, *Derren Brown: The Push I Official Trailer [HD] I Netflix*, 2018, https://www.youtube.com/watch?v=doFpACkiZ2Q&feature=emb_title.

33. Herbert C. Kelman, "Compliance, Identification, and Internalization Three Processes of Attitude Change:," *Journal of Conflict Resolution*, July 1, 2016, https://doi.org/10.1177/002200275800200106.

34. B. Mullen, "Effects of strength and immediacy in group contexts: Reply to Jackson." Journal of Personality and Social Psychology, https://doi.org/10.1037/0022-3514.50.3.514

35. Russell D. Clark III, "Effect of number of majority defectors on minority influence." Group Dynamics: Theory, Research, and Practice, https://doi.org/10.1037/1089-2699.5.1.57

36. Patricia Pliner et al., "Compliance without Pressure: Some Further Data on the Foot-in-the-Door Technique," *Journal of Experimental Social Psychology* 10, no. 1 (January 1, 1974): 17–22, https://doi.org/10.1016/0022-1031(74)90053-5.

37. Robert Cialdini et al., "Reciprocal Concessions Procedure for Inducing Compliance: The Door-in-the-Face Technique," *Journal of Personality and Social Psychology* 31 (February 1, 1975): 206–15, https://doi.org/10.1037/h0076284.

38. Edward E. Jones, *Ingratiation: A Social Psychological Analysis*, First Edition (Appleton-Century-Crofts, Inc, 1964).

39. Mark Whatley et al., "The Effect of a Favor on Public and Private Compliance: How Internalized Is the Norm of Reciprocity?," *Basic and Applied Social Psychology - BASIC APPL SOC PSYCHOL* 21 (September 1, 1999): 251–59, https://

doi.org/10.1207/S15324834BASP2103_8.

40. Herbert C. Kelman, "Compliance, Identification, and Internalization Three Processes of Attitude Change:," *Journal of Conflict Resolution*, July 1, 2016, https://doi.org/10.1177/002200275800200106.

41. Jerry M. Burger et al., "What a Coincidence! The Effects of Incidental Similarity on Compliance:," *Personality and Social Psychology Bulletin*, July 2, 2016, https://doi.org/10.1177/0146167203258838.

42. Dan Ariely, *Predictably Irrational, Revised and Expanded Edition: The Hidden Forces That Shape Our Decisions. Chapter 2: The Fallacy of Supply and Demand*, Revised and Expanded ed. edition (New York, NY: Harper Perennial, 2010).

43. Christina Steindl et al., "Understanding Psychological Reactance," *Zeitschrift Fur Psychologie* 223, no. 4 (2015): 205–14, https://doi.org/10.1027/2151-2604/a000222.

44. Brad J. Sagarin et al., "Dispelling the Illusion of Invulnerability: The Motivations and Mechanisms of Resistance to Persuasion," *Journal of Personality and Social Psychology* 83, no. 3 (2002): 526–41, https://doi.org/10.1037/0022-3514.83.3.526.

45. Arend Hintze et al., "Risk Aversion as an Evolutionary Adaptation," October 23, 2013.

46. "Adaptability: How Students' Responses to Uncertainty and Novelty Predict Their Academic and Non-Academic Outcomes. - PsycNET," APA PsycNET, accessed November 25, 2020, https://doi.org/10.1037/a0032794.

47. Abraham H. Maslow, Bertha G. Maslow, and Henry Geiger, *The Farther Reaches of Human Nature. Chapter 2: Neurosis as a Failure of Personal Growth*, n.d.

48. Steven M. Albert and John Duffy, "Differences in Risk Aversion between Young and Older Adults," *Neuroscience and Neuroeconomics* 2012, no. 1 (January 15, 2012), https://doi.org/10.2147/NAN.S27184.

49. John Kaag, *Hiking with Nietzsche: On Becoming Who You Are*, 1st edition (New York: Farrar, Straus and Giroux, 2018).

50. Bernard Reginster, *The Affirmation of Life: Nietzsche on Overcoming Nihilism*, 0 edition (Harvard University Press, 2009).

51. Rodica Ioana Damian et al., "Sixteen Going on Sixty-Six: A Longitudi-

nal Study of Personality Stability and Change across 50 Years," *Journal of Personality and Social Psychology* 117, no. 3 (September 2019): 674–95, https://doi.org/10.1037/pspp0000210.

52. L. -G Öst et al., "One vs Five Sessions of Exposure and Five Sessions of Cognitive Therapy in the Treatment of Claustrophobia," *Behaviour Research and Therapy* 39, no. 2 (February 1, 2001): 167–83, https://doi.org/10.1016/S0005-7967(99)00176-X.

53. Lissa Rankin M.D, *The Fear Cure: Cultivating Courage as Medicine for the Body, Mind, and Soul. Chapter 4: Uncertainty Is the Gateway to Possibility*, n.d.

54. Friedrich Nietzsche, *Twilight of the Idols: Or How to Philosophize with a Hammer*, trans. Duncan Large, n.d.

55. Geraldine O'Sullivan, "The Relationship Between Hope, Eustress, Self-Efficacy, and Life Satisfaction Among Undergraduates," *Social Indicators Research* 101, no. 1 (March 1, 2011): 155–72, https://doi.org/10.1007/s11205-010-9662-z.

56. Marcus Aurelius, *Meditations*, 1st edition (CreateSpace Independent Publishing Platform, 2018).

57. R. Blaug, *How Power Corrupts: Cognition and Democracy in Organisations. Chapter 2: Psychologies of Power*, n.d.

58. Olena Antonaccio and Charles R. Tittle, "Morality, Self-Control, and Crime*," *Criminology* 46, no. 2 (2008): 479–510, https://doi.org/10.1111/j.1745-9125.2008.00116.x.

59. David Myers, *Exploring Social Psychology*, n.d.

60. James Clear, *Atomic Habits: An Easy & Proven Way to Build Good Habits & Break Bad Ones. Chapter 2: How Your Habits Shape Your Identity (and Vice Versa)*, Illustrated edition (New York: Avery, 2018).

61. Daryl J. Bem, "Self-Perception Theory, Development of Self-Perception Theory Was Supported Primarily by a Grant from the National Science Foundation (GS 1452) Awarded to the Author during His Tenure at Carnegie-Mellon University.," in *Advances in Experimental Social Psychology*, ed. Leonard Berkowitz, vol. 6 (Academic Press, 1972), 1–62, https://doi.org/10.1016/S0065-2601(08)60024-6.

62. Danica Mijović-Prelec and Drazen Prelec, "Self-Deception as Self-

Signalling: A Model and Experimental Evidence," *Philosophical Transactions of the Royal Society of London. Series B, Biological Sciences* 365, no. 1538 (January 27, 2010): 227–40, https://doi.org/10.1098/rstb.2009.0218.

63. David D. Burns, *Feeling Good: The New Mood Therapy. Chapter 5: Do-Nothingism: How to Beat It*, n.d.

64. "Praise for Intelligence Can Undermine Children's Motivation and Performance. - PsycNET," accessed November 25, 2020, https://psycnet.apa.org/doiLanding?doi=10.1037%2F0022-3514.75.1.33.

65. "Implicit Social Cognition: Attitudes, Self-Esteem, and Stereotypes. - PsycNET," accessed November 25, 2020, https://doi.apa.org/doiLanding?doi=10.1037%2F0033-295X.102.1.4.

Chapter 9

1. Kentaro Fujita, Ariana Orvell, and Ethan Kross, "Smarter, Not Harder: A Toolbox Approach to Enhancing Self-Control," *Policy Insights from the Behavioral and Brain Sciences* 7, no. 2 (October 1, 2020): 149–56, https://doi.org/10.1177/2372732220941242.

2. Christian Tornau, "Saint Augustine," in *The Stanford Encyclopedia of Philosophy*, ed. Edward N. Zalta, Summer 2020 (Metaphysics Research Lab, Stanford University, 2020), https://plato.stanford.edu/archives/sum2020/entries/augustine/.

3. David Dubner, "Willpower and Ego Depletion: Useful Constructs?," *Counseling & Wellness: A Professional Counseling Journal* 5 (February 2016), https://openknowledge.nau.edu/2338/.

4. Matthew T. Gailliot and Roy F. Baumeister, "The Physiology of Willpower: Linking Blood Glucose to Self-Control," *Personality and Social Psychology Review* 11, no. 4 (November 1, 2007): 303–27, https://doi.org/10.1177/1088868307303030.

5. Mischel Walter, *The Marshmallow Test: Understanding Self-Control and How To Master It. Chapter 2: How They Do It*, n.d.

6. "Nietzsche and Psychology: How to Become Who You Are," *Academy of Ideas* (blog), February 21, 2017, https://academyofideas.com/2017/02/nietzsche-psychology-become-who-you-are/.

7. David L. Watson and Roland G. Tharp, *Self-Directed Behavior: Self-Modification for Personal Adjustment. Chapter 5: Antecedents*, n.d.

8. "The Complete Guide to Self-Control," Scott H Young, September 30, 2019, https://www.scotthyoung.com/blog/2019/09/30/self-control/.

9. David L. Watson and Roland G. Tharp, *Self-Directed Behavior: Self-Modification for Personal Adjustment. Chapter 7: Consequences*, n.d.

10. Daniel H. Pink, *Drive: The Surprising Truth About What Motivates Us. Chapter 2: Seven Reasons Carrots and Sticks (Often) Don't Work* (New York: Riverhead Books, 2011).

11. T. E. Moffitt et al., "A Gradient of Childhood Self-Control Predicts Health, Wealth, and Public Safety," *Proceedings of the National Academy of Sciences* 108, no. 7 (February 15, 2011): 2693–98, https://doi.org/10.1073/pnas.1010076108.

12. "Neuroreality: The New Reality Is Coming. And It's a Brain Computer Interface.," Futurism, accessed November 25, 2020, https://futurism.com/neuroreality-the-new-reality-is-coming-and-its-a-brain-computer-interface.

13. Anne-Marie Willis, "Ontological Designing," *Design Philosophy Papers* 4 (June 1, 2006): 69–92, https://doi.org/10.2752/144871306X13966268131514.

14. Benjamin Hardy, *Willpower Doesn't Work: Discover the Hidden Keys to Success. Chapter 2: How Your Environment Shapes You*, n.d.

15. Epictetus, *Enchiridion*, XXXII, trans. George Long, n.d.

16. Nicholas A. Christakis and James H. Fowler, "The Spread of Obesity in a Large Social Network over 32 Years," *New England Journal of Medicine* 357, no. 4 (July 26, 2007): 370–79, https://doi.org/10.1056/NEJMsa066082.

17. M. J. Howes, J. E. Hokanson, and D. A. Loewenstein, "Induction of Depressive Affect after Prolonged Exposure to a Mildly Depressed Individual," *Journal of Personality and Social Psychology* 49, no. 4 (October 1985): 1110–13, https://doi.org/10.1037//0022-3514.49.4.1110.

18. Walter Mischel and Nancy Baker, "Cognitive Appraisals and Transformations in Delay Behavior," *Journal of Personality and Social Psychology* 31, no. 2 (1975): 254–61, https://doi.org/10.1037/h0076272.

19. Monique Boekaerts, Paul R. Pintrich, and Moshe Zeidner, eds., *Handbook of Self-Regulation. Chapter 15: Attentional Control and Self-Regulation*, n.d.

20. Stacey Long et al., "Effects of Distraction and Focused Attention on Actual and Perceived Food Intake in Females with Non-Clinical Eating Psychopathology," *Appetite* 56, no. 2 (April 1, 2011): 350–56, https://doi.org/10.1016/j.appet.2010.12.018.

21. Ashley E. Mason et al., "Reduced Reward-Driven Eating Accounts for the Impact of a Mindfulness-Based Diet and Exercise Intervention on Weight Loss: Data from the SHINE Randomized Controlled Trial," *Appetite* 100 (May 1, 2016): 86–93, https://doi.org/10.1016/j.appet.2016.02.009.

22. W. Mischel, E. B. Ebbesen, and A. R. Zeiss, "Cognitive and Attentional Mechanisms in Delay of Gratification," *Journal of Personality and Social Psychology* 21, no. 2 (February 1972): 204–18, https://doi.org/10.1037/h0032198.

23. Fjolvar Darri Rafnsson, Fridrik H. Jonsson, and Michael Windle, "Coping Strategies, Stressful Life Events, Problem Behaviors, and Depressed Affect," *Anxiety, Stress, & Coping* 19, no. 3 (September 1, 2006): 241–57, https://doi.org/10.1080/10615800600679111.

24. Shireen L. Rizvi, *Chain Analysis in Dialectical Behavior Therapy. Chapter 3: Getting to Know the Target Behavior*, 1st edition (The Guilford Press, 2019).

25. David L. Watson and Roland G. Tharp, *Self-Directed Behavior: Self-Modification for Personal Adjustment. Chapter 2: Forethought: Planning for Success*, 10th edition (Australia: Cengage Learning, 2013).

26. Raymond G. Miltenberger, *Behavior Modification: Principles and Procedures. Chapter 4: Reinforcement*, 6th edition (Boston, MA: Cengage Learning, 2015).

27. Dan Ariely and Klaus Wertenbroch, "Procrastination, Deadlines, and Performance: Self-Control by Precommitment," *Psychological Science* 13, no. 3 (May 1, 2002): 219–24, https://doi.org/10.1111/1467-9280.00441.

28. Xavier Giné, Dean Karlan, and Jonathan Zinman, "Put Your Money Where Your Butt Is: A Commitment Contract for Smoking Cessation," *American Economic Journal: Applied Economics* 2, no. 4 (October 2010): 213–35, https://doi.org/10.1257/app.2.4.213.

29. Jinfeng Jiao and Catherine A. Cole, "The Effects of Goal Publicity and Self-Monitoring on Escalation of Goal Commitment," *Journal of Consumer Behaviour* 19, no. 3 (2020): 219–28, https://doi.org/10.1002/cb.1806.

30. John Raglin, "Factors in Exercise Adherence: Influence of Spouse Participation," *Quest* 53 (August 1, 2001), https://doi.org/10.1080/00336297.2001.10491752.

31. James Clear, *Atomic Habits: An Easy & Proven Way to Build Good Habits & Break Bad Ones. Chapter 17: How an Accountability Partner Can Change Everything*, Illustrated edition (New York: Avery, 2018).

32. "Focusmate - Distraction-Free Productivity," Focusmate, accessed November 25, 2020, https://www.focusmate.com.

33. "Change Your Habits and Life with Pavlok," Pavlok, accessed November 25, 2020, https://pavlok.com/.

34. Robert Soussignan, "Duchenne Smile, Emotional Experience, and Autonomic Reactivity: A Test of the Facial Feedback Hypothesis," *Emotion (Washington, D.C.)* 2, no. 1 (March 2002): 52–74, https://doi.org/10.1037/1528-3542.2.1.52.

35. Katherine L. Milkman, Julia A. Minson, and Kevin G. M. Volpp, "Holding the Hunger Games Hostage at the Gym: An Evaluation of Temptation Bundling," *Management Science* 60, no. 2 (February 2014): 283–99, https://doi.org/10.1287/mnsc.2013.1784.

36. Timothy D Hackenberg, "TOKEN REINFORCEMENT: A REVIEW AND ANALYSIS," *Journal of the Experimental Analysis of Behavior* 91, no. 2 (March 2009): 257–86, https://doi.org/10.1901/jeab.2009.91-257.

37. Friedrich Nietzsche, *Nietzsche: Daybreak: Thoughts on the Prejudices of Morality*, ed. Maudemarie Clark and Brian Leiter, trans. R. J. Hollingdale, 2nd edition (Cambridge University Press, 1997).

38. Lisa Williams and David desteno, "Pride and Perseverance: The Motivational Role of Pride," *Journal of Personality and Social Psychology* 94 (June 1, 2008): 1007–17, https://doi.org/10.1037/0022-3514.94.6.1007.

39. Abraham H. Maslow, Bertha G. Maslow, and Henry Geiger, *The Farther Reaches of Human Nature. Chapter 23: A Theory of Metamotivation: The Biological Rooting of the Value-Life*, n.d.

40. Edward Deci, Richard Koestner, and Richard Ryan, "A Meta-Analytic Review of Experiments Examining the Effect of Extrinsic Rewards on Intrinsic Motivation," *Psychological Bulletin* 125 (December 1, 1999): 627–68; discussion

692, https://doi.org/10.1037/0033-2909.125.6.627.

41. Mark Lepper and And Others, "Undermining Children's Intrinsic Interest with Extrinsic Reward: A Test of the 'Overjustification' Hypothesis," *Journal of Personality and Social Psychology* 28 (October 1, 1973), https://doi.org/10.1037/h0035519.

42. Teresa M. Amabile, *Creativity In Context: Update To The Social Psychology Of Creativity. Chapter 3: A Consensual Technique for Creativity Assessment*, New edition (Boulder, Colo: Routledge, 1996).

43. Daniel H. Pink, *Drive: The Surprising Truth About What Motivates Us. Chapter 2: Seven Reasons Carrots and Sticks (Often) Don't Work*, n.d.

44. Edward L. Deci, Richard Koestner, and Richard M. Ryan, "Extrinsic Rewards and Intrinsic Motivation in Education: Reconsidered Once Again," *Review of Educational Research* 71, no. 1 (2001): 1–27.

45. Mihaly Csikszentmihalyi, *Beyond Boredom and Anxiety: Experiencing Flow in Work and Play*, 25th Anniversary edition (San Francisco: Jossey-Bass, 2000).

46. Teresa Amabile and Steven J. Kramer, "The Power of Small Wins," *Harvard Business Review*, May 1, 2011, https://hbr.org/2011/05/the-power-of-small-wins.

47. Kjærsti Thorsteinsen and Joar Vittersø, "Striving for Wellbeing: The Different Roles of Hedonia and Eudaimonia in Goal Pursuit and Goal Achievement," *International Journal of Wellbeing* 8, no. 2 (December 8, 2018), https://doi.org/10.5502/ijw.v8i2.733.

Chapter 10

1. Lorraine L. Besser, *Eudaimonic Ethics: The Philosophy and Psychology of Living Well. Chapter 6: An Instrumental Theory of Virtue*, 1st edition (Routledge, 2014).

2. History com Editors, "Aristotle," HISTORY, accessed November 25, 2020, https://www.history.com/topics/ancient-history/aristotle.

3. "Who Was Epictetus? The Slave Who Became The Stoic Philosopher," Orion Philosophy, accessed November 25, 2020, https://www.orionphilosophy.com/stoic-blog/epictetus.

4. Viktor E. Frankl, William J. Winslade, and Harold S. Kushner, *Man's Search for Meaning*, n.d.

5. Charles Huenemann, "Nietzsche's Illness," The Oxford Handbook of Nietzsche, September 1, 2013, https://doi.org/10.1093/oxfordhb/9780199534647.013.0004.

6. "Marcus Aurelius []: The Main Philosopher of Ancient Roman Empire," Rome.us, November 18, 2019, https://rome.us/roman-emperors/marcus-aurelius.html.

7. Aleksandr Solzhenitsyn, *The Gulag Archipelago* (Place of publication not identified: Random House, 2003).

8. Stephen G. Post, "Altruism, Happiness, and Health: It's Good to Be Good," *International Journal of Behavioral Medicine* 12, no. 2 (June 1, 2005): 66–77, https://doi.org/10.1207/s15327558ijbm1202_4.

9. June Price Tangney et al., "Reliability, Validity, and Predictive Utility of the 25-Item Criminogenic Cognitions Scale (CCS)," *Criminal Justice and Behavior* 39, no. 10 (October 1, 2012): 1340–60, https://doi.org/10.1177/0093854812451092.

10. Roy F. Baumeister Ph.D and Aaron Beck, *Evil: Inside Human Violence and Cruelty. Chapter 8: Crossing the Line: How Evil Starts*, n.d.

11. James L. Knoll, "The 'Pseudocommando' Mass Murderer: Part I, The Psychology of Revenge and Obliteration," *Journal of the American Academy of Psychiatry and the Law Online* 38, no. 1 (March 1, 2010): 87–94.

12. Fabienne Glowacz and Michel Born, "Away from Delinquency and Crime: Resilience and Protective Factors," 2015, 283–94, https://doi.org/10.1007/978-3-319-08720-7_18.

13. Neelu Sharma et al., "The Relation between Emotional Intelligence and Criminal Behavior: A Study among Convicted Criminals," *Industrial Psychiatry Journal* 24, no. 1 (2015): 54–58, https://doi.org/10.4103/0972-6748.160934.

14. Friedrich Nietzsche, *Daybreak: Thoughts on the Prejudices of Morality*, n.d.

15. Roy F. Baumeister Ph.D and Aaron Beck, *Evil: Inside Human Violence and Cruelty. Chapter 1: The Question of Evil, and the Answers* (New York: Holt Paperbacks, 1999).

16. Robert Ressler, "Lecture at the University of Virginia, 1993."

17. Harma Meffert et al., "Reduced Spontaneous but Relatively Normal

Deliberate Vicarious Representations in Psychopathy," *Brain* 136, no. 8 (August 1, 2013): 2550–62, https://doi.org/10.1093/brain/awt190.

18. Paul Bloom, *Against Empathy: The Case for Rational Compassion* (New York, NY: Ecco, 2016).

19. Carlo Garofalo et al., "Emotion Dysregulation, Impulsivity and Personality Disorder Traits: A Community Sample Study," *Psychiatry Research* 266 (August 1, 2018): 186–92, https://doi.org/10.1016/j.psychres.2018.05.067.

20. Tamas Bereczkei, "The Manipulative Skill: Cognitive Devices and Their Neural Correlates Underlying Machiavellian's Decision Making," *Brain and Cognition* 99 (October 1, 2015): 24–31, https://doi.org/10.1016/j.bandc.2015.06.007.

21. C. Zlotnick, "Antisocial Personality Disorder, Affect Dysregulation and Childhood Abuse Among Incarcerated Women," *Journal of Personality Disorders* 13, no. 1 (March 1, 1999): 90–95, https://doi.org/10.1521/pedi.1999.13.1.90.

22. Iakovos Vasiliou, "The Role of Good Upbringing in Aristotle's Ethics," *Philosophy and Phenomenological Research* 56, no. 4 (1996): 771–97, https://doi.org/10.2307/2108280.

23. "The Cook and the Chef: Musk's Secret Sauce," Wait But Why, November 6, 2015, https://waitbutwhy.com/2015/11/the-cook-and-the-chef-musks-secret-sauce.html.

24. James Martin, *The Meaning of the 21st Century: A Vital Blueprint for Ensuring Our Future*, (Penguin Group, 2006)

25. Brian Hall, *Silicon Valley - Making the World a Better Place*, 2019, https://www.youtube.com/watch?v=B8C5sjjhsso.

26. "What Is Transhumanism?," What is Transhumanism?, accessed November 25, 2020, https://whatistranshumanism.org/.

Made in the USA
Las Vegas, NV
05 December 2021

36021869R00148